The Rise of Unemployment in Europe

NEW DIRECTIONS IN MODERN ECONOMICS

Series Editor: Malcolm C. Sawyer,
Professor of Economics, University of Leeds, UK

New Directions in Modern Economics presents a challenge to orthodox economic thinking. It focuses on new ideas emanating from radical traditions including post-Keynesian, Kaleckian, neo-Ricardian and Marxian. The books in the series do not adhere rigidly to any single school of thought but attempt to present a positive alternative to the conventional wisdom.

A list of published titles in this series is printed at the end of this volume.

The Rise of Unemployment in Europe

A Keynesian Approach

Engelbert Stockhammer

Vienna University of Economics and Business Adminstration, Austria

NEW DIRECTIONS IN MODERN ECONOMICS

Edward Elgar

Cheltenham, UK • Northampton, MA, USA

Published by
Edward Elgar Publishing Limited
Glensanda House
Montpellier Parade
Cheltenham
Glos GL50 1UA
UK

Edward Elgar Publishing, Inc.
136 West Street
Suite 202
Northampton
Massachusetts 01060
USA

A catalogue record for this book
is available from the British Library

Library of Congress Cataloguing in Publication Data
Stockhammer, Engelbert, 1969–
The rise of unemployment in Europe : a Keynesian approach / Engelbert Stockhammer.
p. cm. – (New directions in modern economics)
Includes bibliographical references and index.
1. Unemployment–Europe. 2. Keynesian economics. 3. Keynes, John Maynard, 1883–1946. General theory of employment, interest and money. I. Title. II. Series.

HD5764.A6S75 2004
331.13′794–dc22 2004048266

ISBN 1 84376 410 5

Printed and bound in Great Britain by MPG Books Ltd, Bodmin, Cornwall

Contents

Acknowledgements

This book started out as a dissertation at the University of Massachusetts at Amherst, which was defended in May 2000. Thereafter, following the standard practice in modern academia, it was disassembled and submitted to academic journals (for details see below). This process involved repeated revising and, occasionally, learning. Only in spring and autumn 2003 were the parts, some of which had changed substantially in the meantime, reassambled and complemented by some missing sections and chapters. Overall, this book took years to write. So I have had a lot of time to accumulate intellectual and personal debts. While this book has only one author, he has benefited from many people's comments, suggestions and criticisms. Since I am not good at saying 'thank you' during my work week, I will use this opportunity extensively to do so.

Let us start with the material basis. In order to produce a book the author has to be reproduced on a daily basis. In a capitalist society this is impossible without some income. Most of my income during the period of working on the dissertation was provided by various teaching jobs at the University of Massachusetts. The Graduate Employee Organization (GEO) and the Economics Graduate Student Organization (EGSO) have fought hard to make these teaching jobs pay a decent wage under decent working conditions. Still, without regular and unconditional financial support from my parents, I would not have been able to get through these years without accumulating debt, next to knowledge. Spring and autumn 1999 I had research jobs at the Vienna University of Economics and Business Administration. Finally, in spring 2000 I received a PERI (Political Economy Research Institute) dissertation fellowship, that allowed me to finish things in a timely manner. Three years later, the manuscript was thoroughly revised in 2003 while I had visiting positions at Sabanci University and Bilkent University.

The intellectual incomes I received during this time are much harder to enumerate than the financial ones. For good reasons, most dissertations first thank the members of the dissertation committee. This is also appropriate in my case. Bob Pollin, as the dissertation chair, has shown a rare combination of encouragement and criticism that enabled me to get started as well as to finish – which mentally are probably the most difficult parts – and has patiently read various drafts. Jerry Epstein has at various stages complemented Bob by helpful and clear, if sometimes sobering, criticisms. Bernie Morzuch has (together with Cleve Willis) not only taken away my initial intimidation by econometrics, but also supported my early journeys through the jungle of the unit root literature. Jens Christiansen has made extensive and friendly comments on various drafts.

Less formally, I have benefited from the interest, encouragement and criticisms by many friends and colleagues. In narrowing down the topic, I benefited from regular meetings with Christine Arnold at Wednesdays in the Haymarket. Jerry Friedman has helped me go on at times when each idea appeared as either too large, too small or too trivial. Among the friends with whom I had frequent discussions at the time were Vamsi (Vamsicharan Vakulabharanam), Dori Posel and Eric Verhoogen.

I spent the year 1999 at Vienna University of Economics, where I was warmly welcomed and could devote much of my energy to research. In particular I benefited from the econometric expertise of Alfred Stiassny; from Dieter Gstach's conviction that my work was an important contribution; from various comments and discussions with Fabio Rumler, Sigrid Stagl, Christian Ragacs, Thomas Grandner and Werner Raza; and finally from regular meetings on financialization with Vanessa Redak and Taha Nasr. Early drafts for various chapters or parts thereof were published as WU Department of Economics Working Papers (nos. 67 and 68) and as Working Papers on Employment and Growth in Europe (nos. 8 and 10).

Back to the University of Massachusetts at Amherst (UMass) in spring 2000 frequent meetings with Bob Pollin and with Özlem Onaran – Monday nights, usually ending up in the Amherst Brewing Company – helped to clarify many points of my work.

Writing a dissertation is not only an intellectual undertaking but also a psychological challenge. Coping with it was made more bearable, or even greatly simplified, by the liveliness of SuZanne Castello, thoughtful walks with Ellen Russell, late Sunday-get-out-of-Thompson-beers with Li Minqi, unpredictable meetings with Xiao Feng and the occasional sarcasm of Erik Olsen. Every Wednesday night I could escape the dullness of Amherst and the burden of dissertation-writing by visiting Doug Fulton, Val Voorheis, Max, 99, Captain Janeway, 7of9, and the Delta Quadrant. Regular e-mail therapy was provided by Nik Hammer and Annemarie Steidl.

Upon completion of my doctorate I joined the Economics Department of the Vienna University of Economics and Business Administration, where the papers of the dissertation were submitted to various journals. Articles based on the materials used in Chapters 2, 4, 5 and 6 have been published in the *Review of Political Economy*, the *International Review of Applied Economics* and the *Cambridge Journal of Economics* respectively. In the process some seven anonymous referees helped me to clarify my arguments. The papers had also been presented at several conferences or workshops, including the annual meetings of the Association of Heterodox Economics, the Eastern Economic Association and the European Association of Evolutionary Political Economy.

Finally in May to November 2003, while I was visiting Sabanci University and Bilkent University, I took the time for the revisions, which included adding a new introductory chapter and a chapter on policy conclusions. These revisions might never have taken place if it had not been for steady encouragement by Robert Pollin and for Ozlem's insistence that a 'real economist' ought to have published a book. Malcolm Sawyer's focused comments on how to revise the manuscript greatly helped the enterprise. Comments by Ozlem Onaran, Malcolm Sawyer, Nik Hammer and Markus Marterbauer have helped to improve the new chapters.

The staff of Edward Elgar and Cathrin Vaughan have patiently helped to iron out the numerous inconsistencies of the manuscripts.

Last but not least, I wish to acknowledge that without Irish stout, Scotch whisky, French cigarettes, Austrian Mohnschnitten and Swiss chocolate, writing this book would not have been half as much fun.

1. The rise of unemployment in Europe: a synopsis

Unemployment in the European Union has risen from a modest level of around 2 per cent in 1970 to 8.3 per cent in 2002, a level unseen since the Great Depression. The social costs of this mass unemployment range from income losses to severe social and psychological problems resulting from not having a job, insecurity about the future and dropping out of social security systems. More than 11 million people are directly affected by this misery, not counting the families and communities of the unemployed. While most politicians claim that the fight against unemployment is one of the top priorities, policy concerns have in fact shifted during the 1980s and 1990s. Preserving price stability and the integration of European countries along neo-liberal lines is what history books will record about these decades, not energetic attempts to create jobs for those who need them.

Obviously this rise in unemployment is but one aspect of the many far-reaching transformations that societies and economies in advanced capitalist countries (ACC) have undergone over the past decades. The most prominent of these, that has also called forth a vigorous social opposition, is globalization (Pollin 2000). The internationalization of trade and capital flows is part of the changes that have taken place in the transition from Fordism to the Neo-Liberal Era.[1] In the 1970s a phase of capitalist development, labelled Fordism, came to an end and with it the institutional structures and social compromises that carried it (Aglietta 1979, Boyer 1990, Bowles et al. 1986). The class compromise between labour and capital that guaranteed wage rises roughly in line with inflation and labour productivity growth through collective bargaining has given way to a decentralization of wage setting and a rise of inequality in many countries. Organized labour is in decline in European countries. The role of the state has been redefined. Full employment is not a goal of macroeconomic policy any more. In the EU, a treaty that is euphemistically called the Pact for Stability and Growth effectively rules out counter-cyclical fiscal policy, and the newly founded European Central Bank is praying to the Holy Grail of price stability when economies are on the verge of recession. While states remain important and powerful actors in the economy commanding 30 per cent to 50 per cent of GDP, their aims are different from in the past.

Equally important is the changing role of the financial sector. The end of the Bretton Woods system led to an era of flexible exchange rates. However within Europe countries soon tried to establish more stable arrangements known as the snake, the European Exchange Rate Mechanism and finally monetary integration and the euro (Eichengreen 1998). But while exchange rates within members of the European Monetary Union have irrevocably been frozen, financial transactions have become liberalized. Externally, the ERM included the abolishment of capital controls. Internally, regulations of banks and other financial institutions have been reduced, competition increased and stock markets fostered. Interest rates have been deregulated and increased substantially and have, importantly, been above growth rates for most of the 1980s and 1990s (Levy and Panetta 1996). The changing role of finance in today's economies is illustrated by the fact that, unlike the 1970s, but similarly to the 1930s, the 1997 crisis in Asian countries emanated from foreign exchange markets and the crises of 2001 took their start in the burst of the speculative bubbles in American and European stock markets.

The shift to the right is also reflected in academia, in particular in Economics. While plenty of critical material exists, the mainstream explanation of unemployment in Europe is one of labour market institutions and 'too high' wages. Derived from what has become known as the NAIRU theory, inflexible labour markets and overgenerous welfare states are blamed for the rise in European unemployment. In order to reduce it, wage push factors have to be manipulated: cutting unemployment benefits, reducing minimum wages, weakening labour unions, doing away with employment protection measures. In short, deregulation of the labour market to bring it closer to a perfectly competitive market. While the policy conclusions derived from the NAIRU theory may suggest that this is a step backwards to pre-Keynesian economics, such a diagnosis of the state of the economic science is unwarranted. It represents a sophisticated mixture of ideas that incorporates Keynesian, classical and, one is tempted to say, even Marxist ideas.

One of the key motives in writing this book was the dominance of the idea that the inflexibility of labour markets is the cause of European unemployment, and that unemployment can only be reduced by curbing the welfare state and weakening social institutions like labour unions which the labour market is embedded in. Building on Post-Keynesian theory, the book develops a Keynesian explanation of the rise of unemployment in the large European countries. Facing the high unemployment of the 1920s in Britain and anticipating the Great Depression, John Maynard Keynes rejected the idea that capitalist economies gravitate smoothly to a general equilibrium where all markets clear, that is where full employment prevails.

Rather, his vision of the functioning of the economy was one where there is an asymmetry in the relation between markets. Equilibrium on the goods market, mostly set by investment decisions which are in part determined by outcomes of financial markets, determines the level of employment. The labour market is dragged along by the development on goods markets. The feedback in case of unemployment is either slow or dysfunctional (a deflationary tendency rather than a decrease in real wages at constant prices).

This book takes Keynesian macroeconomics and growth theory, reviewed in Chapter 2, as its starting point and uses it to analyse the rise of unemployment in the large European economies. In a nutshell, the explanation proposed in this book is the following. Employment growth is determined by demand growth. The path of growth is set by investment decisions. Changes in labour market institutions are unable to explain the rise in unemployment. Econometric evidence on the relative explanatory power of labour market institutions and capital accumulation in explaining labour market variables is presented in Chapter 4. It concludes that capital accumulation determines the development on the labour market. Consequently the question of why capital accumulation has slowed down arises. It will be argued that changes in the relation between the financial sector and the real sector of the economy, a phenomenon to be labelled 'financialization' (discussed in Chapter 5) is at the root of this slowdown.

In the remainder of this introductory chapter we will first establish some stylized facts on the development of the countries that will be investigated later. In particular, the development of unemployment, of growth and capital accumulation, and of income distribution are of interest. Section 2 summarizes the argument developed in the book.

1.1 GROWTH, UNEMPLOYMENT AND INCOME DISTRIBUTION: SOME STYLIZED FACTS

Table 1.1 summarizes the growth rates of the business sector GDP for France, Germany, Italy, the UK and the USA, which are the countries the analysis in the following chapters will be based on. As in the following tables, five-year averages are given, to smooth out business cycle fluctuations. For our purpose the figures can be interpreted as trend growth rates. The period after the Second World War is sometimes called the Golden Age of capitalism as growth rates reached historically unprecedented levels in the advanced capitalist countries. Growth rates were above or close to 4 per cent in all economies except the UK until the early 1980s. In the 1970s most economies entered a period of crisis. The precise date of the crisis is subject

Table 1.1 Growth of business GDP

	France	Germany	Italy	UK	USA
1960–64		4.63	6.22	3.14	4.78
1965–69	5.95	4.05	7.30	2.07	4.18
1970–74	4.78	2.91	4.28	3.03	3.90
1975–79	3.69	4.07	4.92	3.26	5.28
1980–84	1.43	0.89	1.30	2.31	3.26
1985–89	3.67	3.15	3.34	4.79	3.80
1990–94	0.60	1.62	0.97	1.99	2.59
1995–99	2.66	1.86	1.89	3.16	4.53
2000–02	3.29	2.11	2.12	2.76	3.49
	France	Germany	Italy	UK	USA
1960–74	5.63	3.79	5.77	3.04	4.16
1975–84	2.42	2.09	3.18	2.18	3.73
1985–99	2.34	1.54	2.17	3.14	3.45

Note:
Germany adjusted for unification
UK starts 1961–64, France: 1963–74

Source: OECD Employment Outlook dataset.

to debate. Commonly the first oil price shock in October 1973 is taken as a watershed; some authors date the start of the crisis in the late 1960s. This crisis did not at once articulate itself as a crisis of average growth rates although most countries witnessed the worst recession since the Second World War in the mid-1970s. As a consequence, to be discussed below, unemployment rates shot up in the second half of the 1970s. The immediate expression of the crisis, however, was the acceleration of inflation, in many countries to double-digit numbers. While initially economic policy reacted in a Keynesian fashion, by the late 1970s or early 1980s most governments and, importantly, most central banks changed their policy stance. In what proved to be a watershed in twentieth-century history, neo-conservatives, most famously Ronald Reagan and Margaret Thatcher, came to power and over the next decade promoted neo-liberal, market-oriented reforms with an often explicitly anti-labour flavour. More immediately, monetary policy turned restrictive and interest rates were increased dramatically. As a consequence ACCs (advanced capitalist countries) experienced a recession in the early 1980s, sometimes called the Volcker crisis – named after Paul Volcker who became head of the Federal Reserve in 1979 and engineered the increase in interest rates. The sharp drop in growth can be seen clearly in Table 1.1, with growth rates falling as low as 0.89 per cent in Germany for the 1980–84 period. Only the USA, which experienced a pronounced upswing in the mid-1980s, saw a growth rate above 3 per cent. The second half of the 1980s witnessed a long boom, in Europe also spurred by German unification (1990), reflected in a recovery of growth rates which however stayed well below the pre-1970s levels. By that time, the neo-liberal restructuring of economy and society was well under way. In the 1990s ACCs experienced a recession in the first half and a prolonged boom in the second half. The latter was not least fuelled by a speculative bubble on stock markets that finally burst in 2000. This is beyond the scope of this book that discusses the rise of unemployment from the 1960s to the 1990s.

The following tables also offer summary statistics for the periods 1960–74, 1975–84 and 1985–99. This roughly corresponds to the period of Fordism, the period of crises and the Neo-Liberal Era respectively. The periodization obviously is somewhat arbitrary. In particular there is no reason to presume that the periodization would be the same for all the countries. This is most transparent in the political sphere: Ronald Reagan came to power in 1980, Margaret Thatcher in 1979, Helmut Kohl in 1982, the French Socialists abandoned their Keynesian experiment in 1984. Other than by numerical convenience, the 1975 and 1985 dates are attractive in that they allow for an equal number of years in the Fordist and in the Neo-Liberal Eras. By this periodization the recession of the early 1980s is not counted part of the Neo-Liberal Era. While this may overestimate the growth performance that the neo-liberal revolution delivered, it conversely ensures that this period is not downward biased by the initial recession that inaugurated it. The final stage of the boom at the turn of the century is excluded as is the present recession.

After the Fordist Era growth rates dropped significantly in all countries except the UK and failed to recover in the Neo-Liberal Era. In the continental European economies, growth rates in 1985–99 were less than half what they were in 1960–74. In the UK, growth recovered to a level slightly above the 1960–74 level. Judging from the indicator of business GDP growth one may get the impression that the crisis never ended. Looking at unemployment rates the picture is similar.

In the Keynesian explanation of the rise in unemployment, capital accumulation will play a prominent role. It is generally the latter which sets the pace for growth in Keynesian growth theory. Capital accumulation rates, that is the growth rates of non-residential business sector capital stock, are a measure of productive capacity and are summarized in Table 1.2. The pattern is similar to that of GDP growth. Accumulation rates were high in all countries except the UK, roughly 4–5 per cent in the 1960–74 period. In

Table 1.2 Capital accumulation in the business sector

	France	Germany	Italy	UK	USA
1960–64		7.00	6.48		3.01
1965–69	4.80	6.57	4.70	1.98	4.74
1970–74	6.09	5.81	5.01	1.81	4.06
1975–79	4.37	3.93	3.85	1.58	3.70
1980–84	3.03	2.94	2.98	1.06	3.17
1985–89	3.68	2.99	3.11	2.52	2.59
1990–94	3.23	3.01	2.77	2.44	1.82
1995–99	2.77	1.69	3.03	3.12	3.66
2000–02	3.02	1.50	3.29	3.34	3.54
	France	Germany	Italy	UK	USA
1960–74	4.93	5.74	5.16	1.94	3.99
1975–84	3.70	3.50	3.45	1.35	3.48
1985–99	2.54	2.34	2.50	2.34	2.55

Note: France, UK: 1962–74

Source: OECD Employment Outlook dataset.

the 1975–84 period accumulation declined, with drops of 1–2 per cent in the continental European countries and 0.5 per cent in the USA. This decline continued in the 1985–99 period. In the continental European countries and the USA accumulation rates dropped, roughly by another 1 per cent. The UK differs in that it had exceptionally low accumulation rates in the Fordist Era of 1.94 per cent. This is half the value for the USA, and even less compared to the European countries. In the 1975–84 period accumulation fell to 1.35 per cent and subsequently improved to 2.34 per cent in the 1985–99 period. While this is higher than in the 1960–74 period, it is still, together with Germany, the lowest value.

The five-year averages tell a similar story of an almost continuous decline, with the UK being an exception. The USA, the UK and Italy experienced an increase of accumulation in the second half of the 1990s, whereas France and Germany did not. Thus while it is possible that the trend of declining capital accumulation has been reversed, it is far from certain and we will only know for certain after the current recession.[2]

Table 1.3 summarizes the unemployment rates for the same countries and the same periods. Substantial differences between countries can be observed in all periods. While Germany's unemployment rate was below

Table 1.3 Unemployment

	France	Germany	Italy	UK	USA
1960–64	1.44	0.49	3.46	1.61	5.72
1965–69	2.04	0.67	4.13	1.86	3.84
1970–74	2.71	0.71	4.27	2.53	5.41
1975–79	4.88	2.15	5.09	4.60	7.02
1980–84	7.92	4.44	6.99	9.58	8.32
1985–89	10.08	5.90	9.88	9.47	6.23
1990–94	10.48	6.28	9.57	8.82	6.59
1995–99	11.54	8.41	11.75	7.03	4.93
2000–02	10.49	8.10	11.08	5.93	4.59
	France	Germany	Italy	UK	USA
1960–74	2.06	0.62	3.95	2.00	4.99
1975–84	6.40	3.30	6.04	7.09	7.67
1985–99	10.28	6.09	9.73	9.14	6.41

Note: France 1960–64 source BLS

Source: OECD Employment Outlook dataset.

1 per cent until the mid-1970s, Italy's and the USA's unemployment rates were close to or above 4 per cent. However all countries experienced a dramatic increase in the crisis period. Unemployment rates tripled in Germany, France and the UK. In Italy and the USA they more or less doubled. In the 1985–99 period unemployment rates decreased only in the USA. A look at the five-year intervals modifies the picture only slightly. Most of the increase in unemployment happened in the 1980s. Unemployment in the UK decreased slightly in the 1990s, but failed to reach the initial low levels. Rates in France and Italy increased by a small margin, whereas the increase in Germany is largely due to high unemployment in the eastern provinces that joined in 1989. Only the USA had reached unemployment levels in the same order of magnitude as in the Golden Age.

According to standard microeconomic analysis of the labour market, one would expect unemployment if wages are 'too high'. Table 1.4 summarizes the profit share in the business sector[3] and is thus an inverse measure of real wages relative to productivity. A rise in the profit share will occur when wage growth lags behind productivity growth. For the European countries the development of the profit share over time is

Table 1.4 Profit share in the business sector

	France	Germany	Italy	UK	USA
1960–64		36.27		30.97	28.15
1965–69	33.11	36.02		30.66	30.74
1970–74	33.46	33.05		29.172	30.61
1975–79	29.17	32.45	28.68	28.898	32.59
1980–84	28.04	31.86	29.46	29.884	32.21
1985–89	33.41	35.32	33.16	32.030	33.06
1990–94	36.92	33.66	33.40	31.166	33.44
1995–99	38.96	35.85	38.65	33.050	35.12
2000–02	39.15	35.88	38.98		34.59
	France	Germany	Italy	UK	USA
1960–74	33.29	35.11		30.27	29.83
1975–84	28.60	32.15	29.17	29.39	32.40
1985–99	35.16	34.66	33.28	32.08	33.25

Note:
Germany 1985–90 and 1991–94 because of break due to unification.
UK profit share of total economy.

Source: OECD Employment Outlook dataset.

U-shaped, starting out with high levels of profitability followed by a decline in the late 1970s and early 1980s and an increase thereafter. Only the USA experienced a relatively stable increase in the profit share with only a minor reduction in the 1980–84 period.

The development of income distribution is hard to square with any explanation of European unemployment resting on wages being 'too high'. Real wages have declined substantially relative to productivity since the mid-1980s. In fact, in the continental European countries, which experienced high unemployment, a significant redistribution from labour to capital has taken place amounting to some 10 per cent of GDP in Italy and France (from 1980–84 to 1995–99). This decrease in wages (relative to productivity) has not translated into a reduction in unemployment over that period.

Dramatic changes have taken place in the financial sector since the 1970s: the end of the Bretton Woods system of fixed exchange rates, European Monetary Unification, financial deregulation and liberalization, and of late a stock market boom. The liberalization of capital accounts has allowed volatile capital flows in and out of countries that have led to a series of exchange rate crises: the 1992–93 crises affecting several European coun-

Table 1.5 Financial crises in the recent past

Late 1980s	S&L crises in USA
1987	Stock market crash, USA
1990s	Deflation of stock market, Japan
1992/93	EMS crises
1994	Peso crises, Mexico; Turkey
1997	East Asian financial crises (Thailand, Malaysia, South Korea . . .)
1998	Crisis in Russia
2000	Stock market deflation, USA and Europe
2001	Crises in Turkey and Argentina

tries, 1994 in Mexico, 1997 in South-East Asia, a year later in Russia, 2001 in Argentina and Turkey. A list of the major financial crises of the recent past is compiled in Table 1.5

One of the changes in economic policy was the shift in policy priorities of central banks, which switched to anti-inflationary policies in the early 1980s, most famously the FED under Paul Volcker. However the development in Europe was similar, with the Bundesbank having the dominant position in the European Monetary System and forcing other countries, notably France and Italy, to pursue high interest policies. Real interest rates, defined as the interest rates on long-term government securities deflated by the GDP deflator, are summarized in Table 1.6. In 1960–74 real interest rates were below 2 per cent in all countries except Germany and they were substantially below real growth rates in all countries. In the 1970s real interest rates fell significantly due to unexpectedly high inflation rates; in many countries they turned negative at some point. In the early 1980s interest rates in the major economies increased dramatically to above 4 per cent, with Italy following a few years later. Thereafter interest rates remained at these extraordinarily high levels, with only the UK falling below 4 per cent (3.79 in 1995–99).

Only very recently has the FED lowered interest rates to counter the recession and the burst of the stock market bubble. However the ECB has so far not followed to anything like the same extent, despite ailing economies and rising unemployment rates. The overall picture of real interest rates can be summarized as follows: real interest rates were 1–3 per cent in the Fordist Era, fell in the 1970s and increased dramatically in the early 1980s to above 4 per cent. Since then they decreased nowhere substantially until 2001. This means that while interest rates were below growth rates in the Fordist Era, they were consistently higher than growth rates in the Neo-Liberal Era.

High interest rates are thought to depress investment and are therefore

Table 1.6 Real interest rates

	France	Germany	Italy	UK	USA
1960–64	1.78	2.30	−0.57	2.52	2.70
1965–69	2.89	3.90	2.51	2.67	1.85
1970–74	1.08	1.97	−2.54	0.50	0.95
1975–79	−0.04	3.24	−3.24	−2.94	0.76
1980–84	4.20	4.83	0.87	3.17	5.59
1985–89	5.47	4.41	4.34	4.33	5.52
1990–94	5.75	4.29	6.47	4.71	4.26
1995–99	4.53	4.45	4.04	3.79	4.23
2000–02	4.08	4.24	3.04	2.95	3.84
	France	Germany	Italy	UK	USA
1960–74	1.93	2.75	−0.18	1.85	1.77
1975–84	2.08	4.04	−1.19	0.12	3.17
1985–99	5.61	4.35	5.40	4.52	4.89

Source: OECD Economic Outlook database.

an obvious candidate for explaining the slow growth and accumulation performance in the Neo-Liberal Era. Ball (1994, 1999) has forcefully argued that differences in labour market performances can to a large extent be explained by differences in monetary policies. In the argument to be developed below, the change in interest rates is but one symptom, though an important one, for the structural changes that have taken place between the real sectors of the economy and the financial sector. In Chapter 5 more quantitative measures of theses changes will be discussed. Here only one more indicator central to the econometric work will be discussed.

One of the important changes that can be observed is that non-financial businesses themselves are becoming increasingly active on financial markets. Table 1.7 summarizes the ratio of financial income (interest income, dividend income and rents) to the operating surplus of non-financial businesses. This reveals substantial differences between countries and a dramatic rise in the financial income share of non-financial business in all countries. The USA and UK start out around or below 20 per cent in the 1960s and increase to levels above or close to 50 per cent. France and Germany start at much lower levels, below 10 per cent. Whereas the figures for France increase to close to Anglo-Saxon levels, the German financial share of NFB doubles, but remains comparably low at around 14 per cent. Financial activity of non-financial businesses has thus increased substantially.

Table 1.7 Financial income as share of operating surplus for NFB

	France	Ger (W)	Italy	UK	USA
1960–64		3.76			17.14
1965–69		4.79		20.11	16.86
1970–74	9.21	6.79		46.74	29.17
1975–79	16.38	6.40		44.67	32.74
1980–84	30.01	9.94	26.85	35.56	49.40
1985–89	24.99	9.23	19.84	32.50	52.04
1990–94	41.46	13.47	19.73	47.19	56.66
1995–99	45.97	16.45	9.98	34.02	

Note:
Break in series with 1995 due to change in OECD National Accounts.
Germany is West Germany before 1995 and Germany thereafter.

It will be argued that the increase in financial investments and income from them went hand in hand with changes in the attitudes towards running a firm. Firms are increasingly regarded as just one investment opportunity, in competition to others. Thus, one would expect systematic changes in investment behaviour.

1.2 THE RISE OF EUROPEAN UNEMPLOYMENT: A KEYNESIAN APPROACH

The rise of unemployment in Europe, in particular the Northern countries, from levels close to or below 2 per cent (in the 1960s) to values close to 10 per cent (after 1980) marks a fundamental social change of the past decades. It constitutes one of the characteristics of the Neo-Liberal Era in Europe. While politicians pay lip service to the reduction of unemployment, actual policy priorities have shifted over the same time towards price stability and balanced budgets.

This is most clearly expressed in the various treaties that have marked the path of European Monetary Unification, which dominated much of European politics in the 1980s and 1990s. While the Amsterdam Treaty reiterates the policy goal of 'high employment' and asks member states to report on the labour market performance and policies, these provisions remain toothless and complementary to those policy goals that constitute the core of the political agenda: price stability and fiscal austerity. Unambiguous numerical goals were set for inflation and budget deficits in the Maastricht Treaty, a document mostly written by central bankers

(Eichengreen 1993), and it was these goals that were to dominate the fiscal policy of the 1990s. Not meeting these convergence criteria would have meant exclusion from Monetary Unification. The Amsterdam Treaty wrote these criteria in stone and established punitive payments (not yet applied) for countries whose budget deficits exceed 3 per cent of GDP in the absence of a strong recession (defined as GDP growth below −2 per cent). While these provisions have not yet been applied, they certainly had a strong impact on economic policies.

Labour market policies not only lack similar clear goals and sanctions, but also are not considered a vital prerequisite for European integration. Moreover, reducing unemployment is conceived to be beyond the scope of fiscal or monetary policy. The European Commission, the European Central Bank and most member countries seem to think that labour market rigidities are to blame for European unemployment. However, 'we should realize that, apart from what one may believe on this issue, the evidence produced by economists concerning the blame that can be put on these rigidities is weak' (Bentolina 1997, p. 73).

In this book a Keynesian approach to explaining the rise of European unemployment is revisited, both theoretically and empirically, and contrasted with the NAIRU approach. The proposed Keynesian approach is one that views unemployment as a result of various demand shocks, mostly crystallizing in business investment. In fact, capital accumulation, that is business investment in relation to capital stock, has decreased substantially in Europe, and more so than in the USA. Finally the book ventures into the explanation of this slowdown of accumulation. It is argued that financial deregulation has strengthened the position of shareholders and owners within corporations leading to shift in management priorities from growth to profits.

1.2.1 Keynesian Theories

Motivated by the experience of prolonged mass unemployment in Britain throughout the 1920s and the Great Depression, Keynes developed a theory of effective demand, according to which output and consequently employment are determined by investment expenditures and other autonomous types of expenditures like exports and government investment. Unlike what he labelled 'classical' theory, he rejected the self-adjusting ability of the market economy for several reasons. First, because there is no feedback from unemployment that guarantees that wages will fall. On the labour market money wages, that is nominal wages, are set by employers or in negotiations with labour unions. An increase in unemployment will weaken labour unions and thus reduce money wages, but whether this also decreases real wages, depends on prices. If, as is likely in a recession, firms cut prices, real wages need not fall. Second, an important part of effective demand depends on investment decisions. These involve decisions regarding the distant future, about which rational expectations often cannot be made. In a fundamental sense the future is open and therefore uncertain. In such a context, investment decisions not only depend on rational factors but also on investor sentiment, or what Keynes famously labelled 'animal spirits' of investors. Third, financial markets, namely stock markets, are prone to mood swings because investors are trying to anticipate the public's evaluation of the decisions. Thus financial markets will be, at least at times, a source of destabilization.

While Keynes sought to develop a general theory that would include the classical (what would today be called 'neo-classical') theory as a special case in the situation of full employment, Keynesian ideas were soon absorbed into the newly constructed mainstream economics, as a special case itself. Pioneered by Hicks (1937) Keynesian arguments were valid in the case of wage or price rigidities or in some extraordinary circumstances like the liquidity trap. In the long run in particular, the economy would obey the classical principles and the market system guarantees full employment and an efficient allocation of resources. The ISLM version of Keynesian economics became part of the standard macroeconomic textbooks, most notably that of Samuelson, and provided the basis for what has often been called the 'Neo-classical Synthesis'. This approach, elaborated theoretically among others by Paul Samuelson, Franco Modigliani and James Tobin, was mainstream economics and dominated economic policy until the 1970s. At that time it came under attack by a succession of new versions of classical economics – Monetarism, Rational Expectations, New Classical Economics – all of which emphasized the self-regulatory properties and the efficiency of the market system. They criticized the Synthesis generation of Keynesians for the ad hoc way of introducing rigidities in wages or prices. From the 1980s onwards they also dominated economic policy-making.

Since then a new generation of Keynesian economics has emerged, often called New Keynesians, that share the individualistic approach of neoclassical economics, but use it to provide support for Keynesian propositions like rigid prices and wages (R. Gordon 1990). They also use information asymmetries to demonstrate how market economies fail to deliver efficient outcomes in the face of informational asymmetries (Stiglitz 1987). The NAIRU theory that will be discussed below is an example of such a New Keynesian theory. Politically the New Keynesians are hard to classify. While the NAIRU theory is mostly used to give policy recommendations hardly distinguishable from neoclassical ones, other New

Keynesian theories, like the Noise Trader theory of financial speculation, are much more damaging for conventional economics. While Gregory Mankiw is economic adviser to George W. Bush, Stiglitz was adviser to Bill Clinton and famously attacked the IMF after his resignation from the World Bank Economics Department.

Many of the close collaborators of Keynes were dissatisfied with the Neo-classical Synthesis early on and sought to extend Keynes's theory of the determination of output and employment from the short to the long run. The most famous of these include J. Robinson, M. Kalecki and N. Kaldor. They developed theories of growth and distribution which emphasized the central role of investment decisions, even in the long run, and that saving propensity of a society depends on income distribution. As investment equals savings in the equilibrium condition for the goods markets, growth and income distribution are thus intrinsically linked.

The role of unemployment in Post-Keynesian growth theories is discussed in Chapter 2. The crucial difference between Robinsonian growth theories and Kaleckian theories is that the Robinsonian models assume full capacity utilization. Thus they are true long-run models, where adjustments have taken place; in particular, excess capacity has been eliminated. In these models, autonomous investment expenditures and the savings propensity of capital income determines growth as well as distribution. Thus there is no role for unemployment to determine either income distribution or output. Employment passively follows the economic trend. Therefore there is no equilibrium rate of unemployment to which the economy reverts.

Kaleckian models, which have received renewed interest since the early 1980s, allow for changes in capacity utilization reflecting firstly, the shorter time horizon of these models and secondly, the greater emphasis Kaleckians put on imperfect competition. In imperfect competitive environments firms will set prices and the price mechanism will therefore cease to clear the goods market. Thus changes in capacity utilization exist as a result. Moreover firms will want to keep excess capacity such as to deter entrance. As Marglin and Bhaduri (1990) have shown in a seminal paper, in such a model, profit-led as well as demand-led regimes can exist. An increase in profits and decrease in wages will have a positive effect on investment, but a negative one on consumption (since workers have a higher consumption propensity than capitalists). Depending on the relative size of the effect a change in the profit share has on investment and on consumption, growth will either be profit-led or wage-led.

The Kaleckian growth models allow for an effect of unemployment on income distribution, since flexible capacity utilization gives an additional degree of freedom. While Kalecki emphasized such an effect, that we will call the reserve army effect, he did not discuss its consequences for his growth models nor have his followers analyse it. In both the profit-led as well as the wage-led regimes, a well-defined short-run equilibrium exists. However, a long-run equilibrium rate of unemployment appears only in the profit-led regime. In the wage-led growth regimes the equilibrium of the labour market is unstable and therefore does not serve as an attractor for actual unemployment. Unemployment does not revert to a long-run equilibrium position but rather follows wherever short-run demand shocks push it.

In the profit-led regime, a stable equilibrium rate of unemployment exists in the long run and employment therefore cannot be thought of as passively responding to demand: it exerts a genuine feedback onto the goods market. This equilibrium rate of unemployment is similar to the NAIRU in that it depends on exogenous wage and profit claims. However, it differs fundamentally from the NAIRU in that it does depend on autonomous investment expenditures. Investment can affect unemployment directly through the demand effect as well as indirectly through increasing productive capacity.

Keynesians stress the role of demand factors in the determination of unemployment not only in the short run. Keynesian growth theories are centred around capital accumulation and the labour market follows where accumulation leads (to paraphrase a quotation by J. Robinson). However, differences exist. In the Robinsonian full capacity models no feedback from unemployment to accumulation exists, whereas Kaleckian models allow for such feedback, for example in the form of a reserve army effect. If demand is profit-led there exists a stable equilibrium rate of unemployment, which depends on capital accumulation. In the wage-led regime, there is no stable equilibrium rate of unemployment and actual unemployment is determined by accumulation. All these models assume unemployment persistence as growth or accumulation only affect the change in unemployment.

1.2.2 The NAIRU Story of European Unemployment

The NAIRU theory is nowadays the mainstream explanation of the rise in European unemployment. It identifies the inflexibilities of labour markets as the culprits for the rise in unemployment and has been embraced by organizations such as the OECD and the IMF. Much of the policy recommendations of the EU are also based on this theory. Chapter 3 discusses the NAIRU theory. At the core of this theory is a trade-off between inflation and unemployment. At any time there will be only one rate of unemployment that allows for a stable rate of inflation, thus the name 'Non-Accelerating Inflation Rate of Unemployment'. In this sense, the NAIRU is an equilibrium rate of unemployment to which the system is assumed to revert. How then is the NAIRU determined and what are the mechanisms that ensure actual unemployment will gravitate towards the NAIRU? Throughout this book the NAIRU model will be distinguished from the NAIRU story. By NAIRU model we designate a broad class of models that accept the inflation–unemployment trade-off, whereas the NAIRU story of European unemployment is one particular, albeit popular, interpretation of European unemployment. In particular the NAIRU story claims that the NAIRU is exogenous and that it serves as a strong attractor for the system, whereas there are NAIRU models that have an endogenous NAIRU and ones where it is a only weak attractor.

The NAIRU theory is a macroeconomic theory of the labour market that takes wage bargaining as its starting point. Unlike standard neo-classical labour market analysis, the real wage is not a mechanism that adjusts to clear the labour market and ensure full employment. Rather, nominal wages are the outcome of a bargaining process between firms and labour unions. Thus the nominal wage depends, given certain expectations about future inflation, on the respective bargaining strength of the two sides, and unemployment negatively affects the power of labour. Prices are thought to be set by firms with market power and depend on aggregate demand. If the real wage implied by wage bargaining and by price setting are inconsistent, unexpected inflation has to occur. With inflation expectations fulfilled there will only be one level of unemployment at which the income claims of labour and capital are consistent. Consequently, the government can affect actual unemployment in the short run by expansionary fiscal or monetary policies that lead to unexpected inflation.

One important issue is whether such a decrease in actual unemployment has a lasting effect on the NAIRU itself. This phenomenon is called hysteresis or unemployment persistence. While there is little disagreement about the existence of hysteresis in European economies, its magnitude and economic significance are subject to debate. While Ball (1994, 1999) and Blanchard and Summers (1988) argue that hysteresis is strong enough for actual unemployment to determine equilibrium unemployment and governments therefore can effectively influence the NAIRU by changing actual unemployment, others like Layard et al. (1991) argue that demand policies have no long-run effect on equilibrium unemployment. In fact, what is at stake here is how exogenous the NAIRU is to economic performance and to the history of unemployment. A related question is whether the NAIRU depends on economic variables like the capital stock or the rate of interest. While some authors (for example Rowthorn 1995, 1999a,b; Sawyer 2001) provide models and empirical evidence that the NAIRU does depend on capital accumulation, others (for example Layard et al. 1991) rule these cases out.

What we will label the NAIRU *story* of European unemployment is a version of the NAIRU *theory* that treats the NAIRU as exogenous to economic variables. The NAIRU thus depends on neither past actual unemployment nor on capital accumulation, but is determined by labour market institutions that increase the bargaining power of labour unions, or more generally insiders. These factors are also called wage-push factors as they increase the wage demands of workers. They typically include minimum wages, duration and generosity of unemployment benefits, firing restrictions and unionization of the labour force. The NAIRU story claims that the rise of unemployment in Europe is due to changes in these wage-push factors.[4]

In terms of policy conclusions the NAIRU story is remarkably close to standard neo-classical arguments. It is frictions and inflexibilities in the labour markets that are to blame for unemployment and that consequently have to be done away with. Thus curbing unemployment benefits, reducing job protection measures and decreasing minimum wages are the standard recommendations, such as put forward by the OECD.[5] However, this similarity in terms of policy conclusion must not conceal the theoretical differences. The NAIRU model, as well as the NAIRU story, are New Keynesian theories. They reject the notion of a real wage being set on the labour market as an outcome of the interaction between labour supply and labour demand. Rather, the nominal wage is the outcome of wage bargaining and prices are set by oligopolistic firms. Consequently unemployment is an equilibrium phenomenon. Labour market institutions like minimum wages increase equilibrium unemployment in the NAIRU theory, whereas in a neo-classical model they increase unemployment because the labour market will not be in equilibrium. The NAIRU theory is thus substantially more sophisticated and realistic than the neo-classical model, and the NAIRU story, while deriving essentially identical policy conclusions, does so from a different theoretical, namely New Keynesian, background.

1.2.3 The NAIRU Story versus the Keynesian Approach: The Empirical Picture

The NAIRU story, stressing labour market institutions and wage-push factors, and the Keynesian approach, stressing capital accumulation, demand factors and unemployment persistence, are thus competing theories in explaining the rise in unemployment. A look at the stylized facts is enough to raise doubts about the NAIRU story. The fall in the wage share, documented in Table 1.4, is hard to square with the NAIRU story that implies an outward shift of the wage-setting function and thus an increase rather than a decrease of real wages. Chapter 4 takes an econometric approach to test the empirical explanatory power of the two approaches.

The empirical work in the NAIRU tradition can roughly be divided into two groups. First, there are estimations of wage-setting and price-setting curves within countries. These two approaches largely coincide with an Atlantic divide on what the NAIRU theory seeks to explain. The first approach, using time series data, estimates wage and price-setting functions, sometimes as a reduced form of an enriched price-setting function. This allows for an *ex post* calculation of the NAIRU implicit in wage and price setting, but it is mostly an explanation of inflation.[6] As is obvious from the Symposium on the NAIRU in the *Journal of Economic Perspectives*, the NAIRU is considered unsatisfactory (mostly in the USA context), if it fails to explain inflation properly. Second, there are regressions explaining unemployment by data on labour market institutions. These attempt, mostly by using cross-country data, to explain actual unemployment via the NAIRU, which is understood to be determined by labour market institutions.

It is this second literature that constitutes the NAIRU story's substantial attempt to explain the rise in European economies. Nickell (1997) and (1998) are probably the most prominent examples of the cross-country approach. He regresses unemployment rates on wage-push variables such as unemployment benefits, employment protection measures, union density, the level of collective bargaining and coverage of bargaining, the tax wedge and active labour market policies. Scarpetta (1996) and the IMF (2003) take a similar approach, but estimate panel regressions and stress the importance of labour market variables and their interactions.

Keynesians have also produced substantial empirical research, stressing the importance of capital accumulation[7] and unemployment persistence. Glyn (1998) analyses the relation between employment growth, structural change and accumulation from the late nineteenth century to the 1990s. He finds that capital accumulation plays an important role in job creation in the non-agricultural sector. Sarantis (1993) estimates a reduced form unemployment function derived from a neo-Kaleckian growth model by means of a panel approach. He explains unemployment by capital accumulation as well as other demand variables. Neither of them controls for wage push variables. Rowthorn (1995) shows that the change in the average growth rate in employment between 1960–73 and 1973–92 is correlated to the change in average capital stock growth rates over the period in a cross-country regression. Arestis and Biefang-Frisancho Mariscal (1998) propose a NAIRU model with variable work effort and hysteresis where the capital stock matters and provided econometric evidence for the UK that the capital stock does affect unemployment and in particular long-term unemployment. Ball (1994 and 1999) stresses the role of hysteresis and the effects of monetary policy. He examines the recessions of the early 1980s and 1990s, and the recovery of the mid-1980s, and shows that the successful countries that managed to decrease their initially high unemployment (the Netherlands, the UK, Ireland and Portugal) pursued expansionary monetary policy.

The explanatory power of the NAIRU story and a Keynesian approach that stresses capital accumulation are evaluated in Chapter 4. This is done in a time series context for the major European economies (France, Germany, Italy and the UK) and the USA. The results of this econometric exercise clearly support the Keynesian approach. Capital accumulation is (statistically significantly) related to unemployment, whereas there is no consistent (statistically significantly) relation between wage-push factors and unemployment. This is true for a variety of specifications.

Based on these results the explanation of the rise in European unemployment suggested is that the rise in unemployment was driven by demand shocks, expressed in lower rates of private capital accumulation (Rowthorn 1995, Marterbauer and Walterskirchen 2000). Demand shocks have long-lasting effects since unemployment persistence is high (Ball 1997, Fritsch and Logeay 2002). Labour market institutions play a minor role, if any, in explaining the rise of unemployment. Nor does unemployment react much to changes in wages (Stockhammer and Onaran 2004). This conclusion regarding the role of labour market institutions is shared by Madsen (1998), Baker et al. (2002) and Ball (1999). Moreover, OECD (1998a, 1999a) present evidence suggesting that minimum wages and employment protect measures are unlikely to be main causes in explaining unemployment. Blanchard and Wolfers conclude: 'labor market institutions do not appear able to explain the general evolution of unemployment over time' (Blanchard and Wolfers 2000, p. 2).

1.2.4 Financialization and the Slowdown of Accumulation

Having established a link between accumulation and unemployment, the obvious question is how to explain the slowdown in accumulation. This is a difficult task however. Explaining investment expenditures has proven a long-lasting challenge to the economics profession (Ford and Poret 1991). From a Keynesian point of view this is unsurprising, as Keynesians emphasize the role of 'animal spirits', that is the non-rational, creative aspect in investment decisions. Thus investment will exhibit a stable relation to other economic variables only to some extent. While some Keynesians have drawn the conclusion that investment expenditures are fundamentally unpredictable (Vickers 1992, Heye 1995), others have been in the forefront of empirical investment research (Kalecki 1969, 1971).[8] However, an emphasis of the role of animal spirits does not imply that investment is inexplicable, rather that it is hard to explain in the short run. Structural changes in the economy would certainly affect investment expenditures and one of the important developments in the Neo-Liberal Era is the changing role of the financial sector.

The changes in the financial sector have their roots in government policies as well as private behaviour. Partly pressured by supranational organizations such as the IMF or the OECD, countries have liberalized their capital accounts and deregulated their financial systems domestically (Epstein and Schor 1992). Capital controls were abolished, interest ceilings (on deposits) were lifted, credit allocation schemes abandoned. In parallel new financial institutions were created (most famously the Money Market Mutual Funds in the USA in the 1970s) and financial institutions crossed their traditional boundaries. As a consequence new actors appeared on the financial scene, like institutional investors, pension funds and hedge funds.

While the various macroeconomic effects of these developments are felt throughout the economy, their overall effect is hard to assess and has created a rich literature. The following is thus a selective list of debates.

The effect on income distribution is rather unambiguous: incomes from financial wealth, that is interest income, dividends and capital gains, also called rentiers' income, has increased dramatically since the 1970s (Epstein and Power 2003, Power et al. 2003a,b).

Most countries have experienced shifts from bank-based financial systems to market-based ones (Grabel 1997, Schaberg 1999). This shift to market-based financial systems, however, is not reflected in financial markets playing an increasing role in the (net) finance of investment. Rather, in aggregate non-financial businesses finance themselves out of retained earnings (Mayer 1988). At the same time markets play an increasingly important role in corporate finance as firms start to engage in financial transactions, on the one hand to hedge against various risks, in particular exchange rate risks, and on the other hand because financial investment is more profitable than physical investment.

The area where the shift to market-based financial systems is most clearly felt is corporate governance. Hostile takeovers fuelled by new financial instruments have created a market for corporate control and led to a wave of mergers and acquisitions (OECD 1998b, Froud et al. 2000). As a consequence firms try to follow the rules set by financial markets and aim at 'creating shareholder value', that is pursue policies that guarantee rising share prices and high dividends. Of course these development have not affected all countries equally. While the UK has had a market-based financial system for a long time, continental European countries are traditionally classified as bank-based economies (Demirgüc-Kunt and Levine 2001). Among these France has probably experienced the most pronounced shift towards a market-based system, and Germany has been the most resilient and maintained strong bank-based structures. The USA, while also considered a market-based system, used to have a heavily regulated financial sector that was deregulated radically in the 1980s.

A succession of financial crises has illustrated the potential instability of liberalized financial markets and led to theories of asset price speculation. Behavioural finance (Shiller 2000), Noise Trader theories (Shleifer and Summers 1990, Shleifer 2000) and a revival of Minskyan theories (Skott 1995) all suggest that financial markets are inherently unstable.

The stock market boom of the 1990s also sparked new interest in the wealth effect in consumption. Several empirical studies presented evidence for the existence of an economically significant effect of wealth on consumption expenditures (Boone et al. 1998), though many questions regarding the precise mechanisms and the relative effects of financial and real estate property remain open (Poterba 2000, Case et al. 2001).

There have been some attempts to explore the macroeconomic dynamics of the effects of financial markets and shareholder value orientation on business decisions. Boyer (2000) has offered the most complete formal macroeconomic treatment of what he called a 'finance-led accumulation regime'. He posits changes in investment behaviour, a redistribution from labour to shareholders that gives rise to a stock market boom, which in turn fuels consumption expenditures and analyses under which conditions such a finance-led growth regime can be stable. Aglietta (2000) offers a similar analysis, but without a formal model, and assigns a greater role to productivity gains through the 'new economy'. Neither of the authors offers a detailed analysis of changes in investment behaviour. Smithin (2002) proposes a model that stresses the negative effect of the increase of rentiers' income on firms' funds that are disposable for investment.

A theory of the effect of financialization on the investment behaviour of non-financial businesses is proposed in Chapter 5. Financialization will be defined as the engagement of non-financial businesses on financial markets. These financial activities are interpreted as reflecting a shift in the firm's objectives and a rising influence of shareholder interests in the firm. Thus a narrow concept of financialization is used that has the advantage of allowing us to derive a testable hypothesis. The argument is based on the Post-Keynesian theory of the firm, which for our purposes has to be developed further, stressing the conflict of interest between management and shareholders.

The corporate governance literature takes as its starting point that managers have goals other than profit maximization. They may wish to increase their income, prestige or power, which is expressed in their desire for many subordinates and 'the pursuit of market share and growth at the expense of profitability' (OECD 1998b, p. 17). It is typically argued that in the Fordist period management was relatively independent and able to pursue these goals. Notably this was also the time of growing power of labour unions. In a firm with strong stakeholders like organized labour and governments committed to full employment, firms can be expected to have bias towards growth.

During the 1980s and 1990s shareholders reclaimed their position in the firm. Through the establishment of a market for corporate control and through incentives (performance-related pay schemes, stock options) shareholders sought to realign management's interests with their own. Downsizing in the name of 'creating shareholder value' became the key business term of the 1980s and 1990s (Lazonick and O'Sullivan 2000). Simultaneously firms shredded their identity as pure industrial enterprises and moved towards profit centres that readily engage in financial activity if the latter is more promising than the former.

As implied in the OECD quotation above, there is a trade-off between profits and growth of a firm that is also stressed in the Post-Keynesian theory of the firm. In fact, if there is a profit-maximizing level of investment, there has to be a trade-off between profits and investment beyond this point. If such a trade-off holds, a shift of management priorities from growth to profits will decrease investment expenditures.

Chapter 5 proposes a formal model of the formation of management objectives based on the relative power of management and shareholders. The conclusion of this model is that an increase of shareholder power leads to a decrease in desired investment. Chapter 6 presents an econometric test of this model. For the estimations of the hypothesis an indirect measure of shareholder value orientation is used – the activity of non-financial businesses on financial markets. The interest and dividend income, for short: rentiers' income, of non-financial businesses serves as a proxy for financialization. It measures to what extent non-financial businesses have acquired rentier status and the hypothesis is that this corresponds to a change in management priorities.

This measure is included in a standard investment regressions for the USA, the UK, France and Germany. The results confirm the importance of financialization. In the USA and France the financialization variable has strong explanatory power; in the UK it has in some specifications, but not in all. In Germany, where shareholder power is less developed, we fail to find an effect. Overall the central finding is that the more firms are engaged in financial activities, in fact the more they earn from financial activities, the less they invest in physical capital.

1.3 CONCLUSION

Fordism, the accumulation regime of the post-war era, which was characterized by a compromise between capital and labour, by a growing and activist state, by a regulated financial sector and by low real interest rates, went into crisis in the 1970s. With the Neo-Conservative revolution of the early 1980s labour relations changed in favour of capital, expressed in a rising profit share. Equally the welfare state was curbed, the financial sector deregulated and real interest rates rose. At the same time growth rates and accumulation rates fell and unemployment increased to levels unprecedented in postwar history.

The Keynesian explanation we propose regards the fall in capital accumulation as the main culprit for the rise in unemployment. The reason for the slowdown in accumulation is located in the changes in the financial sector. Not only have real interest rates exceeded growth rates, but shareholder value orientation has shifted management priorities away from growth. Non-financial businesses themselves have become investors on financial investment. It was demonstrated that this went hand in hand with a decrease in physical investment.

By way of conclusion some policy implication of this analysis will be outlined in Chapter 7. Above all, a policy that recognizes and does justice to the externalities to capital investment is called for. Thus investment decisions have effects well beyond the firm that is investing. Correspondingly, investment decisions have to be made, not only taking into account the firm or even their shareholders financial return, but their entire social effects. Consequently Keynes famously suggested the socialization of investment. The policy proposals are centred around three areas:

1. Within the firm, broader social groups, often summarized as stakeholders such as organized labour, NGOs and communities need to be represented in the decision-making bodies. The German model of codetermination may serve as a starting point for this.
2. The structure and growth of the financial sector have to be regulated and directed such that they serve the needs of the real sectors of the economy and such that financial development (and reaping profits thereof) does not become an end in itself. This will include measures increasing the transparency of financial transactions and accounts, but also an adaption of tax systems to highly liquid and, indeed, often unstable financial markets. A security transaction tax such as proposed by Pollin et al. (2002) may be a starting point for such a reform of the tax system.
3. The state sector for the economy has to be empowered financially as well as legally such that it is capable of fulfilling its economic functions.

These functions include not only the pursuit of price stability, but also stabilization (which is all the more important in times of frequent financial crises), and policies aimed at full employment and an equitable income distribution. Financially a securities transaction tax would be an important step towards modernizing tax systems. A reduction of real interest rates would go a long way in increasing states' finances. Legally, treaties like the euphemistically called Pact for Stability and Growth have to be revised such that governments can effectively pursue policies that aim at growth, stability and full employment.

NOTES

1. Various authors have proposed different labels for these periods, but most agree on the periodization. For example Marglin and Bhaduri (1990) refer to the Golden Age rather than Fordism, thus making a reference to Joan Robinson. Setterfield and Cornwall (2002), presenting an analysis in the spirit of Kaldor, use the terms Golden Age and Age of Decline. The term 'Fordism' goes back to the French Regulation School and in particular Aglietta (1979), who highlighted the use of Taylorist work organization and wages roughly growing in line with labour productivity. This term is preferred because it tells more about the social structures than 'Golden Age'. 'Neo-Liberal Era' is used because it highlights characteristics of the period: the political origins of the period and the focus on pro-market policies. However, nothing of importance hinges on the names for the periods.
2. Figures for the National Accounts are revised as statistical agencies process data. Thus data for the past three years should be interpreted cautiously. This is all the more true for the OECD Economic Outlook dataset that is used as a data source here, because it uses forecasts where actual values are not available.
3. Remarkably the OECD has discontinued reporting the profit share in the Economic Outlook dataset. Presumably this is done because of methodological difficulties, in particular the treatment of unpaid family workers and the self-employed. While there are undoubtedly problems, these problems are certainly less serious than those associated with other series that the OECD publishes in the same data set, in particular the output gap and the NAWRU (Non-Accelerating Wage Rate of Unemployment). These latter, in addition, rest on econometric analysis based on certain theoretical models, whereas the profit share requires none of these. Thus it is hard to believe that the inclusion of variables in the data set reflects solely the reliability of data. Rather it seems to be a question of which variables are considered interesting and the analysis of functional income distribution is not high on the OECD's analytical agenda. The data in Table 1.3 have been calculated based on the earlier definition of the Profit Share in the Business Sector (OECD 2002).
4. Note that while the NAIRU story argues that the NAIRU is exogenous to demand in the long run, it exclusively focuses on wage-push factors in determining the NAIRU, but usually ignores 'profit-push' factors, that is factors that increase the mark-up exogenously.
5. This, however, is not to say that all the recommendations by the OECD are backed by the empirical research in the NAIRU tradition. In particular the OECD encourages the decentralization of collective bargaining. However nearly all the research in the NAIRU tradition finds that a higher degree of centralization of collective bargaining is associated with lower unemployment (Nickell 1998, IMF 2003).
6. See *Journal of Economic Perspectives* 1997 Symposium on the NAIRU as an illustration.
7. It is worth noting that this view is not restricted to Post-Keynesians. For example Modigliani et al. (1998) write: 'We believe that one reason for the drastic European decline

in the demand for labor relative to its available supply, and the resulting rise in unemployment has been a decline in investment relative to full-capacity output.'

8. The core of Keynesian macroeconomics is that investment expenditures are independent in the sense that they do not adjust passively to savings decisions. The notion that investment is the driving force in the economic growth process has been emphasized by J. Robinson (1956, 1962), and Marglin (1984) regards an independent investment function as the key feature of Keynesian growth theory. What this 'independence' exactly means, however, is subject to debate. While Kalecki devoted much of his energy to developing different investment functions, estimating them and analysing their macroeconomic implications, Vickers (1992) concludes that investment is fundamentally unpredictable.

2. Profits and unemployment: is there an equilibrium rate of unemployment in the long run?

2.1 INTRODUCTION

Most of the literature on European unemployment is built on the premise that there has been an increase in the long-run equilibrium rate of unemployment, the NAIRU. This increase in the NAIRU, so the story goes, is caused by wage-push factors like an overgenerous welfare state, long and durable unemployment benefits and job protection measures. In short, by labour market inflexibility, which translates into real wage rigidity. In this chapter we develop a Post-Keynesian growth model that explicitly treats the labour market and allows for an effect of unemployment on income distribution. This will allow us to investigate the claims of the NAIRU theory.

In particular we seek answers to the following questions. Is there an equilibrium rate of unemployment in the long run? If so, can it be reduced by increasing labour market flexibility? Is it independent of demand?

The chapter is organized as follows. In the remainder of this introduction, the core features of the NAIRU model are summarized and the differences to our own assumptions are clarified. In section 2, Keynesian growth models are discussed, with a particular focus on the distinction between Robinsonian (full-capacity) models and Kaleckian (excess-capacity) models. The Marglin-Bhaduri model is the most modern formulation of the latter and forms the basis for the growth model to be developed in section 3. We add an employment function (Okun's law) and a distribution function according to which unemployment and the profit share are positively related. Then we examine the short-run and long-run equilibrium conditions and check their stability. Section 4 concludes.

2.1.1 The NAIRU Model: A Preview

The NAIRU theory is discussed in depth in Chapter 3. However, the predominance of the NAIRU model in the debate of European unemployment forms the motivation for the alternative Post-Keynesian model we will propose in the following chapters. Therefore we will summarize the core features of the NAIRU here and contrast the crucial assumptions where our model differs.

In the NAIRU model, effective demand determines actual unemployment in the short run. The deviation of the actual unemployment from the equilibrium unemployment determines unanticipated inflation. In the short run the system therefore has Keynesian features, but only because of the difference between expected and actual prices and wages. Since their expectations have been frustrated, people will alter their behaviour and adjust to higher price levels. The long run is here defined as the state where expectations are fulfilled. Income claims then are equilibrated through the rate of unemployment. There will be only one level of unemployment that renders income claims of workers and capitalists consistent. Any attempt by fiscal or monetary policy to move unemployment away from this equilibrium level is doomed. It will temporarily lower unemployment, thus causing inflation which through the real balance effect undermines demand until the equilibrium rate of unemployment is reached again. The NAIRU depends on wage-push factors and the mark-up, but not autonomous demand.

In the long run the model has neoclassical features, but a non-clearing labour market. It is neo-classical in the sense that the labour market dominates the goods market. The goods market adjusts passively to the corresponding 'natural' output level through the real balance effect. Note that the NAIRU plays a twofold role in this model: in the short run it determines inflation (in conjunction with actual unemployment), in the long run it determines actual unemployment and output.

To clarify, let us summarize the most important features of the NAIRU model:

1. Unemployment has an effect on real wages.
2. Distribution does not effect the level of demand.
3. The real balance effect has an expansionary effect.
4. In the long run the system is anchored in a long-run equilibrium rate of unemployment.
5. The long-term equilibrium rate of unemployment is independent of demand factors.
6. Higher wage flexibility and lower bargaining power of workers reduce unemployment.

We accept the first point. The effect of unemployment has, in our view, incorrectly been neglected by Keynesians. We reject the second point. Income distribution has a double effect on demand. Wage income and profit income do have different savings propensities; profits are an important inducement (and a source of finance) for investment. We reject the third point (the real balance effect), a standard assumption in Keynesian models. The model we develop is a model of the real economy. Points four to six are not assumptions, but propositions that we will investigate in our model.

2.2 POST-KEYNESIAN GROWTH THEORIES

The aim of this section is to provide an overview of Post-Keynesian growth theories. Since the mid 1980s there has been a renewed interest in growth theories, but of a distinctly non-Keynesian flavour. New growth theory focuses on the contribution of knowledge and innovation to economic growth while having a neo-classical macroeconomic underpinning. Demand plays no independent role and, more to the point, savings determine investment. The principles of Keynesian economics seem to have been forgotten. Contrary to this, the present chapter discusses the basics of Keynesian growth models. At the very core of these models are an independent investment function and saving propensities that differ between income classes (Kaldor savings equation). Thus the distribution of income between capital and labour plays a crucial role.

Post-Keynesian growth models however are not easily accessible. In particular, there is not a single Post-Keynesian model, but a whole variety, with different, sometimes contradictory assumptions. For example Kaldor assumes full employment, which has been denounced as 'more neo-classical than neo-Keynesian' (Marglin 1984, p. 534). Kaleckians emphasize the role of variable capacity utilization, whereas this has not been an issue for Robinson's equilibrium analysis. (These differences are summarized in Table 2.1.) The aim of this chapter is to provide an overview and a structure for the varying models.[1]

Two major groups of Post-Keynesian growth models are distinguished: one going back to Joan Robinson and another originating from Michal Kalecki. Both are Keynesian in that they have an independent investment function and Kaldor saving function. The difference lies in that the Robinsonian model assumes full capacity utilization whereas the Kaleckian model does not. This difference turns out to be crucial. In Robinsonian models income distribution is an endogenous variable and higher profits go together with faster growth. Kaleckian models on the other hand, having an additional degree of freedom through variable capacity utilization, need to be complemented with an exogenous theory of income distribution and allow for regimes where higher wages lead to higher growth.

Table 2.1 Varying assumptions in Post-Keynesian growth models

		Employment	
		Full employment	Unemployment
Capacity	Full capacity	Kaldor (1960)	Robinson (in equilibrium)
	Excess capacity		Kalecki

The section is structured as follows. First the basic short run Keynes-Kalecki model with exogenous investment demand, which serves as a benchmark for the subsequent growth models, is developed. Second the case for independent investment is made and some clarifications as to the notion of the long run are provided. Third, the basic Robinsonian model is presented. Fourth the rationales for variable capacity utilization is introduced and the Kaleckian model incorporating variable capacity utilization summarized. To simplify the exposition we focus on the goods market only.

2.2.1 The Principle of Effective Demand in the Short Run

At the core of Keynesian macroeconomics is the principle of effective demand, that is, that investment determines savings. In contrast to classical and neo-classical economics the variable adjusting savings and investment is aggregate income and not the rate of interest:

> The Keynesian models . . . are designed to project into the long period the central thesis of the General Theory, that firms are free, within wide limits, to accumulate as they please, and that the rate of saving of the economy as a whole accommodates itself to the rate of investment that they decree.
>
> (Robinson 1962, p. 82)

2.2.1.1 Investment

To develop a theory of growth, Keynesian models then need an explicit theory of investment. This is dealt with in the next section. Here, dealing with the short run, we merely posit that investment is exogenously determined, which can be justified on the grounds that investment projects take time to be realized. In other words, this period's investment expenditures are determined on last period's investment decisions. Thus investment demand in the short run simply is:

$$I = \bar{I} \tag{SR 1}$$

2.2.1.2 Saving

Different types of income are associated with different savings propensities. This can be argued on microeconomic as well as on institutional grounds. Since workers typically have lower incomes than capitalists they will consume a higher share of their income. This would be the microeconomic argument. However, Kaldor insisted that the reason for the different saving propensities lies in the difference between workers and firms, not workers and capitalists. Firms will withhold part of the profits in order to finance investment (Kaldor 1957, Kaldor 1956).

For convenience, we will later assume that the saving propensity out of wage income is zero, which was the original proposition of Kalecki and can be substantiated empirically (for example Bowles and Boyer 1995). However the crucial assumption is that the saving propensity out of profits is higher than that out of wages.[2] Hence the saving function will typically have the form:

$$S = s_w (Y - R) + s_R R$$

Kaldor savings function, where Y is income, R profits, S savings and s_W and s_R the saving rates of wage and profit income respectively.

And in the simplified form, where saving occurs out of profits only:

$$S = s_R R \tag{SR 2}$$

2.2.1.3 Wages and the labour market

The labour market in Keynesian models is unlike other markets: the labour market equilibrium is not an equilibrium in the usual sense of market clearing. The number of workers employed depends on the level of economic activity, that is the equilibrium in the goods market; and wages are understood as conventional wages, either in nominal (Keynes) or in relative (Kalecki) terms, rather than as the outcome of market clearing. While Keynes and Kalecki agree on the rejection of the neo-classical market clearing on the labour market and have other similarities, their theories differ in ways that do translate into crucial differences for long-run analysis. In a nutshell, in Keynes, with money wages given, macroeconomic conditions determine income distribution, whereas in Kalecki the income distribution is given by the institutional setting.

Keynes assumed given money wages. Workers and capitalist cannot bargain over real wages, but only over nominal wages (Keynes 1936, p. 13). These are thought to be determined by the respective income positions of different groups of workers. Hence the idea of a real wage equilibrating the labour market is rejected, because real wages are not, and cannot in a decentralized economy be, subject to wage bargaining. A cut in money wages will lead to a decrease in nominal demand and, as a consequence, in the price level. Real wages are the *ex post* outcome of nominal wage agreements and prices determined on the goods market, strongly effected by aggregate demand. Wage cuts are therefore more likely to result in a deflationary spiral rather than in expansionary real wage reductions. Implicit in this argument is that prices adjust faster to lower demand than investment to the potentially higher profits if prices remained at their pre-wage cut level (as pointed out by Kalecki 1936 in an early review of the General Theory) and that the price level does not have by itself an expansionary effect through a real balance effect. Hence the asymmetry between inflation and deflation and Keynes's recommendation to pursue inflationary policy if real wages are 'too high'.

Kalecki is explicitly assuming imperfect competition and mark-up pricing by firms. For him the profit share, and inversely the wage share, are determined by firms' mark-up. The mark-up is determined by the degree of monopoly, which in turn is determined by the degree of competition, the extent of non-price competition and the organizational strength of labour. Hence the real or relative income distribution is determined by structural factors, that are fixed in the short run. As for Keynes, a change in money wages has little real effect for Kalecki, since firms will lower their prices accordingly and thereby re-establish the conventional income distribution. In either case, changes in money wages translate into changes in the price level rather than changes of the real wage.

It is worth emphasizing that a conventional wage is not *eo ipso* in contradiction with the wage being equal to the marginal product of labour. Marginal productivity wages are just another way of stating the profit maximization condition, if standard production functions are assumed (which many Post-Keynesians are unwilling to do). In any case, the neo-classical chain of causation is reversed: in a Keynesian model it is the conventional wage in combination with demand factors determining the marginal productivity of labour instead of the other way round.[3]

2.2.1.4 The simple short-run model

Putting savings (or inversely consumption) and investment together, we get equilibrium income:

$$Y = I + wN + C_R$$

$$Y = I + (1 - \pi)Y + (1 - s_R)\pi Y$$

where Y, I, w and N, following conventional notation, denote income, investment, wages, and employment respectively and $\pi \equiv R/Y$, the exogenously given profit share, and C_R the consumption by capitalists. At the equilibrium level of income we get the Kaleckian multiplier

$$Y^* = \frac{1}{s_R \pi} \bar{I} \qquad \text{(SR 3)}$$

2.2.1.5 Key findings

The two results that will provide the yardstick to evaluate Keynesian growth models are firstly, the inverse relationship between the savings propensity and output, and secondly, the inverse relationship between the profit share and output. Both the savings propensity and the profit share appear in the denominator of the equilibrium value of income. Savings in this model are a leakage; the smaller the leakage, the higher output will be. A similar argument applies to the profit share. Since profits are associated with a higher savings propensity they exhibit higher leakages than wage income (which is assumed to be fully consumed).

The question of how, if at all, the Keynesian argument of effective demand can be maintained in the 'long run' is contested. Before diving into the discussion of long-run Keynesian models we will briefly review the investment function.

2.2.2 A Keynesian Theory of Investment

Unlike neo-classical economics, Keynesian economics regards accumulation, or investment, as the variable that drives the growth process. In neoclassical growth theory, investment effectively ceases to exist in the long run, with the capital stock adjusting passively to changes in relative prices and output growth. Moreover, in many models people are assumed to save in capital goods and therefore the demand for investment coincides with the supply of savings. Contrary to this, in Keynesian economics investment is understood to be determined independently from savings. This presupposes that investment is not normally constrained by the availability of savings,[4] but by the possibility of mobilizing credit (Pollin 1997). Usually this analysis of the real sector is complemented by assuming a flexible financial system and an endogenous money supply. Thus the structure of the financial system becomes important. Unlike in neoclassical theory, internal and external finance are treated asymmetrically. For small firms especially it is often difficult to obtain credit. For the purpose of this chapter, however, we will ignore financial issues.

Though the 'independent investment function' is at the core of Keynesian economics, there is no agreement on the precise form of the investment function. In the most general formulation investment is determined by the present value of the expected future income stream – where 'expected' is the critical word. Since the future is fundamentally uncertain and open, there is no objective way of forming expectations, rather it is animal spirits, conventions and psychology that determine profit expectations and thus investment spending. Hence the crucial question in Keynesian theory of investment becomes, what determines expectations about future revenues? And, how can a realistic investment function thus be modelled?

2.2.2.1 Uncertainty (Shackle, Vickers)

To some Keynesians the formation of expectations is a genuinely creative act, hence investment cannot be predicted:

> . . . intended (designed, *ex ante*) investment is a laws to itself, dependent (if at all) on too elusive and involved a skein of subtle influences, too eagerly clutching at the straws of suggestion whirled along by 'the news', to be ever captured in any intelligible, let alone determinable equation. It is not really the shapes of the curves, but their broad bodily shifts and deformation, that contain the meaning of the argument. (Shackle quoted in Vickers 1992, p. 446).

Thus one current of Keynesians holds that investment demand is simply unpredictable, continually subject to sudden shifts. This does not allow for a meaningful long-run theory, but it privileges short-run analysis. Since we are interested in the former, we do not follow this line of thought. Uncertainty is a condition of human behaviour and not the end of the story on investment.

2.2.2.2 From uncertainty to conventions and institutions (Crotty)

Crotty (1990, 1992) argues that Keynes combined his argument of fundamental uncertainty with a theory of conventional behaviour. Since people are forced to act in an uncertain world, they will adopt and submit to conventions of behaviour, rules of thumb and the like, not the least because they cannot tolerate admitting that they 'simply don't know' what the consequences of their actions will be. Furthermore, institutions and long-term contracts will be established to mediate and soften unpredictable shocks and an uncertain future. Once established, such conventions and institutions give rise to periods of continuity, order and stability – for certain periods – but may violently break down at other times. Hence Keynesian economics has to be 'institutionally specific and historically contingent' (Crotty 1992, p. 495). Much the same is true for a Keynesian investment function.

2.2.2.3 Long-run equilibrium and historical time

In the analysis of long-run steady state conditions uncertainty ceases to play a central role. Since steady states reproduce themselves, there is nothing to be uncertain about. Asserting uncertainty will then not do the job of guaranteeing an independent investment function – if we subscribe to the standard view of what the long run is. For Keynesians this has been a reason to criticize the notion of the long run rather than to give up the independent investment function. In particular Joan Robinson has argued that the standard notion of the long run operates in a framework of logical time that is inadequate for a realistic growth theory because it does away with the unpredictability of the future that economic agents are confronted with at any point in time.

To elaborate, in neo-classical economics the notion of a long-run equilibrium refers to a theoretical point where all adjustment processes have taken place – including the adjustment to optimal capital stock – subject to some deep parameters like preferences or technology. The strong Keynesian assertion is that investment may cause forces that push the economy on a growth path that is inconsistent with the long-run equilibrium in logical time. For this to happen these 'forces', that is demand effects, unleashed by investment have to be stronger than the forces that pull the economy towards its long-run equilibrium, that is relative factor prices.[5] This assumption will be maintained throughout this chapter.

For the purpose of this chapter it might have been helpful to use the term 'medium run' rather than the long run, to draw attention to the differences from the conventional usage of the notion of the long run; however since it is a rather unfamiliar term, we will stick with the more familiar notion of the long run. The time horizon we have in mind is a period of a few decades, certainly of the movements between, not within business cycles. Note that for practical purposes most economists refer to five-year averages, that is values that are not due to business cycles, as long-run values. In this sense the Keynesian growth theories discussed here undoubtedly qualify as long-run theories, because they seek to explain economic growth beyond the business cycle. Another minimalist definition of the long run is that the capital stock is endogenous. With this definition, again, Post-Keynesian theory falls under the category of growth theory.

2.2.2.4 Important influences on expected profits (and hence investment)

Even if the investment function has to be institutionally specific, Keynesian economics has identified some key factors that will enter investment function, though with historically varying weights (Mazier et al. 1993). Four factors appear most frequently in the literature:

- Current or past profits as a proxy of future (expected) profits.
- Demand growth (the accelerator).

- The availability of finance, which either brings us back to profits as the source of inside finance or to the structure of the financial system (bank-based financing versus capital market-based financing).
- The rates of return of financial investment, which is the alternative to the acquisition of additional physical capital.

Other factors that are sometimes included are competitive pressure and technological progress. In Chapter 5 we will explore the effects of different relations between shareholders and management as a potential influence on investment. For the purpose of this chapter, which is comparing Robinsonian and Kaleckian growth models, we will focus on the first two factors, profits and demand, since they are determined endogenously in the model whereas the other factors operate as institutional shift variables.

2.2.3 Post-Keynesian Growth I: Robinson Growth (RG)

The growth model considered here goes back to Robinson (1956, 1962) and Kaldor (1957, 1960). Being a Keynesian model, the assumptions of an independent investment function and of a Kaldor savings function are maintained. Implicitly it is assumed that the economy is operating at full capacity; the importance of this will become clear later. Investment depends on profits. The main difference in the formulations by Kaldor and Robinson is that the former assumes full employment. The investment spending then ceases to determine the level of output, but determines the distribution of income (most explicitly in Kaldor 1960). The profit share has to adjust such that the necessary savings are provided. Contrary to this, Robinson insists on the simultaneous determination of accumulation and profits, with full employment as a mere coincidence. What unites both models is the mechanism of adjustment: changes of prices relative to wages. Money wages are given and prices adjust such that the level of profits generates the savings necessary to finance investment. Hence, this model has also been labelled the inflationist model of growth (Lavoie 1992).

We continue to assume that saving comes exclusively out of profits; for convenience s denotes the saving propensity out of profits, $s=s_R$. As for investment, one part of it consists of autonomous investment and the other is a positive function of current profits. What we call autonomous investment here, captures influences other than through profits, which include factors that may be endogenous in other models.[6] Since we are dealing with steady state analysis, current profits are a perfect expectation for future profits. For simplicity, we use a linearized form of the investment function.[7] Since we are dealing with a dynamic model, savings and investment are normalized by the capital stock. Table 2.2 summarizes a simple linear Robinsonian growth model $r \equiv R/K$ denotes the rate of profit.

Table 2.2 A linear Robinsonian growth model

Investment	$g^I = \frac{I}{K} = a + br$	(RG 1)
Savings	$g^S = \frac{S}{K} = sr$	(RG 2)
Equilibrium condition	$g^I = g^S$	(RG 3)

Since we have three equations and three unknowns (g^I, g^S and r) the system can be solved. The corresponding equilibrium values are (we use $g^* = g^I = g^S$):

$$r^* = \frac{a}{s-b} \qquad \text{(RG 4)}$$

$$g^* = a + \frac{ab}{s-b} \qquad \text{(RG 5)}$$

$s - b > 0$ is necessary to guarantee a positive profit rate. This is also the standard stability condition in Keynesian growth models, already noted in Robinson (1956). It asserts that savings are more sensitive to income than investment, if not the system will explode. In what follows we will assume that this condition holds.

The derivatives with respect to the saving propensity of capital income and autonomous accumulation are:

$$\frac{\partial r^*}{\partial s} = \frac{-a}{(s-b)^2} < 0 \qquad \text{(RG 6)}$$

$$\frac{\partial r^*}{\partial a} = \frac{1}{(s-b)} > 0 \qquad \text{(RG 7)}$$

$$\frac{\partial g^*}{\partial s} = \frac{-ab}{(s-b)^2} < 0 \qquad \text{(RG 8)}$$

$$\frac{\partial g^*}{\partial a} = \frac{s}{(s-b)} > 0 \qquad \text{(RG 9)}$$

This long-run model preserves one of the Keynesian insights of the short run and inverts the other: a higher saving propensity lowers the rate of growth, but higher growth goes together with lower wages. Observe that equilibrium growth, here proxied by the rate of growth of the capital stock, has savings in the denominator. Hence the negative relation between saving propensity and growth (RG 8). The other key finding of the short run however is not maintained. Higher growth rates are associated with higher profitability. Unlike the short run, there is no exogenous income distribution. Hence the causality does not run from income distribution to accumulation but the other way. If capitalists invest more, that is if autonomous investment increases, they will receive higher profits (see RG 7).

This is not a surprise. Since full capacity utilization was assumed (implicitly), the economy is at its production possibility frontier, which at the same time is the profit–wage frontier. Thus there is a clear trade-off between wages and profits. Further, since saving only occurs out of profits, the latter have to rise to allow for higher accumulation. The savings equation holds the key: rewriting it as a profit function ($r = g/s$), it becomes evident that (1) for a given saving propensity, higher growth and higher profits go hand in hand, and (2) for a given level of growth, the lower the propensity to save, the higher the profit rate has to be.

In other words: being on the production possibility frontier, real wages have to be reduced in order to redirect resources from the production of consumption goods to capital goods. Changes in the profit rate are the mechanism by which savings adjust to investment. The way this redistribution from wages to savings takes place (though not modelled explicitly here) is through inflation. Economically, if the demand for investment goods rises, their price will rise too, which initiates an inflationary process through which wages, fixed in money terms, get eroded.

2.2.3.1 A variation without consequences: the accelerator

One might argue that the reason for the result that higher profits and higher accumulation go hand in hand is due to the fact that there is no accelerator term in the investment function. To illustrate that the crucial assumption is the one of full capacity utilization, and not the lack of an accelerator term in the investment function, we will modify the investment function by incorporating a demand variable.

$$\text{investment} \quad g^I = \frac{I}{K} = a + br + cg \qquad \text{(RG 2')}$$

where c is the accelerator and g the equilibrium growth rate.

The equilibrium values then are:

$$r^* = \frac{a}{s(1-c) - b} \qquad \text{(RG 4')}$$

$$g^* = a + \frac{ab}{s(1-c) - b} \qquad \text{(RG 5')}$$

Thus, again, higher accumulation is possible only with a higher profit rate. The point of this exercise was to clarify that it is not the accelerator itself that allows higher wages to be conducive to growth, but that this mechanism works only in conjunction with flexible capacity utilization.

Within the Post-Keynesian debate two main criticism against the Robinsonian approach have been articulated. First, that the assumption of exogenous money wages is not meaningful beyond a short-run analysis. The longer the time horizon of the analysis, the greater the ability to bargain over real wages. However, the model presented above has no room for an exogenous determination of the distribution of income. There are only three equations and three unknowns, thus the system is determined. Thus income distribution is determined in the goods market, with no room for the labour market or institutional factors to influence it. Second, higher growth is possible only at a higher profit rate, which is the exact opposite of the short-run model. This latter criticism led to renewed interest in the Kaleckian growth model in the 1980s.

2.2.4 Post-Keynesian Growth II: Kaleckian Growth (KG)

The model presented here has a long line of history: it goes back to Kalecki (1971) and Steindl (1952), and was reformulated recently by Rowthorn (1982) and Dutt (1984). The version presented here is based on Marglin and Bhaduri (1990). The Marglin-Bhaduri model is more general and includes the earlier neo-Kaleckian models by Rowthorn and Dutt as special cases. The difference is seemingly technical, using the profit rate rather than the profit share, but has important implications. We will return to the Rowthorn-Dutt model in a digression later.

The key difference between the Kaleckian model and the Robinson type model is variable capacity utilization. This may sound unfamiliar in a growth model, and will therefore be discussed in some more detail in the next section. The effects of this assumption are important. Income distribution is then not determined by investment, but is set autonomously. A reduction in the profit share can foster growth because the consumption propensities of workers will cause an increase in output and capacity utilization. If the capacity effect on investment is stronger than the profit effect then accumulation will speed up.

2.2.4.1 Variable capacity utilization

There can be no doubt that capacity utilization varies over the business cycle. Changes in output are not so much caused by changes in the equipment and workers hired, but by changes in their productivities (both capital and labour productivity move procyclically) as determined by demand.

However growth models usually employ a full capacity assumption on the grounds that excess capacity would be costly to maintain and thus competed away.

It was Steindl (1952), building on Kalecki's work, who argued forcefully that this need not be true in an economy dominated by monopolistic competition. The existence of excess capacity will be the rule rather than the exception in such an economy.[8] Oligopolists certainly have the power to maintain idle capacity, since they are price setters. Facing a reduction in demand they can keep up prices while reducing only quantities. But why should they maintain these idle capacities?

By now, various justifications have been given (an overview is provided by Lavoie 1992, pp. 124ff). The most prominent reason is uncertainty. Firms will hold excess capacity to maintain flexibility in the face of unexpected events, much the same way households hold cash (Steindl 1952). Second, oligopolists may keep excess capacity as a deterrent to entry by new or outside firms. Third, there may be a variety of technical reasons such as indivisibilities in the production process (Kurz 1990) that may make it impossible to tailor machines to match production exactly. Or, if overworking machines makes them deteriorate quickly, it may be rational to keep excess capacity. Finally, excess capacity may be a result of the irreversibility of many investment projects (Crotty 1992). Since they cannot be undone easily, idle capacity may be existing simply because it is too expensive to remove it, and can be put back to use if demand suddenly increases.

2.2.4.2 The model

The Kaleckian growth model[9] introduces variable capacity utilization. Thus we have one more variable to explain and the model is closed by setting income distribution exogenously. A simple linear Kaleckian growth model[9] is summarized in Table 2.3.

Table 2.3 A linear Kaleckian growth model

Investment	$g^I = \frac{I}{K} = a + b\pi + cz$	(KG 1)
Savings	$g^S = \frac{S}{K} = s\pi z$	(KG 2)
Equilibrium condition	$g^I = g^S$	(KG 3)

where
z capital productivity (Y/K) interpreted as capacity utilization
π profit share R/Y

Assuming constant technology we can interpret capital productivity as a measure of capacity utilization.[10] The saving function is basically unaltered ($S=s_R R$), but is expressed now as a function of the profit share and capacity utilization.

The investment function now consists of an autonomous part, and reacts positively to profits and to capacity utilization. The profit share is used as a measure of profitability to highlight the distributional influence on investment (more on this below).

Since we are not interested here in any specific formulation of the theory of distribution we will, for now, assume that the profit share is exogenously given. It could of course be endogenized, for example as a function of capacity utilization as in Marglin and Bhaduri (1990). In the next section we propose a way to integrate the labour market into this model.

$$\text{income distribution} \quad \pi=\bar{\pi} \tag{KG 4}$$

The equilibrium values and some comparative statics are:

$$z^*=\frac{a+b\pi}{s\pi-c} \tag{KG 5}$$

$$g^*=a+b\pi+c\frac{a+b\pi}{s\pi-c} \tag{KG 6}$$

$$\frac{\partial z^*}{\partial \pi}=\frac{-bc-sa}{(s\pi-c)^2}<0 \tag{KG 7}$$

We are able to sign equation (KG 7) if we assume $a>0$, that is that autonomous accumulation is positive. This could hardly be otherwise. If capitalists do save part of their income, then there have to be autonomous expenditures to allow for investment equals savings.

$$\frac{\partial g^*}{\partial \pi}=b+c\frac{\partial z}{\partial \pi} \tag{KG 8}$$

Note that (KG 8) cannot be signed a priori. We thus get the following interesting result: an increase in the profit share will decrease capacity utilization, but its effect on capacity growth, that is the growth of capital stock, is ambiguous. There will be a positive capacity effect and a negative profit (share) effect on investment. What the net effect will be cannot be answered a priori. Thus, two regimes are possible depending on the relative strength of capacity and profit effects in the investment function. If the capacity effect outweighs the profit effect, growth is wage-led. If the profit effect is stronger than the capacity effect, growth is profit-led.

Table 2.4 Wage-led and profit-led regimes

Wage-led regime	Profit-led regime
$b < c\dfrac{\partial z}{\partial \pi}$	$b > c\dfrac{\partial z}{\partial \pi}$
$\dfrac{\partial g}{\partial \pi} < 0$	$\dfrac{\partial g}{\partial \pi} > 0$

2.2.4.3 A digression

Earlier versions of the Kaleckian model, for example Rowthorn (1982) and Dutt (1984), used the profit rate rather than the profit share in the investment function. The question whether the profit rate or the profit share is used in the investment function may sound like a technical detail, but it is not. As we will see, it automatically gives rise to a wage-led regime. If the investment function is written as:

$$\text{investment} \qquad g^I = \frac{I}{K} = a + br + cz \qquad \text{(KG 2')}$$

this is tantamount to assuming that the capacity effect always outweighs the profit effect. We can rewrite the investment function as:

$$g^I = a + b\pi z + cz = a + (b\pi + c)z$$

Solving this the system now (and leaving the profit share exogenous) we get

$$g^* = a + \frac{a(b\pi + c)}{s\pi - b\pi - c} \qquad \text{(KG 6')}$$

as the equilibrium growth and

$$\frac{\partial g}{\partial \pi} = \frac{-acs}{(s\pi - b\pi - c)^2} < 0 \qquad \text{(KG 8')}$$

as the derivative of growth with respect to the profit share, which is negative.

The intuition behind this result is as follows: if higher capacity utilization rates at a given profit rate induce higher investment, this implies that capitalists are not bothered by lower profit shares. Since we assumed that profit rates are constant and that capacity utilization increased, profit shares must have fallen. Hence a redistribution from profits to wages will affect investment through the capacity effect (caused by the higher consumption propensity of wage incomes), but through the profit effect only if the profit rate falls.

2.2.4.4 Summary

Since capacity utilization is introduced as a new variable, the Kaleckian model has one more degree of freedom, which is filled by a profit share equation, here taken to be fixed exogenously. The current model has three equations in three unknowns. Hence the wage share can rise now, increasing capacity utilization and even raising the profit rate. An increase in wages (in the wage share to be exact), can push the economy towards the profit–wage frontier: distribution is not a zero sum game any more. However wage increases will only have this effect if the capacity effect on investment (accelerator) is stronger than the profit effect.

2.3 IS THERE AN EQUILIBRIUM RATE OF UNEMPLOYMENT IN THE LONG RUN? A KALECKIAN APPROACH

The Post-Keynesian growth models discussed above concentrate exclusively on the goods market and, by design, fail to analyse the labour market and the feedback unemployment may have on distribution. This relation between the goods markets and the labour markets is what we turn to in this section. In particular, it is examined whether actual unemployment is anchored by some long-run equilibrium rate of unemployment.

These questions pose themselves in a very different form in the Robinsonian model and in the Kaleckian one. The Robinsonian growth model is essentially closed and there is no room for a feedback from labour markets, other than the extreme cases. In the Kaleckian model, on the other hand, since income distribution was assumed to be exogenous, there is room for unemployment and its effects on income distribution to be incorporated.

The main part of this section will propose and analyse a simple Kaleckian growth model that is augmented by an employment function and a distribution function. A reduced form of the Marglin-Bhaduri model is taken as a starting point, since it is the most flexible of these growth models. Throughout our analysis we will therefore have to distinguish between profit-led and wage-led regimes. We will carefully analyse the equilibrium values, their existence and whether they are stable, for each of these regimes. The questions we seek to answer are whether there exists a stable long-run equilibrium rate of unemployment and, if so, what it depends on.

This section is organized as follows. First the role of unemployment in the Robinsonian model is briefly discussed. Second the barebone Kaleckian model *cum* labour market is presented. Third the equilibrium conditions in the short run are analysed. Fourth the long run is discussed, and, fifth, our findings with respect the question whether there exists a long-run equilibrium rate of unemployment are summarized.

2.3.1 Unemployment in the Robinsonian Model

It is no coincidence that our discussion of Post-Keynesian growth models so far has got by without mentioning labour markets. The Robinsonian growth model is centred around the equilibration of savings and investment through changes in the income distribution. Labour markets play a secondary role and there is no adjustment mechanism that guarantees the gravitation of the economy to a full employment level. However, this is not to say that Robinson (1956, 1962) neglected to realize the implications that her growth model would have for secular movements of unemployment – far from this, the relation between the warranted rate of growth given by the goods markets and the natural rate, that is the one that would guarantee stable unemployment, is used to derived a rich variety of macroeconomic regimes.

Employment follows the growth on goods market passively, that is employment grows in line with economic growth. Thus unemployment will either constantly grow or fall unless the growth rate determined on the goods market happens to coincide with the growth late of the labour force. The latter was labelled the natural rate of growth by Harrod. This situation of a coincidence of actual growth and natural growth at the level of full employment was labelled the 'Golden Age' by Robinson and considered unlikely to materialize.

More likely, macroeconomic regimes would occur where the two rates differ and thus unemployment would continuously increase or decrease for prolonged periods of time (until animal spirits, investment policies or savings propensities changed). Remarkably there is no feedback from the level of unemployment to income distribution, that is there is no reserve army effect. This is a central feature of the Robinsionian model, since its underlying theory of income distribution is one where income distribution is determined on the goods market via investment decisions and saving differentials.

However, a constant rise and fall in unemployment are not symmetrical. Whereas unemployment can rise for prolonged periods, it cannot fall for too long (unless the initial level of unemployment was exceptionally high) without running into an 'inflation barrier'. The inflation barrier is normally the level of full employment, though according to the institutional setting, in particular the power of organized labour, it can also be reached earlier. At the inflation barrier the desire of capitalists to invest is inconsistent with workers' willingness and ability to accept the implied real wages. The result will be inflation, even hyperinflation.

Thus the feedback from the labour market to the goods market is weak, indirect and asymmetric. Rising unemployment has simply no feedback, nor has shrinking unemployment *per se*. Only once the level of full employment is reached, or a little earlier, then this inflation barrier puts an effective stop to further accumulation. Below full employment, however, there is no feedback. Thus there cannot be a tendency towards full employment. More generally there cannot be an equilibrium rate of unemployment, since there is no adjustment mechanism that would bring it about.

It may seem unrealistic to assume that unemployment could rise or fall over prolonged periods without having profound repercussions on macroeconomic variables. Marglin (1984) argued that Keynesian and Marxian growth theories should do away with the notion of a well-defined labour supply – in particular in the context of growth theory. Over periods of decades there are reserves that the capitalist sector can tap into. Historically these have been hidden unemployment in agriculture, (initially) low female labour market participation and migrant workers. Conversely in the case of rising unemployment, other sectors of the economy will absorb these unemployed workers, or at least part of them. Thus there is no rigid labour supply over longer time periods, at best it is endogenous.

Having a shorter time horizon in mind than Marglin, the following sections will propose a different route. A simplified Kaleckian model will be used to incorporate an effect of unemployment on income distribution, that is a reserve army effect, and analyse the macroeconomic dynamics this gives rise to.

2.3.2 Growth, Distribution and Unemployment: A Simple Kaleckian Model

Let us assume a minimalist demand function g:

$$g_t = a_0 + a_1\pi_t \tag{2.1}$$

where g and π are growth and profit share respectively, with their subscripts denoting time. This is a simplification compared to the Marglin-Bhaduri model, but still captures its essence by allowing for wage-led and profit-led regimes.[11] a_1 is our shorthand for equation (KG8). The sign of a_1 can be either positive or negative, giving rise to a profit-led or wage-led regime respectively. a_0 captures the effects of all other variables influencing growth.

Note that if we follow the Kaleckian line of reasoning (2.1) is an IS-curve. Equation (2.1) can be also derived from other theories. Moreover, a negative correlation between growth and inequality is a stylized fact in growth theory (Temple 1999), although there is no agreement why. The political economy of growth argument is that high inequality leads to political instability which decreases investment (Alesina and Perotti 1996) or blocks the appropriate use of productive resources (Rodrik 1998).

Distributional equilibrium, a result of wage bargaining (see for example Sen and Dutt 1993) is given by

$$\pi_t = d_0 + d_2 u_t \tag{2.2}$$

where u is the unemployment rate. By equation (2.2) we capture the disciplinary effect unemployment has on wages, or what we call the reserve army effect. d_2 will be positive. This is consistent with the wage curve (Blanchflower and Oswald 1994).

The change in the unemployment rate is given by

$$\Delta u_t = n - g_t \tag{2.3}$$

where n is the growth of the labour force, assumed to be constant. (2.3) is a version of Okun's Law, without technical progress. In the language of Harrod, g is the warranted rate of growth and n the natural rate of growth. Taylor (1996) chooses to incorporate unemployment differently into the Marglin-Bhaduri model. He has unemployment as a function of capacity utilization rather than of growth. Ideally we would like to have both effects in the model, but this turns out to complicate matters a lot. With respect to European unemployment the dependence on growth is empirically more relevant. As a stylized fact, Europe experienced a shift of the employment – capacity utilization trade-off, rather than a movement along it (Bean 1994, Rowthorn 1995).

Equations (2.1)–(2.3) summarize the model. The goods market equilibrium determines the change in the rate of unemployment, rather than the level of unemployment. Therefore the full effects of unemployment on the goods market will only be felt in the long run.

In the short run, that is with a given rate of last year's rate of unemployment, the profit function becomes:

$$\pi_t = d_0 + d_2 u_{t-1} + d_2(n - g_t) \tag{2.4}$$

Note that our notion of the short run (and accordingly of the long run) here differs from the one employed in the NAIRU model. There the short run describes a state where expectations may diverge from actual values. Here it designates a state where past values of unemployment are taken as given.

2.3.3 Short-Run Equilibrium

Solving (2.1) and (2.4) we get

$$g_t{}^{**} = \frac{a_0 + a_1(d_0 + d_2u_{t-1} + d_2n)}{1 + a_1d_2} \tag{2.5}$$

and

$$\pi_t{}^{**} = \frac{d_0 - d_2a_0 + d_2u_{t-1} + d_2n}{1 + a_1d_2} \tag{2.6}$$

Equations (2.5) and (2.6) give the short-run equilibrium of the goods market. Note that both of them depend on last year's unemployment rate.

2.3.3.1 Stability in the short run

We interpret both the growth function (g(π), equation 2.1) and the profit share function (π(*g*), equation 2.4) as equilibrium loci. The former is a goods market equilibrium curve, the latter a bargaining equilibrium. We expect any disequilibrium values of g and π to have a tendency to return to their respective equilibrium loci, $g(\pi)$ and $\pi(g)$. This gives an adjustment behaviour of the following form:

$$\dot{g} = \lambda_g\,(g(\pi) - g)$$

$$\dot{\pi} = \lambda_\pi\,(\pi(g) - \pi)$$

where $g(\pi)$ and $\pi(g)$ are equations (2.1) and (2.4) respectively and we assume both λ_g and λ_π to be positive. We then get the Jacobian:

$$J = \begin{bmatrix} -\lambda_g & \lambda_g a_1 \\ -\lambda_\pi d_2 & -\lambda_\pi \end{bmatrix} \tag{2.7}$$

For the equilibrium to be stable trace$(J)<0$ and det$(J)>0$ have to hold.

$$tr(J) = -\lambda_g - \lambda_\pi < 0$$

$$det(J) = \lambda_g\lambda_\pi(1 + a_1d_2)$$

Signing these expressions is straightforward for *tr*(*J*), which is negative, but not for *det*(*J*). Here we have to distinguish three cases, the profit-led regime and two wage-led regimes.

I. profit-led regime: $a_1 > 0$
then the equilibrium is always stable since $1 + a_1 d_2 > 0$ holds.
In the wage-led regime $a_1 < 0$ the equilibrium will be stable if

$$1 + a_1 d_2 > 0 \qquad (2.8)$$

holds, or: $a_1 < -1/d_2$.

Since $a_1 = \partial g/\partial\pi|_{IS}$ and $-1/d_2 = \partial g/\partial|\pi_{\pi^*}$ the stability condition requires that theπ-curve is steeper than the *IS*-curve. Graphically, the g^*-curve has to be flatter than the π-curve (see Figure 2.1). Intuitively, a flat *g*-curve means that growth does not react strongly on income distribution and a steep π-curve means that distribution does not react strongly on unemployment.

The two wage-led cases therefore are:
II. short-run stable wage-led regime: $a_1 < 0$ and $1 + a_1 d_2 > 0$, and
III. short-run unstable wage-led regime: $a_1 < 0$ and $1 + a_1 d_2 < 0$.

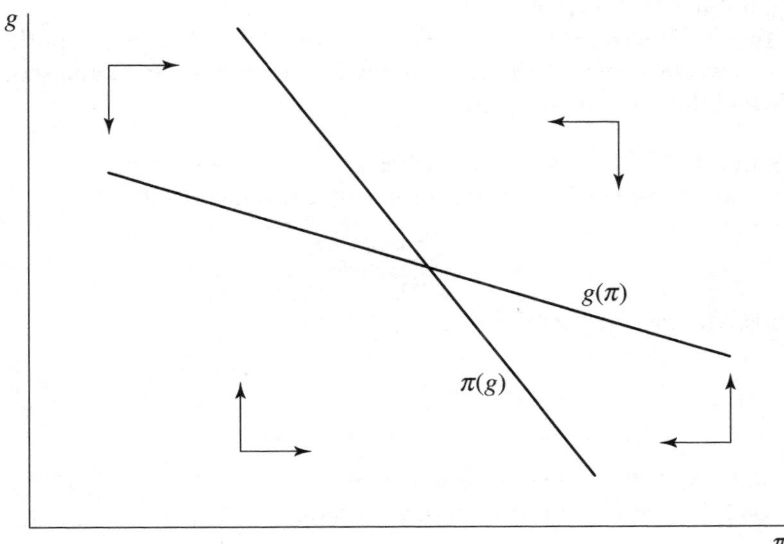

Figure 2.1 Stability in the short run

2.3.3.2 Unemployment in the short run

Having a stable equilibrium on the goods market does not imply a stable unemployment rate. Equation (2.9), derived from (2.3) and (2.5), gives the short-run rate of unemployment:

$$u_t^{**} = \frac{n - a_0 - a_1 d_0}{1 + a_1 d_2} + \frac{1}{1 + a_1 d_2} u_{t-1} \tag{2.9}$$

2.3.4 The Long Run

In the long run, the equilibrium rate of unemployment is:

$$u^{***} = \frac{n - a_0 - a_1 d_0}{a_1 d_2} \tag{2.10}$$

the corresponding long-run equilibrium values of π and g are:

$$\pi^{***} = \frac{n - a_0}{a_1} \tag{2.11}$$

$$g^{***} = n \tag{2.12}$$

(2.12) is unsurprising, since only the equality of warranted and natural rate of growth will allow for a stable rate of unemployment, that is for an equilibrium rate of unemployment.

Two questions arise: first whether the equilibrium values are positive, that is whether there is an economically meaningful solution, and second whether they are stable.

2.3.4.1 Existence of long-run equilibria

First, a positive equilibrium rate of unemployment exists if

$$\frac{n - a_0}{a_1} > d_0 \tag{2.13}$$

holds. Moreover for π to be positive,

$$\frac{n - a_0}{a_1} > 0 \tag{2.13$'$}$$

2.3.4.2 Stability of long-run equilibrium

Second, for stability it turns out that the term

$$\frac{1}{1 + a_1 d_2} \tag{2.14}$$

that is the coefficient of u_{t-1} on u_t is crucial. For convergence towards a stable equilibrium point the absolute value of equation (2.14) has to be less than unity (a detailed discussion of difference equation (2.9) can be found in the Appendix). Again, we will have to distinguish three cases.

Case I, the profit-led regime: $a_1 > 0$.

Note that a profit-led regime requires $n > a_0$, in words: natural growth has to exceed autonomous growth, for a positive profit share to exist.

In the profit-led regime, the denominator of (2.14) is positive and greater than unity, hence the overall expression will be positive and less than unity. Thus the unemployment rate will converge to the equilibrium value.

Case II, a stable (short-run) wage-led regime $a_1 < 0$ and $1 + a_1 d_2 > 0$ (see case II above and equation (2.8) holds).

A positive equilibrium rate of unemployment exists if $n - a_0/a_1 > d_0$ (that is (2.13) holds). The LHS has negative denominator, thus it will be negative unless autonomous accumulation exceeds the natural rate of growth. (The RHS is always positive, therefore a negative LHS is sufficient for no positive equilibrium rate of unemployment rate to exist.) A positive rate of unemployment can thus exist only if autonomous accumulation exceeds the growth of the labour force.

However, if this equilibrium exists it will not be stable. Since the denominator of equation (2.14) is positive, and a_1 is negative, the denominator has to be less than unity. Thus the overall expression (2.14) will be greater than unity. Thus the unemployment rate will not converge, but explode.

Note that, while the economy is moving along a series of stable short-term equilibria, there exists no stable long-run equilibrium, if an equilibrium exists at all.

Case III, an unstable (short-run) wage-led regime $a_1 < 0$ and $1 + a_1 d_2 < 0$ (equation (2.8) does not hold).

Whether this case has a stable long-run equilibrium depends on whether $|1 + a_1 d_2| > 1$. However this is a rather academic exercise since this regime is unstable in the short run and in order to test for long-run stability we have to presuppose that short-run equilibrium values hold.

2.3.4.3 A graphical presentation

The result that the short-run condition for stability is at the same time the long-run condition for instability in the wage-led case may appear counter-intuitive. Thus a graphical presentation may be helpful at this point.

Figure 2.2 presents a short-run stable equilibrium. Assume that $n > g$ at this equilibrium, thus unemployment is rising. In the next period the profit function will shift out because the bargaining power of capitalists increased. Because in a wage-led regime higher profits will lead to lower growth, the gap between natural growth (n) and warranted growth (g) will

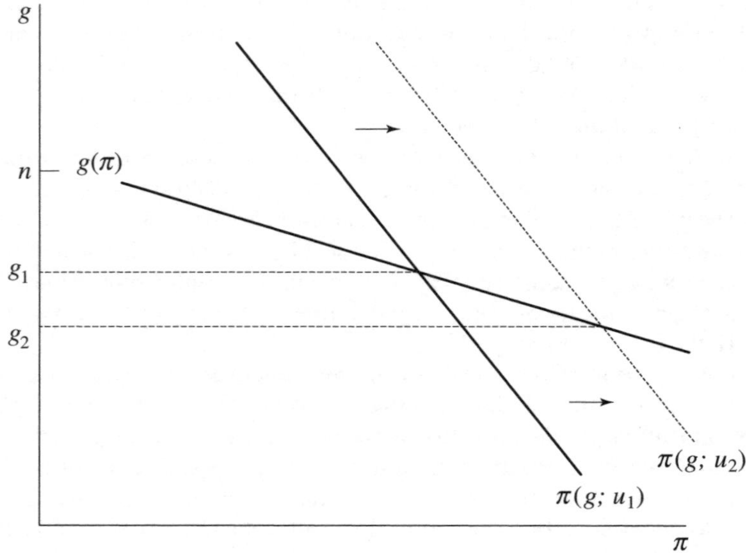

Figure 2.2 Instability of the wage-led regime in the long run

increase even more, leading to more unemployment and higher bargaining power for capitalists. The system will thus move away from equilibrium.

2.3.5 Is There an Equilibrium Rate of Unemployment?

The NAIRU theory posits that unemployment reconciles the income claims of workers and capitalists. If actual unemployment deviates from the NAIRU, it will inevitably return there and drag economic activity along with it. For an equilibrium rate of unemployment to exist in an economically meaningful way, it has to exist *and* be stable. We are now in a position to investigate the claims of the NAIRU model and summarize our results.

The model we used allows for wage-led as well as for profit-led demand regimes. The goods market and the labour market were linked through Okun's law, and unemployment had a positive effect on the profit share. Profit-led and wage-led regimes exhibited very different properties with respect to their long-run behaviour. We sought to establish under what conditions a long-run equilibrium rate of unemployment exists and is stable. Here we will analyse how changes in wage flexibility, the bargaining positions, and autonomous growth affect unemployment. For obvious reasons, we will only look at stable equilibrium solutions. (For unstable solutions comparative statics make no sense since after a shock the system will not gravitate to the new equilibrium position.)

A profit-led demand regime is stable on the goods market in the short run and exhibits a unique equilibrium rate of unemployment and, associated, an equilibrium growth rate, towards which the actual growth rate will converge. This regime seems consistent with the NAIRU, though with different mechanisms for the convergence process at work (profit-led growth rather than real balance effect). It in fact is consistent with the NAIRU story in that there is a stable equilibrium rate of unemployment. More similarities exist when we look at the comparative statics of the equilibrium unemployment rate.

An increase in the unemployment elasticity of wages will lead to a decrease in the long-run rate of unemployment. A higher value of d_2 will increase profits and therefore growth, translating into lower unemployment:

$$\frac{\partial u^{***}}{\partial d_2} = \frac{-a_1(n - a_0 - a_1 d_0)}{(a_1 d_2)^2} < 0 \tag{2.15}$$

An exogenous increase in the bargaining power of capitalists, that is a decrease of union density, will lead to lower unemployment. Again it operates through higher profits inducing higher growth:

$$\frac{\partial u^{***}}{\partial d_0} = \frac{-a_1}{a_1 d_2} < 0 \tag{2.16}$$

A change in autonomous growth, which may be interpreted as autonomous accumulation or exogenous expenditures by the government, will affect equilibrium unemployment. This of course is inconsistent with the NAIRU theory. This finding may be surprising, since the equilibrium growth does not change. Exogenous growth does fully crowd out endogenous accumulation. But it has an indirect effect. Since overall growth is given in equilibrium by the growth of the labour force, higher exogenous growth will inevitably take the place of previously endogenous accumulation. Endogenous accumulation is induced by profits in our model. Since less accumulation is needed now, less profits are needed and therefore less unemployment to generate these profits in the bargaining process:

$$\frac{\partial u^{***}}{\partial a_0} = \frac{-1}{a_1 d_2} < 0 \tag{2.17}$$

Therefore the profit-led case is consistent with the NAIRU story as far as the labour market is concerned. Decreasing workers' bargaining power and increasing wage flexibility will reduce unemployment. However, the equilibrium rate of unemployment is not independent of demand. Changes in autonomous growth will affect unemployment even in the long run.

A wage-led regime can exhibit a stable short-run equilibrium, but this does not lead to a stable long-term equilibrium. If the goods market is stable in the short run, unemployment, and inversely growth, will explode in the long run. In this case there is no equilibrium rate of unemployment that governs the economy in the long run. Kalecki's dictum that the long run is but a succession of short-run equilibria holds true.

Let us be more explicit about what determines unemployment. We will do the comparative statics for the short-run equilibrium rate of unemployment:

$$\frac{\partial u^{**}}{\partial d_2} = (-a_1)\frac{(n - a_0 - a_1 d_0) + u_{t-1}}{(1 + a_1 d_2)^2} \tag{2.18}$$

This expression will be positive if

$$(n - a_0 - a_1 d_0) + u_{t-1} > 0$$

that is there exists a certain level of unemployment below which increases in wage flexibility will decrease unemployment. But the higher past unemployment is, the more unlikely it is that an increase in wage flexibility has a negative effect on unemployment. In other words, wage flexibility cannot cure high levels of unemployment:

$$\frac{\partial u^{**}}{\partial d_0} = \frac{-a_1}{(1 + a_1 d_2)} > 0 \tag{2.19}$$

$$\frac{\partial u^{**}}{\partial a_0} = \frac{-1}{(1 + a_1 d_2)} < 0 \tag{2.20}$$

Standard Post-Keynesian arguments are confirmed by our model in the wage-led case. Insufficient wage flexibility is not the cause of high unemployment, weakening workers' bargaining power will increase unemployment and autonomous growth reduces unemployment.

An unstable wage-led regime, that is a wage-led regime that exhibits an unstable goods market in the short run, may have an equilibrium value towards which it would gravitate, if it were on short-run equilibria.

2.4 CONCLUSION

The chapter examined the existence and stability of a long-run equilibrium rate of unemployment in a NAIRU framework and in a Keynesian growth model. In the NAIRU model the equilibrium rate of unemployment determines unanticipated inflation in the short run and actual unemployment and output in the long run. The real balance effect plays the pivotal role in the transition from the short run to the long run. As to the Keynesian model we take the Marglin-Bhaduri (1990) model as our starting point and complement it by Okun's law for the labour market and a wage curve type relation for distribution. The distinction between wage-led and profit-led demand regimes is one of the interesting features of the Marglin-Bhaduri model and indeed turns out to be crucial for the long-run equilibrium rate of unemployment.

In the profit-led regime, there is a stable equilibrium rate of unemployment that, NAIRU-like, determines growth. Standard NAIRU arguments concerning the labour market apply, that is increases in wage flexibility and weakening workers' bargaining power will decrease unemployment. However, contrary to the NAIRU model, the long-run equilibrium rate of unemployment is not independent of demand. Changes in autonomous growth will affect unemployment in the long run. The policy conclusions of this scenario are straightforward. The standard prescription for labour market reforms would work – but so would active demand policy.

In the wage-led regime, the rules of the game change. The equilibrium rate of unemployment is not stable. The long run is thus but a succession of short-run equilibria. Therefore the goods market dominates the labour market even in the long run. More wage flexibility will not decrease unemployment, neither will weakening workers' bargaining position – both will work in the opposite direction, leading to higher unemployment. Demand policy will be effective.

The implication for the interpretation of the rising unemployment rates in Europe is that they need not be caused by a rise in the equilibrium rate of unemployment, but could be due to a lack of effective demand. If the economies are wage-led, rising unemployment rates cannot be interpreted as a rising NAIRU since no equilibrium rate of unemployment will exist in the long run. Rather, European economies may be trapped in a vicious cycle of falling growth rates, rising unemployment and rising profit share. The empirical evidence supports such a view. From the mid-1970s to the mid-1990s we do observe rising unemployment, rising profit shares and low, if not falling, growth rates in most European countries. Moreover, Bowles and Boyer (1995), testing a version of the Marglin-Bhaduri model for major OECD countries, find that while individual countries are likely to be profit-led because of exports, collectively they are weakly wage-led.[12] Interventions on the goods market through monetary or fiscal policy, then, could not only increase employment but, if growth could be raised above the natural growth rate, they could make use of a virtuous circle of self-generating employment increases.

Obviously, our closed private economy model is too primitive to explain the behaviour of any real economy. Its purpose was to clarify the role of unemployment in the long run in NAIRU models and Keynesian models. Such clarifications are important if future empirical Keynesian work on European unemployment wants to challenge the mainstream NAIRU story of European unemployment.

NOTES

1. Post-Keynesian growth theories, of course, are too big a subject to be comprehensively summarized in a short chapter. Setterfield (2002) is an up-to-date collection of essays that survey Post-Keynesian growth theories, which also includes Kaldorian approaches not discussed above.
2. Pasinetti (1962) proposed an extension of the saving function, where workers receive part of the profit income, according to their share in the capital stock, as represented by their savings. This modification complicates the analysis, but does not modify the results, at least of the Robinsonian model, in any crucial way (Marglin 1984), hence it is ignored here.
3. Sticking closer to Keynes, and not the simplified model presented here, we should say that the conventional nominal wage, together with factors of effective demand that determine the price level, determine the real wage, and thus the marginal product of labour.
4. This is, of course, only true as long as output has not reached its maximum possible level, which in the Keynesian view is the normal state of things. More formally, we assume: $Y < \bar{Y}$, where $\bar{Y}$ is potential output.
5. We wish to be unambiguous on this point: the Keynesian theory of investment in the context of long-run analysis is incompatible with the neo-classical investment theory that regards investment merely as an adjustment to optimal capital stock. If the notion 'independent investment function' is to have any meaning, it does imply that there is more to investment than this adjustment, for example institutional factors, medium-run exogenous influences on profit expectations, long-lasting memories of traumatic economic experiences like the Great Depression and so on. There has to be more to investment than factor optimization. However, the independent investment function is not inconsistent with factor costs and substitution playing a role. It only is asserted that this is not the only factor (besides desired output).
6. In Chapter 5 we investigate the process of financialization, that is the changing relation between management and shareholders that through affecting management priorities can have an effect on investment.
7. Marglin (1984) presents a formal analysis of the Kaldor-Robinson variant of Keynesian growth theory. A brief digression on substitutability may be clarifying. Since Harrod and Domar, Keynesian growth models have become associated with fixed proportions in production. This is misleading, since the general mechanism of the Keynesian model is not affected by the substitutability. For example Marglin concludes: 'in short, continuous substitution resolves the "knife edge" problem of Evsey Domar . . . by imparting a positive slope to the saving function. But continuous substitution does nothing for Harrod's problem of opposition between warranted and natural growth rates. . . . Opposition between warranted and natural rates of growth arises from the existence of an investment demand function' (Marglin 1984, p. 190).
8. Similar ideas about the pervasiveness of excess capacity or slack can be found in Hirschman (1970) and Leibenstein (1966). However neither of them develops this into a theory of variable capacity utilization in a macroeconomic model.

9. As noted, the model presented here is the model proposed by Marglin and Bhaduri (1990), which we regard as the most flexible and rich version of the Kaleckian growth models. However it is not clear whether this does full justice to the fathers of the model. Marglin and Bhaduri do not primarily interpret this model as a growth model, but focus their analysis on the short run, that is changes in capacity utilization. However, they do establish the distinction between profit-led and wage-led growth that will become important later in our discussion.
10. Note a technical difference. Marglin and Bhaduri use $Y/\bar{Y}$ as capacity utilization and $\bar{Y}/K$ as a technology variable. We collapse both expressions into one and, by assuming constant technology, interpret Y/K as capacity utilization (where $\bar{Y}$ is potential output).
11. Note that equation (2.1) is a reduced form of the goods market equilibrium in the Marglin-Bhaduri model, that is a linearized form of equation (KG 6). Capacity utilization is not explicitly treated in our model, which simplifies formal analysis a lot, but makes interpretation a little tricky, in that with any change in growth, capacity utilization will also change.
12. An individual country can pursue a beggar-thy-neighbour policy that will give rise to a profit-led regime, that is wage reduction will increase output via net exports. However, this strategy cannot be pursued successfully by all countries at the same time. Hence the seemingly contradictory finding that individual countries are profit-led, while all of them together are wage-led.

3. The NAIRU theory, the NAIRU story and Keynesian approaches

3.1 INTRODUCTION

Major European countries have experienced double-digit unemployment rates since the 1982/83 recession, associated with high individual as well as social costs. It is widely recognized that creating more employment is one of the foremost policy priorities as witnessed by recent declarations of the European union that recognizes the promotion of 'economic and social progress and a high level of employment and to achieve balanced and sustainable development' (Consolidated Version of the Treaty of Amsterdam, Article 2 p. 11) as its policy goal.

Most of the policies designed to combat unemployment focus on the labour market, or what is often called 'employability'. For example Siebert argues 'that institutional changes affecting Europe's labor markets over the last 25 years are a central reason for Europe's poor labor market performance' (Siebert 1997, p. 39) and consequently: 'Indeed, the specter of unemployment that is haunting Europe will not be exorcised unless governments are prepared to undertake major reforms of the institutional set up of the labor market' (Siebert 1997, p. 53).

This approach has been taken up by governments and supranational organizations in their recommendations on labour market policy. The OECD offers a detailed list on how to increase labour market flexibility (OECD 1997b), advising governments to reduce and shorten unemployment benefits, reduce employment protection, and decentralize collective bargaining. More modestly, EU member countries have agreed to 'review and, where appropriate, refocus their benefit and tax system and provide incentives for unemployed or inactive people to seek and take up work' (EU Employment Guidelines 1999).

This approach, the theoretical underpinnings of which are provided by the NAIRU theory, is in stark contrast to a Keynesian approach that stresses demand deficiency in explaining unemployment. In the context of European unemployment, this means that the specific economic policies that came with European monetary unification are highlighted. 'One experience that the euro countries have shared in common in the last few years, and generally not shared with others, has been the very restrictive aggregate demand policies, both fiscal and monetary' (Modigliani et al. 1998, p. 168). In part as a consequence thereof, in part for reasons related to changes in the financial systems, investment expenditures have been sluggish. This low pace of investment is a key reason for rising unemployment to Keynesians.

This chapter reviews the literature on European unemployment, thereby contrasting the NAIRU explanation and Keynesian approaches. The core mechanisms and assumptions of the NAIRU model, distinguished from a particular explanation of the rise in European unemployment that we will call the NAIRU story, are discussed. Furthermore, the empirical work it has given rise to is reviewed.[1] We will contrast the NAIRU story with Keynesian explanations. Keynesians emphasize the persistence of unemployment and the role of capital accumulation.

3.2 THE NAIRU MODEL AND THE NAIRU STORY

> Unemployment must reconcile the income claims of firms and workers. The aggregate demand relation, as usual, plays no other role in equilibrium than to determine the price level or the rate of inflation. (Blanchard 1990, p. 70)

The NAIRU theory is at the same time a theory of inflation and of unemployment, the link between the two being the real balance effect. The NAIRU is determined by labour market institutions, and inflation by the difference between actual unemployment and the NAIRU. In the long run unemployment will coincide with the NAIRU, the mechanism causing this adjustment is the real balance effect that translates the increase in inflation into a reduction of demand.

This dual theory of inflation and unemployment, combined with different economic developments, has led to a certain divide across the Atlantic in the interpretation of the NAIRU theory. In the US context, the NAIRU is first of all understood as a theory of inflation, leading to an intense debate around the (expectations-augmented) Phillips curve. In the European context, while many studies on the relation between unemployment and inflation exist, the focus has shifted to the question of why unemployment has risen, and has led to numerous studies explaining differences in unemployment rates by labour market characteristics.

This section is structured as follows. First we look at the origins of the NAIRU, that is the natural rate of unemployment (NRU) and the difference between the two concepts. Second, a simple NAIRU model is presented.

Thus the key mechanisms operating are highlighted. Third, the NAIRU story, a specific interpretation of the rise of European unemployment that is based on the NAIRU model, is discussed. Fourth, the empirical work in the NAIRU tradition is reviewed.

3.2.1 The NAIRU and the Natural Rate of Unemployment (NRU)

Friedman (1968) and Phelps (1968) laid the cornerstone for what later became the NAIRU. To wit, Friedman provided a catchy name – the Natural Rate of Unemployment (NRU) – and Phelps the analysis. Phelps achieved his case for a vertical long-run Phillips curve and an equilibrium rate of unemployment by introducing two elements: a search model of unemployment and the expectations-augmented Phillips curve. Assuming hiring and firing costs as well as search costs, optimizing firms will want to pay wages above the market clearing wage in order to create an incentive for workers to stay (instead of looking for other jobs). Thereby firms avoid parts of the costly hiring procedures. The resulting equilibrium wage rate will give rise to unemployment.

Phelps's second ingredient is the expectations-augmented Phillips curve. The original Phillips curve, which relates inflation and the rate of unemployment, was based on a bottleneck theory of inflation. Faster growth will create certain bottlenecks in the production process, either on the goods or labour markets, that give rise to a one-time increase in the rate of inflation. The expectations-augmented Phillips curve relates the change in the rate of inflation and the rate of unemployment. Therefore, an increase in employment will lead to a permanent increase in the inflation rate. Consequently, unemployment can only be pushed below the inflation-neutral level at the cost of exploding inflation.

Friedman (1968) does not offer a rigorous analysis, but broad claims and an analogy. Given certain frictions, the Walrasian system will ground out an equilibrium rate of unemployment, labelled the 'natural rate of unemployment' in analogy to Wicksell's natural rate of interest. Friedman's definition of the natural rate as well as the description of the forces that will push actual unemployment towards its natural level are cryptic.

> At any moment in time there is some level of unemployment which has the property that it is consistent with equilibrium in the structure of real wages . . . The 'natural rate of unemployment' . . . is the level that would be ground out by the Walrasian system of general equilibrium equations, provided that there is embedded in them the actual structural characteristics of the labor and commodity markets, including market imperfections, stochastic variability in demands and supplies, the costs of gathering information about job vacancies, and labor availabilities, the costs of mobility and so on. (Friedman 1968, p. 8)

Asserting that the economy does gravitate to the NRU, Friedman goes on to explain that attempts to influence unemployment will result only in higher inflation. His arguments are similar to those of Phelps: people's inflationary expectations will be based on past inflation rates. Unexpected inflation can thus increase the labour supply in the short run and therefore output, but once people realize that inflation is higher than expected, real variables, including the rate of unemployment, will return to their equilibrium level and prices will increase.

The empirical support for the NRU was weak. Friedman presents no evidence at all, Phelps reports some regression results. However these are bogus by modern standards. The one regression reported in the main body of the text has a DW statistics of 0.15, which is called 'fearsome' by Phelps (1968, p. 695). This is hardly an overstatement. Following Newbold and Granger (1974) Phelps's results can well be qualified as spurious. If two time series with unit roots are regressed onto each other, the estimated coefficients as well as the associated t-values are random variables (more discussion of unit roots in time series econometrics can be found in section 6.3). Phelps regression results in the Appendix fail to report the DW statistics.

While the original NRU concept did lead to similar policy conclusion as the NAIRU theory, there is an important difference in the theoretical foundation. NRU is still founded in a Walrasian world. Markets clear unless impediments, for example minimum wages, or transaction costs, that is search costs, are introduced. The labour market has no intrinsic feature that would prevent it from clearing. The NAIRU model, on the other hand, is founded on bargaining models, that is there is an intrinsic conflict of interest between workers and firms that is mediated not by the market but by a bargaining process. We will return to this issue in our discussion of Post-Keynesian theories.

> The crucial difference between these concepts relates to their micro foundations. Friedman's natural rate is a market-clearing concept, whereas the NAIRU is the rate of unemployment which generates consistency between the target real wage of workers and the feasible real wage determined by labour productivity and the size of a firm's mark up. Since the NAIRU is determined by the balance of power between workers and firms, the micro foundations of the NAIRU relate theories of imperfect competition in the labour and production markets. (Snowdon et al. 1994, p. 323)

3.2.2 The NAIRU Model

Table 3.1 summarizes a stylized macroeconomic NAIRU model following Lindbeck (1993) and Nickell (1998). The model consists of the following

Table 3.1 The NAIRU model

Demand	$y=\alpha_0-\alpha_3 p$	N1
Employment function	$e=\varphi_0-\varphi_3 y$	N2
Price setting	$p=\epsilon_0+w^e$	N3
Wage setting	$w=\gamma_0-\gamma_5(n-e)+p^e$	N4
Unemployment	$u\equiv n-e$	N5
Short run		
Adaptive expections and price setting after wage setting	$p^e=p_{-1},\ w=w^e$	N6
Short-run unemployment	$u=\dfrac{\varepsilon_0+\gamma_0}{\gamma_5}-\dfrac{\Delta p}{\gamma_5}$	N7
Long run		
Fulfilled expectations	$p=p^e,\ w=w^e$	N8
NAIRU	$u^*=\dfrac{\varepsilon_0+\gamma_0}{\gamma_5}$	N9

(all variables in logs)
- y output
- p prices
- e employment
- w wages
- n labour force
- u unemployment

functions. Demand depends on some exogenous factors and the real money supply. Thus demand is a negative function of the price level (equation N1). Employment is a function of output (N2). Prices are set as a mark-up on expected labour unit costs (N3). The mark-up reflects factors like the market power of the firm and the normal rate of profit. Wage setting depends on the expected price level and exogenous wage-push factors, like unemployment benefits (N4).

In our presentation of the NAIRU model, we will not elaborate on factor substitution and the micro foundations for the behavioural functions. This does not do justice to those who developed the NAIRU model, derived from the usual maximizing assumptions (see for example Layard et al. 1991, Phelps 1994), but allows us to focus on the key mechanism of the model. Neither factor substitution nor any particular microeconomic foundations (insider – outsider, efficiency wage, union bargaining for example) are essential for the NAIRU model, because the core mechanism is the equilibration of competing income claims through unanticipated inflation and unemployment.

In the short run, effective demand determines unanticipated inflation and thus determines actual unemployment. To be more precise: demand determines the deviation of actual unemployment from equilibrium unemployment. Assume that prices are set after wages and that people have adaptive expectations with respect to the price level (both are standard assumptions; N6). Unemployment then is a function of the change in the price level (N7), which results from fiscal and monetary policy. In the short run, the system therefore has Keynesian features, but only because of the difference between expected and actual prices.

Since their expectations have been frustrated in the short run, people will alter their behaviour and adjust expectations to the higher price level. For equilibrium in the long run, expectations have to be fulfilled (N8), and income claims are thus equilibrated through the rate of unemployment. There will be only one level of unemployment that renders income claims of workers (γ_0) and capitalists (ϵ_0) consistent. Any attempt by fiscal or monetary policy to move unemployment away from this equilibrium level is doomed. It will temporarily lower unemployment, thus causing inflation, which through the real balance effect undermines demand until the equilibrium rate of unemployment is reached again. Hence in the long run the NAIRU depends on wage-push factors and the mark-up, but not autonomous demand (N9). In the long run the model thus has neo-classical features, but a non-clearing labour market. It is neo-classical in the sense that the labour market outcome is unrelated to exogenous goods market variables. Rather, the goods market adjusts passively to the corresponding 'natural' output level through the real balance effect.

One weak point in this model is the central role that the real balance effect (or the Keynes effect) plays. If prices decrease, this will lead to an increase in demand and thereby realign actual to equilibrium unemployment. Keynesians have long doubted the existence of such an effect and indeed proposed that it may have the opposite sign. Since inflation reduces the debt burden of firms (Fisher effect), it may well have an expansionary effect. Empirically such a negative effect of inflation on growth is doubtful. In fact at moderate levels of inflation, roughly below 20 per cent, inflation is positively correlated with growth (Bruno and Easterly 1998). Sawyer (2001, 2002) highlights conceptual problems for the NAIRU theory that follow from the lack of a reliable adjustment mechanism.

However, this chapter will not dwell on the real balance effect for two reasons. First, a more realistic version would probably argue that the adjustment to unexpected inflation does not take place via a real balance effect, but that it is the Central Bank's interest policy that is depressing demand in the face of accelerating inflation. While such an argument certainly is palpable, it attributes significant power to the Central Bank. Actual unemployment will not be determined by the NAIRU, but by what the Central Bank thinks the NAIRU is. This is inconsistent with the NAIRU hypothesis. Second, at the core of what we call the NAIRU story of European unemployment is the claim that wage-push variables determined the rise in actual unemployment. It is the validity of this empirical claim that is examined.

Before we move on, let us summarize the important features of the NAIRU model:

- Unemployment has a disciplinary (negative) effect on nominal wage demands and real wages.
- Unemployment in the short run is determined by demand.
- Real wages, or income distribution, do not affect the level of demand.
- The adjustment from the short-run equilibrium to the long-run equilibrium takes place through the real balance effect.
- In the long run the system is anchored in a long-run equilibrium rate of unemployment.
- The long-run equilibrium rate of unemployment does not depend on demand or the history of unemployment.
- The model has Keynesian features in the short run, but neo-classical features in the long run.

3.2.3 The NAIRU Story and its Policy Implications

The standard NAIRU story of European unemployment then is that wage-push factors, mostly welfare state related (γ_0 in Table 3.1), caused unemployment. Wage inflexibility caused by labour market rigidities that empowered insiders has caused a rise in the NAIRU (Krugman 1994, Siebert 1997). Among the most frequently cited causes for unemployment are long and durable unemployment benefits, job protection measures, high social security contributions (or more generally: the tax wedge), strong unions. This story, that is a change in γ_0 within the NAIRU model, leads to an increase in the rate of unemployment (see N9), with the mark-up being constant. This however is at odds with the stylized facts of European unemployment. Over the long run we do observe a rise in the rate of unemployment and in the profit share (for example Blanchard 1997, Andersen et al. 1999).

It is necessary to distinguish between the NAIRU model and the NAIRU story regarding European unemployment. The NAIRU model is understood to be a general model of output, employment and inflation that allows for inflation resulting from conflicting income claims. Such models imply that at any point in time there will exist an inflation barrier, the NAIRU, such that if demand took unemployment below that barrier then inflation would tend to rise. The NAIRU story is understood as a specific interpretation of the model. It involves two claims. First that changes in the NAIRU have caused changes in actual unemployment. Thus changes in the NAIRU are understood to be relatively autonomous with respect to changes in actual unemployment and the NAIRU serves as a strong attractor for actual unemployment.[2] Second, that changes in the NAIRU since the 1960s have been due to wage-push factors. Thus changes in wage-push variables are the cause of the rise in European unemployment over the past 30 years. It is this second claim that will be investigated empirically.

The policy recommendations of this story are straightforward: since rigid labour markets and overgenerous welfare states have caused the problem, labour markets have to be deregulated and welfare states curbed. The OECD does therefore recommend in a series of publications (OECD 1997b) the following steps:

- ease employment protection;
- reduce level and duration of unemployment benefits;
- decentralize wage bargaining.

3.2.4 Empirical Work

> While labor market institutions can potentially explain cross country differences today, they do not appear able to explain the general evolution of unemployment over time. (Blanchard and Wolfers 2000, p. 2)

The empirical work in the NAIRU tradition can roughly be divided into estimations of wage setting and price setting curves within countries on the one hand and regressions explaining unemployment by institutional data on the other hand. The first approach, mostly using time series data, allows for a calculation of the NAIRU implicit in wage and price setting, whereas the second, using cross-country data, explicitly attempts to explain actual unemployment via the NAIRU, which is understood to be determined by labour market institutions.

3.2.4.1 Estimations of wage setting and price setting behaviour with time series data

A lot of studies have estimated the price setting and wage setting function by means of time series data, our standard reference is Layard et al. (1991; henceforth: NLJ), other frequently cited studies include: Layard et al. (1983), Bean et al. (1986) and various papers in the same supplement issue of *Economica*; Alogoskoufis and Manning (1988); Gordon and Franz (1993). Referring to Table 3.1, equations N3 and N4 are estimated. In a reduced form this is equivalent to the estimation of the expectations-augmented Phillips curve, the most important recent references here are the contributions collected in JEP (1997).

Note that in this approach unemployment is not the dependent variable. If one seeks an explanation of unemployment, this approach has a fundamental shortcoming. While it allows for the calculation of the NAIRU *ex post*, it does not offer any *ex ante* theory of the NAIRU. In other words, it may tell us with more or less precision what the NAIRU must have been, but not why. No substantial explanation of the NAIRU is offered and, more specifically, no direct link between labour market institutions and the NAIRU can be made. Usually authors proceed in pointing out the differences in wage rigidities, which are interesting in their own right, but in order to be interpreted as an explanation of unemployment a leap of faith is required, that is that wage rigidity causes unemployment.

Some of these issues become particularly apparent in the recent symposium in the *Journal of Economic Perspectives* (1997). An Atlantic divide as to the interpretation of the NAIRU theory seems to have developed. With the exception of Blanchard and Katz (1997), the authors seem to agree that NAIRU is basically a theory of inflation. With some irritation, they notice that the NAIRU changes over time, and they go through great effort to estimate what it must have been and what the precision of the estimate is. However, explanations of the change in the NAIRU are delegated to the end of the paper, offering little more than sensible speculation. This is in sharp contrast to the European literature that has shifted to the *ex ante* explanation of the NAIRU (see below). This literature is not discussed, not even referenced, by the American authors, with the sole exception of Blanchard and Katz.

3.2.4.2 Estimations of unemployment with cross-country data

This second approach is of interest here because the link between unemployment and labour market variables and wage pressure factors is analysed. Variables that are identified as wage-push factors include high and durable unemployment benefits, strong unions, a high degree of job protection and high minimum wages and were shown to be positively correlated with unemployment (OECD 1994).

Nickell (1997) and (1998) gives probably the most careful analysis of the cross-country approach. He regresses unemployment rates on wage-push variables such as unemployment benefits, employment protection measures, union density, level of collective bargaining and coverage of bargaining, the tax wedge and active labour market policy in a cross-country regression usually with one observation per country, but Nickell (1997) also presents a random effect model with two values per country. He concludes:

> Neither measure of labour market rigidity has any impact on total unemployment although protection tends to lower short-term unemployment as expected. Increased generosity of the benefit system is associated with higher unemployment and long duration benefits appear to cause long-term unemployment. Active labour market policies can offset this, however. Unions and high unemployment go together but co-ordination between unions and between firms substantially reduces this relationship. Payroll taxes per se have no impact on unemployment but the total tax burden on labour does seem to have a significant impact. The real interest rate effects are small. (Nickell 1998, p. 810)

Three problems of the cross-section approach can be noted and and we will discuss them in some detail because this approach has proven most influential in terms of policy formation, especially in the form of a contrast USA vs. Europe:

1. The cross-country approach only deals with the differences in unemployment at some point in time, that is it explains differences in unemployment between countries, but not the general rise in unemployment that has taken place over the past two decades. This is widely recognized in the academic debate, if not by politicians. LNJ, after presenting their cross-section regression results, note that 'This analysis does not explain why unemployment has changed over time or why its movement has differed between countries' (Layard et al., p. 56).
2. The robustness of the results have been called into question. By now, for most factors there is also econometric evidence available questioning this effect. For example, OECD (1998) finds no general support for a negative impact of minimum wages, OECD (1999) fails to find evidence that job security caused unemployment. Monastiriotis (1999) shows how sensitive the results are to the specification of the dependent variable. Ball notes: 'There is controversy about whether the OECD and LNJ variables explain cross-country differences in unemployment levels. The developers of the series claim that they do, but others criticize their results as lacking robustness' (Ball 1999, p. 213).
3. Less prominently there is the issue of pooling. Cross-country evidence is able to explain differences between countries, but once it is used for policy prescription it relies on the implicit assumption that mechanisms are the same within a country as between countries. Technically speaking, it is assumed that the countries can be pooled, which is an assumption that usually cannot be tested for in cross-country studies. Thus econometric results may be due to incorrect pooling ('aggregation bias' in the words of Zellner).

3.2.4.3 Combining time series and cross-section data

One common strategy has been, first, to estimate coefficients of persistence or real or nominal wage rigidity by time series data, and in a second step, to try to explain these estimated coefficients by cross-country data on labour market characteristics (Layard et al. 1986, Barro 1988). This exercise aims at providing evidence that wage rigidity is caused by labour market institutions. The main shortcoming of this approach is that the reader has to take for granted that wage rigidity causes unemployment. More specifically, that the rise in European unemployment since 1980 was caused by rigid wages.

A second strategy is to combine cross-section and time series data directly. Layard et al. 1991, Chapter 9 (for the period 1956–88), and Scarpetta 1996 (for the period 1983–93) do so by pooling the data for various countries directly and letting them interact with time invariant institutional variables that have been tested before. LNJ proceed by first estimating wage and price setting functions, second by explaining the structural parameters by labour market institutions, and third, running a pooled regression where labour market institutions interact with the explanatory variables according to the regression results in step two.

Scarpetta (1996), using cross-section and time series data explains the rate of unemployment by the output gap and various cross-country data on labour market institutions. The latter do not vary. He excludes outliers from the sample that would have affected his results. He finds the mainstream story confirmed. One obviously problematic issue is Scarpetta's exclusion of outliers (p. 62). On statistical grounds he excludes various observations that affect his results, for example Portugal, where low unemployment benefits and high unemployment coincided in the early 1980s.

The sophistication of these models turns out to be a liability as much as an asset. The complex interaction of time series and cross-section data makes the testing of implicit pooling restrictions impossible and the model difficult to track, for example three variables are interacted with lagged unemployment and three variables, two of them in linear as well as in cubic form, interact with import prices – in the simpler version of the model. Many of the findings could not be reproduced by other research. As a test of the NAIRU story they are unsatisfactory, since labour market variables enter in a time invariant form.

3.2.4.4 How convincing is the evidence for the NAIRU story?

At first the evidence provided in favour of the NAIRU story may seem impressive. However, Bentolina notes regarding 'labour markets rigidities as the culprits for high European unemployment. We should realize that, apart from what one may believe on this issue, the evidence produced by economists concerning the blame that we can be put on these rigidities is weak' (Bentolina 1997, p. 73). Why? A closer look reveals that the evidence is far from being unambiguous.

Interestingly even a recent IMF (2003) study reports mixed findings in the regression results, though not in the policy conclusions. Performing a panel analysis, they report some NAIRU variables with the expected signs, other like unemployment benefits do not consistently have the expected sign. The study is instructive on several accounts. First, it reports dramatic changes in coefficients once unemployment persistence is allowed for, thus serving as a warning in the interpretation of coefficients from specifications that omit lagged unemployment. Second, when labour market variables are interacted among each other, it turn out that these interacted variables have a negative effect on unemplyment. For example strong labour unions mitigate the positive effect of higher unemplyment benefits. Third, it includes, in one specification, non-labour market variables. Among these the real interest rate and central bank independence have a statistically significant positive effect on unemployment.

Blanchard and Wolfers (2000; henceforth: B&W) explore interaction of shocks and institutions. They pool five-year averages as proxies for long-term values. The shock variables used are the growth rate of TFP, the real interest rate and a labour demand shift variable that is proxied by an adjusted labour share (this last variable can be interpreted in various ways). As labour institution variables they use standard variables but allow for variation. They use two-way fixed effects and report various specifications. Both the shock variables and the institutional variables as well as their interactions are mostly significant with the expected sign. They conclude that the model overall performs very well, however with two worrisome qualifications. First, time invariant measures of institutions perform better than time variant measures. Second, the results of all variables are sensitive to whether LSE (Nickell) data or OECD data are used for unemployment benefits and employment protection. 'Replacing the Nickell measures by alternative, but time invariant measures, substantially decreases the adjusted R^2. Going from the time invariant to the time varying measures further decreases the fit. . . . Luck, or data mining, when the standard set of measures is used?' (B&W 2000, p. 18).

B&W provide a major advancement in the econometric work on unemployment. The role of shocks and their interactions are taken seriously. Of course, their shock variables will be open to debate, for example Ball 1999 argues that monetary policy is the crucial variable and we argue for an independent role of capital accumulation. However, B&W deserve the merit for proposing a model in which there is room for demand shocks to begin with. The major conceptual shortcoming is that in their model there is no room for hysteresis, that is the NAIRU is independent of demand. B&W 2000, since they use five-year averages by definition exclude hysteresis.[3] If hysteresis were important, that is if a change in unemployment in even one year is very persistent, then B&W's regression is misspecified.

Madsen (1998) compares the performance of three general equilibrium models of unemployment with regards to European unemployment in panel data approach with limted use of labour market institutions variables. He concludes that 'the Layard and Nickell model seems unable to explain the increase in European unemployment' (Madsen 1998, p. 862). He also reports that many models fail the tests for pooling. As noted earlier, two OECD studies, surprisingly, find evidence at odds with the NAIRU story. OECD (1999a) finds the strictness employment protection legislation 'has little or no effect on overall unemployment' (OECD 1999a, p. 58) and OECD (1998a) finds that minimum wages have little effect on unemployment. Furthermore Blank (1994) summarizes the findings of an NBER-sponsored research group as that 'there is little evidence that labor market flexibility is substantially affected by the presence of these social protect programs, nor is there strong evidence that the speed of labor market adjustment can be increased by limiting these programs' (Blank 1994, p. 181).

We conclude that the evidence in favour of the NAIRU story is at best weak. Moreover, the omission of explanatory variables of either effective demand or other institutional factors casts doubt on the results. Omitted variables, after all, create bias in the estimated coefficients. The estimated equations may plainly be misspecified. This obviously raises the question of how alternative theories would explain the rise in European unemployment.

3.3 KEYNESIAN APPROACHES

The NAIRU theory lends itself to policy recommendations that are in line with standard neo-classical prescriptions. Labour market reforms, not demand policy, is what is needed to combat unemployment. The NAIRU story correspondingly argues that it has been wrong-headed labour market reforms that led to labour market inflexibility and thus caused the rise in European unemployment. Of course there have been Keynesian reactions to this explanation, but these reaction have been far less unified than the NAIRU approach and range from outright rejection of the NAIRU to extending the NAIRU model by incorporating Keynesian arguments.

One of the main courses for the diversity in Keynesian reaction to the NAIRU model is that the NAIRU model is itself a Keynesian model, albeit a New Keynesian one. In its emphasis on the failure of market clearing the NAIRU theory is New Keynesian. Moreover, some of its arguments, in particular the role of distributional conflict in explaining inflation are also part of the Post-Keynesian repertoire. Thus in the following a variety of Keynesian approaches is presented. What we summarize here under the heading of 'Keynesian' has as the smallest common denominator that demand factors are crucial in explaining the European unemployment performance. Our own theoretical framework is discussed in Chapter 1.

Davidson (1998) offers a Post-Keynesian critique of the NAIRU approach. Emphasizing the pivotal role of uncertainty in a monetary production economy he insists that no labour demand curve, nor its present incarnation in the form of the price setting curve, can be drawn without an assumption about effective demand, because the notion of the marginal product of labour or the marginal revenue product of labour that underlies the price setting curve does not exist prior to the level of effective demand. The labour demand curve therefore depends on the level of effective demand, which in turn is crucially determined by government expenditure and investment. Wage decreases can therefore not bring about an increase in employment unless they increase effective demand. The explanation for high unemployment, for Davidson, is to be found in the shift to a flexible exchange rate system after the breakdown of the Bretton Woods system. Since then:

> exchange rate movements reflect changes in speculative positions rather than changes in patterns of trade. Significant exchange rate movements affect the international competitive position of domestic *vis-à-vis* foreign industries and therefore tend to depress the inducement to invest in large projects with irreversible sunk costs. Since 1973, volatile exchange rates have made entrepreneurs more wary of undertaking large investment projects. (Davidson 1998, p. 819)

Davidson's contribution is welcome because it constitutes a clear Keynesian rebuttal of the NAIRU story, however it remains unsatisfactory because he neither offers empirical analysis of the rise of European unemployment nor does he take very seriously the implications of the fact that the NAIRU analysis is based on a bargaining model of wage formation. Thus he seems to miss the difference between a standard labour supply curve and the wage setting curve. Finally, but this is a question of nuance rather than of substance, he misses that the NAIRU model does have a mechanism of adjustment of effective demand, albeit an old one: the NAIRU model reiterates the old Patinkin solution of the real balance effect.

Pollin (1998) can be regarded as the complement to Davidson in that he discusses the wage setting curve, but remains silent on the price setting curve. Pollin draws attention to the parallels in the NAIRU bargaining model and a Marx-Kalecki theory of income distribution and the reserve army: 'In my view, Marx and Kalecki also share a common conclusion with natural rate proponents, in that they would all agree that positive unemployment rates are the outgrowth of class struggle over distribution of income and political power.' And he goes on:

> Of course, Friedman and the New Classicals reach this conclusion via analytic and political perspectives that are diametrically opposite to those of Marx and Kalecki. To put it in a nutshell, mass unemployment results in the Friedmanite/New Classical view when workers demand more than they deserve, while for Marx and Kalecki, capitalists use the weapon of unemployment to prevent workers from getting their just due. (Pollin 1998, p. 5f)

Pollin hardly addresses the issue of effective demand or, in Davidson's spirit, the negation of the problem of effective demand in the price setting curve. He goes on referring to the issue of USA inflation, but he does not develop further to an explanation of European unemployment. Davidson and Pollin cover the extreme poles of the reactions of Post-Keynesians to the NAIRU theory: harsh criticism of its neglect of demand and approval of its emphasis on distributional conflict. Similar arguments regarding the role of unemployment and distributional conflict in the determination of inflation had been made much earlier by Post-Keynesians under the name of conflict inflation.

3.3.1 Conflict Inflation[4]

Davidson probably underestimates the innovative potential of the NAIRU theory and how far it has moved from the classical model that Keynes had criticized. As mentioned the NAIRU theory is a theory of inflation as well as of unemployment. As a theory of inflation it resembles the conflict inflation theory of Post-Keynesian origin. This theory was formally developed in the 1970s and 1980s, but was already contained in the early writings of J. Robinson (1937) and reflects Post-Keynesians' long-standing conviction that inflation is the outcome of distributional conflict (and not excessive growth in the money supply) and thus has to be combated through incomes policies.

Conflict inflation theory takes as its point of departure income claims of labour and capital, though the model can obviously be extended to include the state and a foreign sector. If the income claims of labour and capital exceed national income, the income claims are inconsistent and inflation will result. Thus the income claims are reconciled nominally. The distributional effects of this inflation depend on the speed and frequency with which wages and prices are adjusted.

The income claims, nominal wage demands by labour and the mark-up set by firms depend on the respective power position, which will depend on various exogenous factors (strength and militancy of labour unions; market power of firms) and demand. For workers a lower level of effective demand results in higher unemployment, for firms it implies lower capacity utilization. Thus a lower level of demand weakens the bargaining position of either side and thus will lead to lower inflation. Inflation in this theory is thus not a monetary phenomenon in the sense of the quantity theory of money, but a real phenomenon, resulting from the distributional conflict between capital and labour.

Such a model will exhibit a rate of unemployment at which inflation is constant, because at this rate of unemployment workers are weakened sufficiently to accept capitalists' income claims. Thus the model exhibits a quasi-NAIRU. However, the similarities between the conflict inflation model and the NAIRU theory are rarely discussed explicitly. Most proponents (for example M. Lavoie) of the conflict inflation model regard it as a theory of inflation rather than unemployment. Though there will at any point in time be a 'quasi-NAIRU', this is where the similarity ends. First, no automatic mechanism between inflation or the price level and output is presumed. In particular, no real balance effect is assumed.[5] Thus there is a mechanism that would ensure that the system gravitates towards the quasi-NAIRU. Second, the quasi-NAIRU is not necessarily assumed to be constant. In particular, it may be influenced by past unemployment, that is subject to hysteresis.

3.3.2 Hysteresis

Most of the discussion of hysteresis focuses on the labour market: insider–outsider, loss of human capital by the unemployed and so on (see Blanchard and Summers 1986, Lindbeck and Snower 1988). We are not interested in the microeconomic foundations of hysteresis, but in its macroeconomic consequences, which are of paramount importance. The standard story of the NAIRU assumes that the NAIRU is independent of demand and history. If hysteresis exists, this does not hold true. Rather than the NAIRU determining actual unemployment, the latter will drag along the former. In other words the causality between the NAIRU and actual unemployment is reversed.

NAIRU proponents have made two arguments as to why hysteresis is not a major problem for the NAIRU theory. First, some models allow for partial unemployment persistence. Second, it has been argued that unemployment persistence is itself a product of labour market inflexibility.

The first strategy has been to admit that there may be a short-run NAIRU distinct from the long-run NAIRU (Layard et al. 1991, Chapter 1). Due to unemployment persistence, the short-run NAIRU will be above the long-run NAIRU after a shock that increased actual unemployment. However as time passes the actual unemployment will gravitate towards the long-run NAIRU. For mainstream NAIRU theorists the distinction between a full hysteresis, that is a unit root in unemployment, and some persistence, that is an autoregressive term less than unity, is of paramount importance. If there is no unit root, eventually the system will come back to the NAIRU. 'In this view there is a short-term "hysteresis", in the sense that past events affect the current short-run NAIRU. But there is no long-term "hysteresis": there is a unique long-run NAIRU. In the end, the unemployment rate always reverts' (Layard et al. 1991, p. 10).

Ball (1999) offers a recent defence of hysteresis that is outstanding on the empirical level, but uncreative on the theoretical part. Ball argues that hysteresis does exist, that its occurrence depends largely on monetary policy and that labour market institutions are overrated. To provide evidence Ball examines in some detail the recessions of the early 1980s and 1990s, and the recovery of the mid-1980s. Further he discusses the success countries that managed to decrease their initially high unemployment – the Netherlands, the UK, Ireland and Portugal – as well as those who failed. Contrary to standard anecdotes, labour market reform did not do the trick of reducing unemployment. Portugal as well as Ireland increased unemployment benefits, whereas half of the failure countries decreased them.

Overall, Ball concludes:

> I argue that the conventional wisdom overrates these factors [institutions such as labor unions, unemployment insurance and firing restrictions]. In explaining rises in unemployment in the early 1980s, I find that unemployment insurance plays a role: both a long duration of benefits and passive macroeconomic policy contribute to hysteresis. However, labor market policies are not important causes of the unemployment successes and failures since 1985. (Ball 1999, p. 191)

Second, some studies have tried to explain differences in unemployment persistence by reference to labour market institutions. LNJ and Scarpetta (1996) do so implicitly or explicitly. However these studies usually do not allow factors other than labour market institutions to affect hysteresis. Bean (1994a) takes a more flexible approach and was unable to confirm the hypothesis that labour market institutions explain the extent of hysteresis. Ball finds in his study that 'whether hysteresis arises depends largely on the response of monetary policy to the recession' (Ball 1999, p. 192).

3.3.3 Accumulation and a Keynesian Story

Sarantis (1993) is probably the first empirical attempt to show the role of capital accumulation for unemployment with a distinctly Post-Keynesian flavour.[6] Sarantis estimates a Kaleckian growth model for ten large OECD economies by means of panel methods for the 1976–89 period. His main concern is the relation between income distribution and employment. He finds 'strong support for the Kaleckian hypothesis that inadequacy of capital equipment is a major source of unemployment' (Sarantis 1993, p. 466). However his paper is hardly referred to in the subsequent Keynesian debate.

Rowthorn (1995) is an important empirical study which demonstrates the role of capital accumulation for unemployment by means of a cross-country estimation. Rowthorn's argument however is only half-Keynesian. He articulates his argument within a quasi-NAIRU framework. Rowthorn (1977) had developed a conflict inflation model inspired by Marx that he later on (Rowthorn 1999a,b) seems to regard as equivalent to the NAIRU model. And he sketches out a rather un-Keynesian theory of investment; however this is not crucial to his argument about unemployment and accumulation.

The core of Rowthorn's theoretical argument is that the mark-up is a function of the existing capital stock. *Ceteris paribus*, that is given output, a higher capital stock leads to a lower mark-up, because of the existence of excess capacity. 'Unemployment reduces the ability of workers to push up wages, while excess capacity limits the ability of firms to raise prices' (Rowthorn 1995, p. 28). Within the NAIRU framework this is a big step forward, because in the standard formulation the mark-up is given as exogenous with no explanation other than a casual reference to the monopoly power of the firm. Conveniently, the issue of the mark-up is ignored in empirical studies. However, the transmission from accumulation to unemployment is not Keynesian, but within a bargaining model: it does not operate through effective demand, but through firms' bargaining position. A lower capital stock increases firms' desired mark-up, which can only be realized in a non-inflationary way if unemployment increases to restrain wage claims. Soskice and Carlin (1988) had made a similar argument, but without econometric evidence.

In his empirical work Rowthorn (1995) shows that the change in the average growth rate in employment between 1960–73 and 1973–92 is correlated to the change in average capital stock growth rates over the period in a cross-country regression. He further investigates the differences of effects of accumulation in the service sector and the manufacturing sector on sectoral as well as total employment growth. He offers no rigorous analysis of the slowdown of accumulation but hints at a rather classical story of investment by arguing that low profitability, high interest rates, and insufficient savings because of high public budget deficits caused the slowdown.

Glyn (1998) gives an overview of the relation between employment growth, structural change and accumulation from the late nineteenth century to the 1990s. Thus his aim is much broader than an explanation of current European unemployment. His analysis presents descriptive statistics as well as panel data regression. His work is also notable in that he disaggregates his analysis for men and women. His findings confirm the central role of capital accumulation. Accumulation plays an important role in job creating in the non-agricultural sector and population growth, though it has a strong effect on employment growth, does not by itself translate into employment growth, that is the coefficient is statistically different from unity. Thus while not directly addressing the issue of European unemployment, Glyn provides important historical back-up for the Keynesian argument that accumulation is crucial for employment growth.

3.3.4 Productivity growth, employment growth, labour relations and hidden unemployment

One of the stylized facts about US vs. European economies during the 1980s and early 1990s (but not thereafter) was that the productivity growth was much higher in Europe than in the USA (whether measured as TFP or labour productivity). This has given rise to explanations of European unemployment that relate productivity growth and job creation. In the 1990s productivity growth famously accelerated in the USA, which gave rise to the debate on the New Economy. Since the mid-1990s the US productivity growth has exceeded Europe's. Thus the theories to be discussed may seem outdated. However such an impression would be misleading. While they certainly do not apply to the period after the mid-1990s, they may enhance our understanding of the earlier decades, that is the period 1975–95.

Appelbaum and Schettkat (1995) start from the observation that in the 1980s employment and output per worker were negatively related between countries, which is in contrast to the Golden Age period, when there was a positive correlation. Moreover, the current negative correlation also holds true for sectors within an economy. Appelbaum and Schettkat interpret this as a structural shift from an industrial economy to a post-industrial economy. In the former, there was a virtuous cycle of high wage increase in all sectors of the economy, driven by high-productivity manufacturing which put pressure on low-productivity sectors, which were growing slowly. This relation has changed. Now it is not the productive sectors that are growing fast, but unproductive service sectors. Appelbaum and Schettkat do not draw policy conclusion but hope for a new Kondratieff cycle.

Buchele and Christiansen (1999a) also accept the inverse relationship between employment growth and output growth across countries (unlike Appelbaum and Schettkat they use differences rather than level and argue that this inverse relation has existed since the 1960s). They regard the overall growth rate as determined by effective demand, which is mostly determined by economic policy. The countries' positions on the Employment–Productivity Trade-Off Schedule are determined by their labour market institutions. European labour market institutions give rise to 'cooperative labour relations' offering job security and rising real wages to workers who under these circumstances have an incentive to contribute to productivity growth (Buchele and Christiansen 1992). Workers, so the presumption of this argument goes, have a specific tacit knowledge of the work process that is hard to mobilize without cooperation on their part. American labour relations on the other hand use the stick, that is the firing threat, rather than the carrot in motivating workers, leading to less loyalty to the firm and hence less active cooperation, therefore lower productivity growth.

Eatwell (1997) elaborates on the same theme from a more Keynesian angle. Following J. Robinson's notion of hidden unemployment he shows that labour productivity is lower in the US service sector compared to its manufacturing sector, than in Europe. International competition enforces comparable productivity levels in manufacturing, but not in services. Both economies are constrained by a lack of effective demand. Since most European countries have an intact welfare state the unemployed refuse to accept low pay and low-quality service jobs, whereas in the USA, lacking a social security system they are pushed into these sectors. Unproductive service sectors therefore serve as a sponge for the hidden reserve army that could easily be mobilized if the economy were hit by a positive demand shock.

Appelbaum and Schettkat, Buchele and Christiansen, and Eatwell talk about the same phenomenon but from a technological angle, a labour relations angle and a demand viewpoint respectively. Appelbaum and Schettkat regard the economy as constrained by the supply side, that is technology, whereas Buchele and Christiansen, and Eatwell, regard it as demand constrained. The analysis I will present therefore is complementary to that by Buchele and Christiansen, and Eatwell, though it has at its focus what they take as given: that the increase in European unemployment was caused by lack of effective demand.

3.3.5 Keynesian Extensions of the NAIRU Model

Given that the line between the NAIRU theory and Keynesian theory is blurred to begin with and that conflict inflation had been a part of Post-Keynesian theories for a long time, some Keynesian authors have tried to integrate Keynesian arguments into NAIRU models. Thus several versions of NAIRU models with hysteresis and capital stock exist. In fact most NAIRU models allow for unemployment persistence in one form or another. For example Nickell (1998) allows for past unemployment to affect wages differently from present unemployment, but his employment function exhibits no unemployment persistence.

Ball (1994, 1999) presents his hysteresis argument within a NAIRU framework. In his model there also exists no long-run hysteresis. However he interprets the relevance of the long run for empirical analysis differently. Analysing unemployment in various countries he allows for hysteresis and explains the different developments in unemployment rates by different monetary policies. Thus for practical purposes the short run matters to Ball. Modigliani et al. (1998) take a similar approach. While they do not develop a formal model, a kind of NAIRU model is underlying their arguments. They emphasize that actual unemployment in Europe is caused by restrictive monetary and fiscal policy. Thus again the short run matters. In addition they note that 'one reason for . . . the rise in unemployment has been a decline in investment relative to full-capacity output' (Modigliani et al. 1998, p. 169).

Recently there also have been efforts to incorporate the capital stock into the NAIRU model. Within the Keynesian literature, three channels, through which capital accumulation may affect unemployment and the NAIRU, may be distinguished analytically. First, there is the traditional demand effect. Through the multiplier investment will affect demand and thus employment; combined with hysteresis it may also affect the NAIRU (Ball 1994, 1999). The model proposed in Chapter 2 is close to this in inspiration. While it is not strictly compatible with the NAIRU model and does not explicitly solve for inflation, it allows for an effect of unemployment on income distribution.

Second, there is limited substitutability, which underlies the Robinsonian growth model in the extreme form of fixed production coefficients. However this restrictive assumption is not necessary. Rowthorn (1999a,b) has shown that even in a Layard-Nickell NAIRU model equilibrium unemployment will depend, among other factors, on capital stock – unless an elasticity of substitution of one is assumed, as Layard et al. (1991) do. Arestis and Biefang-Frisancho Mariscal (1998) propose a NAIRU model with variable work effort and hysteresis where capital stock matters, and provided econometric evidence for the UK that capital stock does affect unemployment and in particular long-term unemployment.

Third there is a bargaining effect. Rowthorn (1995) argues that 'unemployment reduces the ability of workers to push up wages, while excess capacity limits the ability of firms to raise prices' (Rowthorn 1995, p. 28).

Thus an insufficient capital stock will necessitate a higher unemployment rate to equilibrate income claims of workers and capitalists. All three effects are potentially complementary and have been incorporated into NAIRU models. Thus the NAIRU itself may depend on capital accumulation.

3.3.6 Conclusion

The Keynesian contributions to a modern theory of employment and to explaining the rise in European unemployment lack coherence but can potentially be unified and would then pose a powerful alternative to the NAIRU story. The present book is intended as a contribution to such a project.

The contributions of Davidson (1998) and Pollin (1998) cover the range of the challenge this poses to Keynesian economics: combining theories of effective demand and wage bargaining. In Chapter 2 we have proposed a highly simplified model based on Marglin and Bhaduri (1990) that allows for unemployment to affect income distribution. Distinguishing between wage-led and profit-led demand regimes the interaction of the goods market and the labour market were discussed. The model proposed has hysteresis as a natural side-effect, and is thus consistent with Ball (1999), even though we do not attribute as much importance to monetary policy as he does.

Since we have argued that the NAIRU story fails to explain changes in unemployment over time, this defines the ground on which the Keynesian story has to be more successful. The objective of the following chapter is to test the NAIRU story and a Keynesian approach empirically using a time series approach. Since the statistical results within the NAIRU approach may be due to incorrect pooling (aggregation bias), we will carefully test pooling restrictions.

NOTES

1. Due to the enormous volume of literature on the subject, a complete review of the debate around European unemployment and the NAIRU is beyond the scope of this chapter. Moreover, Nickell (1990) and Bean (1994b) offer comprehensive surveys, and collected volumes exist (Supplement issue of *Economica* 1986, Cross 1988, Dreze and Bean 1990). Instead we will focus on issues relevant to the argument put forward in this chapter. The aim is to contextualize its arguments and to clarify its contributions. Furthermore, we will focus on recent developments on the debate. In particular, we will take a look at special issues and symposia (*Oxford Review of Economic Policy* 1995, JEP 1997 on European unemployment, JEP 1997 on NAIRU, and *Economic Journal* 1998)
2. The possibility that a third variable, say demand or the capital stock, is driving both actual unemployment and the NAIRU is either ruled out theoretically or ignored empirically. Needless to say this is not true for all NAIRU models. Some extensions of the NAIRU models will be discussed below.

3. In fact they fail to discuss the phenomenon and do not even reference Blanchard and Summers (1986), nor Ball (1994) to which Blanchard (1994) had contributed a sympathetic discussion.
4. See Rowthorn (1977), Lavoie (1992) and Palley (1996) as examples.
5. Lavoie (2002) and Casetti (2002) propose Kaleckian growth models with conflict inflation, where a higher price level has no effects on demand. In such a model a NAIRU will exist, though it is not mentioned explicitly by either author, but it affects only inflation, but no real variables.
6. There was a debate around accumulation in the 1980s too (Malinvaud 1980, 1982, 1986; Sneessens and Dreze 1986; Bean 1989; Dreze and Bean 1990). The main difference between this New Keynesian approach and the Post-Keynesian approach advocated here is that for the former, developing out of New Keynesian disequilibrium theory, limitations in substitutability of capital and labour and shortage of capital stock were crucial, not an independent investment function.

4. Explaining the rise in European unemployment: an evaluation of the NAIRU story and a Keynesian approach

While the NAIRU theory stresses labour market institutions as the cause for the rise in European unemployment, Keynesian approaches highlight demand deficiency and, more specifically, low capital investment as the key reason. In this chapter some econometric findings regarding the causes of the rise in unemployment are reported. The empirical work will cover the large European countries – Germany, France, Italy and the UK – and, for comparisons, the USA. We focus on the large European countries because they are the ones that experienced the most pronounced increase in unemployment, whereas many small European countries fared remarkably well. Since we are interested in the rise in unemployment, the method employed will be time series analysis. The period of investigation will cover the period from the early 1960s to the mid-1990s.

This chapter presents the empirical tests that are performed to evaluate the explanatory power of the NAIRU model and the Keynesian model. It is structured as follows. First, we present basic specifications of the NAIRU and the Keynesian model. Second, we discuss data sources and the time series properties of the variables. Third, the econometric method utilized is presented. Fourth, the tests for the NAIRU model and, fifth, of the Keynesian model are presented. Section 6 combines the two models. Finally issues of robustness and causality are discussed. Additional tests are to be found in the Appendix.

4.1 BASIC SPECIFICATION OF THE NAIRU AND THE KEYNESIAN MODELS

In this section we present the specification of the NAIRU model and the Keynesian model, each in its basic form; that is prior to any modification to accommodate time series properties that will be discussed below, in order to discuss the choice of variables and the predicted signs. A detailed discussion of the definition of the variables and their development over time is delegated to the next section.

In the NAIRU model, the rate of unemployment equilibrates income claims of workers and capitalists. Thus, the dependent variable in the regression has to be the rate of unemployment. Since what is explained is structural unemployment, that is the NAIRU, we want to control for cyclical fluctuations. The appropriate variable in the NAIRU context is the change in inflation.

Thus the basic specification, which corresponds to (N7) is

$$u_t = \beta_0 + \beta_1 \Delta p_t + \Sigma \beta_{2,i} \gamma_{0,i,t'} + \Sigma \beta_{3,i'} x_{i,t} + \varepsilon_t \tag{4.1}$$

where Δp, γ_0 and x are the change in inflation, wage-push variables and other control variables respectively.

In the Keynesian model capital accumulation is supposed to drive employment growth. We regard the growth of private employment as the appropriate variable to be explained in the Keynesian story, because a stable relation between growth, driven by accumulation, and employment growth is posited.

Thus the simple Keynesian regression is

$$g^e{}_t = \beta_0 + \beta_1 g^*{}_t + \beta_2 \Delta z_t + \beta_3 x_t + \varepsilon_t \tag{4.2}$$

where g is the rate of capital accumulation, z capacity utilization, x control variables.

Equation (4.2) corresponds to equation (2.3) and is a variation on Okun's Law separating out the effect of accumulation and changes in capacity utilization. Note that it implies hysteresis since is formulated in rates of growth.

As discussed in Chapter 3, unemployment hysteresis has played an important role in European unemployment and has been incorporated into NAIRU models, giving rise to a distinction between a short-run NAIRU and a long-run NAIRU. Extending the NAIRU model to allow for hysteresis gives the following regression specification that has become standard in the time series context:

$$u_t = \beta_0 + \beta_1 \Delta p_t + \Sigma \beta_{2,i} \gamma_{0,i,t} + \beta_3 x_t + \beta_4 u_{t-1} + \varepsilon_t \tag{4.3}$$

Several authors have proposed extensions of the NAIRU model where the NAIRU depends on capital accumulation (Sawyer 2001, Rowthorn 1995 and 1999b, Arestis and Biefang-Frisancho Mariscal 1998). This is summarized in the following regression specification:

$$u_t = \beta_0 + \beta_1 \Delta p_t + \Sigma \beta_{2,i} \gamma_{0,i,t} + \beta_3 x_t + \beta_4 u_{t-1} + \beta_5 g^*_t + \varepsilon_t \tag{4.4}$$

This equation is also implied by the model presented in Chapter 2, where the key conclusion was that unemployment depends on capital accumulation and autonomous changes in the bargaining position of labour and capital. Two cases were distinguished. In the wage-led demand regime there was no stable long-run equilibrium rate of unemployment. However, in this case (4.4) corresponds only to the short-run equilibrium rate of unemployment (2.9). In this case the long-run stability conditions are not satisfied and β_4 is expected to be greater than unity. In the profit-led demand regime (4.4) is still the short-run equilibrium rate of unemployment. However a long-run equilibrium rate of unemployment exists (2.10), which is also reasonably approximated by (4.4), since it contains capital accumulation as well as exogenous factors of income distribution.[1]

4.2 DATA ISSUES

This section describes the data sources used and offers plots of the time series of all variables. Descriptive statistics and unit root tests can be found in the Appendix.

For the countries under investigation, no substantial empirical difference exists between the standardized and the national definition of the rate of unemployment. Following conventional practice, we use unemployment rates according to national definitions. Whether unemployment rates exhibit a unit root is subject to debate. Our tests (reported in the Appendix), support the frequent finding of unit roots, that is full hysteresis. What is clear, in any case, is that there are strong persistence effects in unemployment.

The core of the NAIRU explanation is that European unemployment is caused by labour market inflexibility and wage pressure. While a considerable amount of data is now available on a cross-country basis (for example in OECD 1994, Layard et al. 1991), time series data on labour market institutions are still limited. Thus data availability determines the choice of variables. We were able to incorporate a measure of the generosity of unemployment benefits (*RR*), union density (*UD*) and the tax wedge (*TW*). Only for two countries, the USA and France, is minimum wage data available as a time series. Higher unemployment benefits unambiguously increase the bargaining power of workers by increasing their non-employment income. Stronger unions, at least if union density is regarded as a proxy for the unions' ability to mobilize works to back up their wage demand, increase wage claims. Things are less clear for the tax wedge. While it is commonly argued that a higher tax wedge will lead to higher wage demand, assuming that workers care only about their after-tax wages and firms about the before-tax wages, Blanchard (1999) argues that the standard model predicts higher wages, but no effect on unemployment. Since we wish to use the standard variables in NAIRU employment specifications we decided to include the tax wedge. Finally, to control for the oil price shock, the terms of trade (*TOT*) are included. Except for job protection legislation, we therefore have taken into account the most frequently cited wage-push factors.

Inflation is measured by the rate of growth of the GDP deflator (see Figure 4.1). The terms of trade (*TOT*) are import prices divided by export prices. As the measure of the generosity of the unemployment benefit system the OECD gross replacement ratios (*RR*) are used. The OECD series offer comparable time series for most OECD countries that are based on legal entitlements, not actual payments. They count replacement rates for the first five years of unemployment with a higher weight for the first year. Thus the measure takes into account the level as well as the duration of unemployment benefits. *UD* is the net union density from Visser (1996), which excludes retired and unemployed union members. The same union density of course can mean different things in different countries, but in any country a stronger union should increase wage claims and, according to the NAIRU story, unemployment. The tax wedge (*TW*) is the difference between the wage cost paid by the firm and the wage income received by the worker. *TW* is direct taxes on household income plus social security contributions divided by the wage sum. Household income includes capital income, introducing some bias into our measure. However the resulting error ought to be small.

We regard the growth of private employment as the appropriate variable to be explained in the Keynesian story. As the measure for employment growth the rate of growth of private sector employment (*EPG*) is used. Accumulation (*ACCU*) is the rate of growth of the business sector gross fixed capital stock. As the capacity utilization variable we use capital productivity in the business sector, following stylized facts of growth theory that in the long run capital productivity follows no trend. This somewhat unorthodox choice is given preference over the output gap, because the output gap does include a concept of the NAIRU, the OECD NAWRU (non-accelerating wage rate of unemployment), in its calculation and therefore presupposes the existence of a NAIRU. The change of inflation, like in the NAIRU model, while potentially consistent with a Keynesian model, does not appear appropriate for a Keynesian model that does not necessarily have a NAIRU. However, to test for robustness with respect to the measure of capacity utilization, we alternatively use detrended capital productivity of the business sector, the output gap and the change in inflation. All these variables are highly correlated. Unsurprisingly therefore, the choice of the capacity variable has little effect on the accumulation coefficient. But the

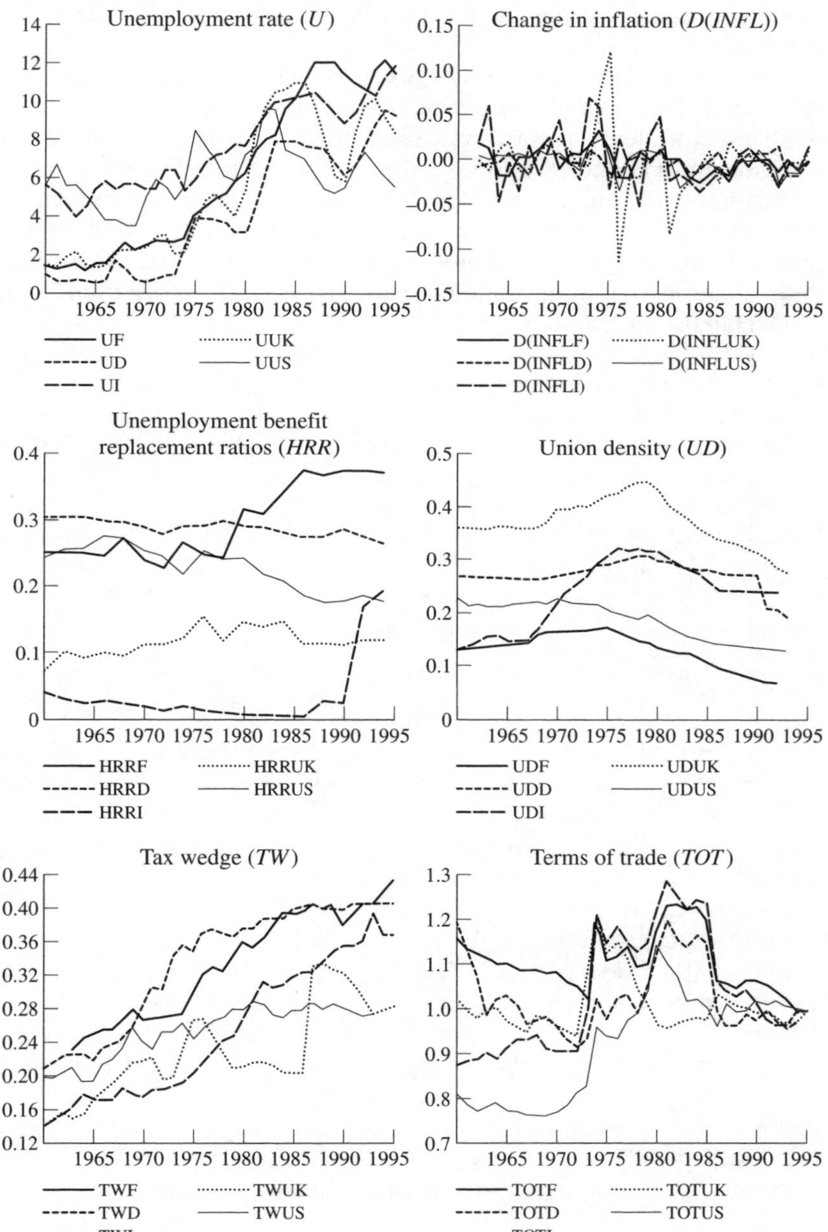

Figure 4.1 Summary plots of variables

robustness of the results is checked by using the output gap and the change in inflation.

EPG is clearly I(0), so is the change in CAPUT (see unit root tests in the Appendix). The order of integration is less clear for ACCU, for which the ADF test indicates I(1) rather than I(0), with trend stationarity not rejected either for most countries. However, the interval −5 to +15 per cent probably captures all values accumulation has taken on historically, making it very unlikely that it is a random walk.[2] Thus we will treat ACCU as if it were I(0), but test the results in an ADL framework (ADL models have desirable properties even in the presence of integrated series (Sims et al. 1990, Hamilton 1994).

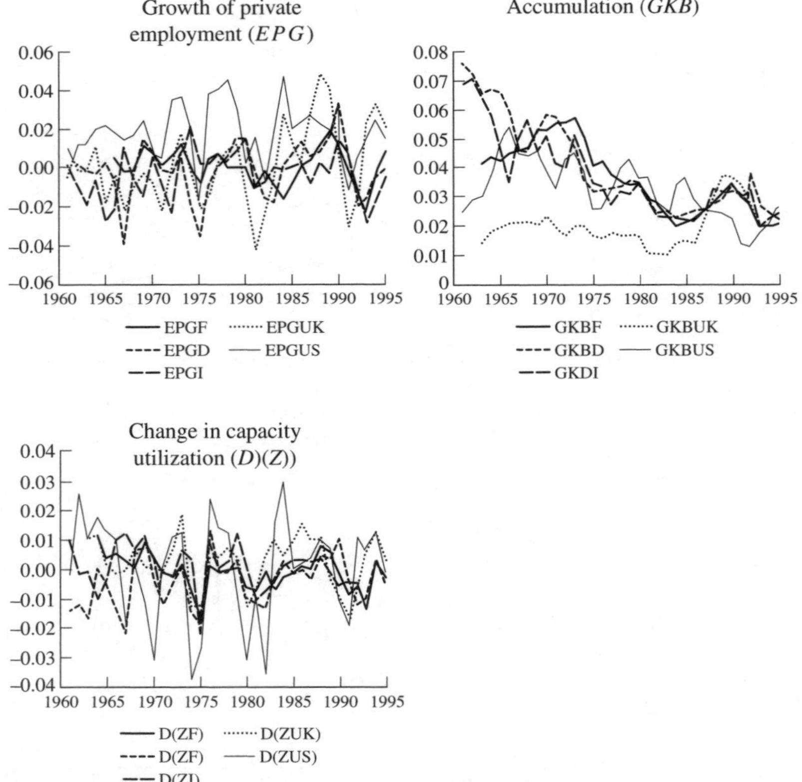

Note: observation for Germany 1991 (unification) deleted for some graphs.

Sources: see Appendix.

Figure 4.2 Summary plots of variables for Keynesian specification

4.3 ECONOMETRIC METHOD

Identical specifications are estimated for all countries which may lead to the neglect of country specificities, but has the advantage that it provides a better test of the validity of the model in question. More technically, it reduces the problem of data mining (Lovell 1983), since we do not customize the specification to get a best-fit regression or high t-values.

Since the five regressions cover the same period, we can make use of the possible correlation of the error terms that may arise from shocks that simultaneously hit all countries. This is exploited by applying Zellner's seemingly unrelated regression (SUR) method. To illustrate this procedure, take the two country case

$$\begin{bmatrix} y_1 \\ y_2 \end{bmatrix} = \begin{bmatrix} \beta_1 \\ \beta_2 \end{bmatrix} \begin{bmatrix} X_1 & 0 \\ 0 & X_2 \end{bmatrix} + \begin{bmatrix} \varepsilon_1 \\ \varepsilon_2 \end{bmatrix}$$

where y_c is the vector of variables to be explained and X_c is a matrix of explanatory variables for country c. For simplicity assume that X_c consists of vectors $x_{c,i}$ where the variable i represents the same variable for various countries c.

Assuming no autocorrelation and heteroscedasticity, the covariance matrix of the error term will have the following form:

$$\begin{bmatrix} \varepsilon_1 \\ \varepsilon_2 \end{bmatrix} * [\varepsilon_1 \quad \varepsilon_2] = \begin{bmatrix} \sigma_{11} & \cdots & 0 & \sigma_{12} & \cdots & 0 \\ \vdots & \ddots & \vdots & \vdots & \ddots & \vdots \\ 0 & \cdots & \sigma_{11} & 0 & \cdots & \sigma_{12} \\ \sigma_{21} & \cdots & 0 & \sigma_{22} & \cdots & 0 \\ \vdots & \ddots & \vdots & \vdots & \ddots & \vdots \\ 0 & \cdots & \sigma_{21} & 0 & \cdots & \sigma_{22} \end{bmatrix}$$

The partitions on the main diagonal reflect the standard assumption of OLS. If the main diagonal elements of the off-diagonal partitions are non-zero, the error terms of both countries are correlated. Estimating two separate OLS regressions is equivalent to assuming that these elements are zero. If they are not, the SUR method, first proposed by Zellner 1962 (for a textbook presentation see for example Greene 1997), using a generalized least square (GLS) procedure, will be appropriate. Thus even if the data cannot be pooled, more efficient estimates can be obtained if the two regressions are treated as a system and if the error terms of the two countries are correlated, that is if $\sigma_{12} \neq 0$.

Pooling in this example imposes the restriction that the two coefficient vectors are identical, that is $\beta_1 = \beta_2$. Pooling is thus a restriction that can be tested (with an F-test). Of course, we need not pool all variables, but could do so for only one variable, that is $\beta_{1,i}=\beta_{2,i}$. We proceed by estimating the equation first by OLS, second by SUR and test for pooling. Third, where appropriate, we also estimate using a restricted, that is pooled SUR. To decide upon pooling we adopt the following procedure. For each variable, we first test for pooling for all countries and, second, for four countries, that is we allow for one exception. If we fail to reject the null hypothesis of no pooling, that is the restriction of identical coefficients, at the 10 per cent level, the pooling restrictions are adopted. Finally we also test all such pooling restrictions simultaneously.

There is one potential practical problem that may arise from using SUR. Since we need the same period of observation for all countries, the country with the least observations dictates the period of investigation.

Since we are dealing with time series data we have to be aware of the problems of spurious regression results that may arise when two variables with unit roots are regressed onto each other (Campbell and Perron 1991, Charemza and Deadman 1997). Unfortunately in finite samples tests cannot distinguish between unit roots and autocorrelation. Miron's conclusion – 'since we can never know whether the data are trend stationary or difference stationary, any result that relies on the distinction is inherently uninteresting' (Miron 1991, p. 212) – may be too pessimistic, but effectively reminds us of the need for flexible modelling that can accommodate time series. Fortunately, autoregressive distributed lag (ADL) models do have desirable statistical properties in the presence of unit roots as well as with stationary data. In particular the estimates of the standard errors of the coefficients are consistent except for the lagged dependent variable (Sims et al. 1990, Hamilton 1994) even if all variables do have unit roots. We will thus test the robustness of our results by means of ADL models, where the ADF tests failed to reject a unit root in variables

4.4 TESTING THE NAIRU STORY

As explained above the basic specification of the NAIRU model is:

$$u_t=\beta_0+\beta_1\Delta INFL_t+\beta_2 RR_t+\beta_3 UD_t+\beta_4 TW_t+\beta_5 TOT_t+\varepsilon_t \quad (4.1')$$

with expected signs: $\beta_1<0$, $\beta_2>0$, $\beta_3>0$, $\beta_4>0$, $\beta_5>0$. Note that this specification does not allow for hysteresis.

The results of this regression are reported in Table 4.1. First we have to

Table 4.1 Specification (4.1), OLS

	Germany	France	Italy	UK	US
R^2	.96	.98	.96	.94	.84
period	63–93	66–92	63–92	63–93	63–93
C	2.36	4.8	2.03	24**	.25
t-value	*.17*	*.8*	*1.49*	*2.56*	*.06*
Δ infl	−21.8**	−12.4*	.28	−4.18	−40.6***
t-value	*2.5*	*1.72*	*.09*	*1.1*	*2.98*
rr	33.7	7.7	−12.4**	4.33	33*
t-value	*.71*	*.92*	*2.57*	*.14*	*1.69*
ud	−30.3*	−20	1.64	−30	−3.2
t-value	*1.77*	*.89*	*.38*	*1.61*	*.32*
tw	10.7	10.6	39.1***	−11.9	−19.8*
t-value	*.86*	*.8*	*12*	*1.31*	*1.73*
tot	.12	−.18	−3.8**	−2.6	8.3**
t-value	*.04*	*.09*	*2.07*	*.52*	*2.18*
dw	1.3	1.75	1.5	1.17	1.92
ADF	2.24	5.38*	4.8	3.32	4.5

Note:
Computations performed with Eviews. Germany: dummy for 1991 (unification) included.
critical values of Engle-Granger cointegrating ADF (30, 6) test:

1%	6.55
5%	5.66
10%	5.23

Source: Charemza and Deadman 1997.

address the question of spurious regression results. The regression passes a frequent rule of thumb, that the Durbin Watson (DW)- statistics exceeds the R-squared, but, except for France, the more rigorous Engle-Granger cointegration test fails to reject the null hypothesis of no cointegration. For Germany, Italy and the UK, the DW-statistics indicate the presence of autocorrelation. Thus we will have to look for better time series specifications, but it is still instructive to look at the results of this first regression. Only for the inflation variable do the results confirm the NAIRU approach. In four countries its sign is negative and in three cases it is statistically significant at conventional levels. For the other variables, looking only at coefficients that are statistically significant at least at the 10 per cent level, the signs do not correspond to the predictions: *RR* is negative in Italy and positive in the USA, *UD* is negative in Germany, *TW* is positive in Italy and negative in the USA. *TOT* is negative in Italy and positive in the

Table 4.2 Specification (4.3), OLS

	Germany	France	Italy	UK	US
r^2	.98	.99	.98	.92	.84
period	62–93	66–92	62–92	62–93	62–93
C	−2.6	−8.1***	1.3	4	−1.1
t-value		*3.09*	*1.58*	*.6*	*.3*
u_{-1}	.7***	.59***	.65***	.9***	.19
t-value	*10*	*4.2*	*4.7*	*6.6*	*1.29*
Δ infl	−21.3***	−12.7*	−6.5**	−8.12	−38.5***
t-value	*2.78*	*1.82*	*2.28*	*1.47*	*2.8*
RR	.54	7.9	−10.3***	−10.1	29.8
t-value	*0*	*1.27*	*3.14*	*.6*	*1.54*
UD	−19.4***	4.3	2.8	4.3	.6
t-value	*3.44*	*.5*	*1.28*	*.7*	*0*
TW	12***	16.1**	14.2**	−.7	−15.2
t-value	*3.35*	*2.24*	*2.46*	*.1*	*1.36*
TOT	4.94***	2.2	−2.2*	−2.3	6.9**
t-value	*3.1*	*1.43*	*1.82*	*.6*	*2.17*
dw	1.91	1.98	1.87	1.13	1.79

Note: Computations performed with Eviews. Germany: dummy for 1991 (unification) included.

USA. We conclude that while the trade-off between unemployment and the acceleration of inflation, the expectations-augmented Phillips curve, is confirmed, the regression clearly fails to explain the changes in the NAIRU.

We have tested different time series specifications, starting with an unrestricted autregressive distributed lag (ADL) model, which gives weak supports to entering the explanatory variables in levels rather than differences. The difference version of (Table 4.1) renders most variables insignificant, and an autocorrelation procedure does not lead to the predicted results.

As a convenient way to correct for autocorrelation in order to improve the reliability of the results, a lagged dependent variable was added on the right hand side (RHS) of the equation. This has the advantage of having an economic interpretation: it measures the extent of unemployment persistence. Thus the second equation to be estimated is:

$$u_t = \beta_0 + \beta_1 \Delta INFL_t + \beta_2 RR_t + \beta_3 UD_t + \beta_4 TW_t + \beta_5 TOT_t + \beta_6 u_{t-1} + \varepsilon_t \quad (4.3')$$

Table 4.3 Specification (4.3), diagnostic tests

	France	Germany	Italy	UK	USA
Testing for structural break: Chow test 1973					
F-value	.36	.57	.86	.69	.94
Prob.	.9	.77	.5	.69	.5
Testing for autocorrelation: Breusch-Godfrey 1 lag					
F-value	.11	.12	.17	7.73	.38
Prob.	.74	.73	.69	.01	.54

Note: null hypothesis is: no serial correlation

Table 4.3 summarizes the results of this regression. With the exception of the UK, autocorrelation of the error term is not a problem now. Since a lagged dependent variable is used the DW critical values do not apply, but the DW-statistics are still suggestive, as the Breusch-Godfrey serial correlation LM test confirms. (The estimates for the UK cannot be improved by an autocorrelation procedure, because the parameter estimates do not converge.) The results are similar to the first regression with the exception of *TW*, which is now positive and significant at least at the 5 per cent level in three continental European countries. The coefficient on the change in inflation is still consistently positive and significant in all but one country. *UD* and *RR* are significant in only one country each, Germany and Italy respectively, with a negative sign. *TOT* has the expected sign in Germany and the USA, but a negative sign in Italy. Unsurprisingly, the lagged unemployment rate is highly significant in all countries except the USA, with values ranging from .59 to .9. Thus persistence is high in these countries, but probably below full hysteresis.

The lack of significance of the labour market variables may be due to multicollinearity among these variables. And a quick look at the correlation among the variables confirms potential collinearity problems: the *TW* and *RR* are correlated with a coefficient above 0.6 in all countries, *TW* and *UD* in France and the USA, *UD* and *RR* only in Germany (Table 4A.8). The tax wedge was dropped from specification (4.3) to check whether this would improve the significance of the other labour market institution variables (Table 4A.9). It did not. *UD* remains insignificant in all countries, *RR* is significant twice but with the 'wrong' sign. However, two other things are remarkable about the results: *TOT* turns out to have the predicted positive sign in three countries at significant levels and the hysteresis term moves closer to unity. Thus multicollinearity does not seem to be the reason for the dismal performance of *RR* and *UD*.

Overall, while the expectations-augmented Phillips relation is confirmed, we fail to find evidence for labour market variables explaining changes in the NAIRU. In particular unemployment benefits and the organizational density of unions do not increase unemployment. Only the tax wedge seems to play the role that it is attributed by the NAIRU theory.

4.5 TESTING THE KEYNESIAN STORY

Accumulation is supposed to drive employment growth in the Keynesian model. To control for cyclical fluctuations, we add the change in capacity utilization. Thus the simple Keynesian regression is:

$$EPG_t = \beta_0 + \beta_1 ACCU_t + \beta_3 \Delta CAPUT_t + \varepsilon_t \qquad (4.2')$$

with expected signs: $\beta_1 > 0$, $\beta_2 > 0$

Table 4.4 summarizes the results of equation (4.2) with a shift dummy starting in 1973.[3] All variables have the expected signs and are highly significant. Accumulation is significant at the 1 per cent level in all countries but Germany, where it is significant at the 5 per cent level. Note that the dummy 1973 is positive in all countries, which may reflect the slowdown in trend productivity growth.

Applying SUR to the regression does improve the significance of the estimates, but does not change the signs of the coefficients. ACCU as well as

Table 4.4 Specification (4.2), SUR

	France	Germany	Italy	UK	USA
const	−0.03***	−0.04***	−0.04***	−0.04***	−0.02***
	−4.76	−2.22	−4.31	−5.63	−3.30
d CAPUT	1.22***	0.95***	0.43**	1.64***	0.59***
	7.59	5.30	2.24	6.30	7.98
ACCU	0.51***	0.65**	0.56***	1.55***	0.87***
	5.30	2.35	3.31	4.70	5.95
T73	0.01***	0.02**	0.02***	0.02***	0.01***
	3.84	1.99	4.78	3.24	4.52
R^2	0.70	0.96	0.42	0.63	0.72
DW	1.82	1.82	1.72	1.94	2.12

Note:
Germany: AR(1) correction and dummy 91 (unification)
Computations performed with Eviews. Germany: dummy for 1991 (unification) included.

CAPUT are significant at the 1 per cent level in all but one country, Germany and Italy respectively. In Germany ACCU is significant at the 10 per cent level. The explanatory power varies between countries. For Italy only 16 per cent of the variation of the dependent variable is explained, in all other countries, more than half of the variation is explained.

These results are fairly robust. Using the output gap as the capacity utilization variable has no effect on the significance of ACCU. Nor does using a lagged dependent variable on the RHS instead of the autocorrelation procedure. Adding a first difference of ACCU is often statistically significant, but does not affect the estimates of ACCU.

Overall, the Keynesian model performs remarkably well. Employment growth is consistently and at high levels of statistical significance correlated with accumulation. However the question remains whether this result still holds once labour market variables are included.

4.6 COMBINING NAIRU AND KEYNESIAN FACTORS

Finally we will add accumulation to equation (4.2), which leads to the following specification:

$$u_t = \beta_0 + \beta_1 \Delta INFL_t + \beta_2 RR_t + \beta_3 UD_t + \beta_4 TW_t + \beta_5 TOT_t + \beta_6 u_{t-1} + \beta_7 ACCU_t + \varepsilon_t \qquad (4.4')$$

Since the Keynesian argument is that accumulation determines employment growth we would expect that the log of capital stock rather than accumulation determines unemployment. However, including both log capital stock and accumulation in the regression makes clear that accumulation is the appropriate specification of the variable. Note that this may affect the interpretation. The log capital stock captures the capacity effects whereas its change, accumulation, captures the income effect.[4]

Equation (4.4) was estimated with SUR in which TW, U_{-1}, $ACCU$ and $INFL$ were highly significant with the predicted signs. Next tests were performed to determine which of these variables could be pooled across countries. As a result we failed to reject pooling for RR (except Italy), for persistence (except for the USA) and for accumulation (except the UK). For other coefficients pooling was rejected (testing pooling for four countries). The results of the unrestricted, that is non-pooled, regression and the test statistics can be found in the Appendix.

Table 4.5 summarizes the results of this restricted SUR. Autocorrelation problems remain for the UK, but are not serious for the other countries.

Table 4.5 Specification (4.4), SUR, pooled after testing

	Pooled	France	Germany	Italy	UK	USA
const		−0.15	3.33**	4.28***	8.69***	−6.13***
		−0.09	*2.02*	*5.55*	*3.60*	*−3.33*
d(infl)		−5.13	−19.06***	−2.45	−6.89**	−32.59***
		−0.99	*−4.02*	*−1.26*	*−2.02*	*−4.80*
RR	−1.41			−7.78***		
	−0.41			*−3.44*		
UD		0.21	−19.25***	−0.76	−10.37**	21.32***
		0.04	*−6.54*	*−0.43*	*−2.40*	*4.81*
TW		11.53***	4.31**	9.08***	24.44***	3.05
		3.27	*2.47*	*5.12*	*5.16*	*0.58*
TOT		0.42	3.82***	−1.97	−4.25**	7.16***
		0.37	*4.05*	*−2.29*	*−1.76*	*4.92*
U(-1)	0.68***					0.40***
	20.02					*5.41*
ACCU	−39.26***				−199.03***	
	−6.98				*−5.78*	
R-squared		0.99	0.98	0.98	0.94	0.87
Adjusted R-squared		0.99	0.97	0.98	0.92	0.83
S.E. of regression		0.38	0.48	0.38	0.95	0.65
Durbin-Watson		1.57	1.98	2.14	1.31	1.89

The results are consistent with the separate NAIRU and Keynesian regressions. The explanatory power of *ACCU* and *TW* are confirmed. Accumulation is highly significant in all countries, *TW* in four out of five, with consistent positive signs. Unemployment persistence can be pooled across European countries giving a value of about two-thirds, whereas for the USA it is around one-third. *INFL* still is consistently negative and statistically significant in three of five countries. The fact that we cannot pool $\Delta INFL$ suggests that the inflation unemployment trade-off varies between countries. The pooled value of *RR* is not significant, whereas the non-pooled value is significant at the 1 per cent level, but with a negative sign. *UD* is significant thrice, once with a positive sign, twice with a negative one. *TOT* is statistically significant in two countries, but with two positive signs (at the 1 per cent level) and one negative sign (at the 10 per cent level).

Second we enter the labour market variables in the Keynesian employment growth regression. This is done in differences:

$$EPG_t = \beta_0 + \beta_1 \Delta CAPUT_t + \beta_2 \Delta RR_t + \beta_3 UD_t + \beta_4 \Delta TW_t + \beta_5 \Delta TOT_t + \beta_6 ACCU_t + \beta_7 T73_t + \varepsilon_t \quad (4.5)$$

To estimate equation (4.5) we use SUR and test what variables could be pooled. We fail to reject pooling for all variables except for *CAPUT*. For *TW* and *TOT* we also fail to reject the hypothesis that all coefficients are simultaneously zero.

Table 4.6 reports the estimation results of specification (4.5) with the above pooling restrictions. Accumulation, the time dummy and the change in capacity utilization are consistently and highly significant. Among the institutional variables, the pooled *RR* and *TW* are significant, the former having a negative sign, the latter a positive. Note that *TW* is significant now despite the fact that when testing restrictions we failed to reject the hypothesis that it was simultaneously zero in all countries. *UD* is significant and negative in non-pooled Germany. *TOT* is not significant.

Table 4.6 Specification (4.5), pooled SUR

	Pooled	France	Germany	Italy	UK	USA
const		−0.03***	−0.03***	−0.04***	−0.04***	−0.01***
		−7.82	*−6.81*	*−9.89*	*−5.71*	*−3.06*
d CAPUT		1.24***	1.06***	0.34*	1.61***	0.54***
		7.64	*6.20*	*1.85*	*5.73*	*7.32*
d RR	−0.11**					
	−2.49					
d UD	0.14		−0.76			
	1.49		*−2.21*			
d TW	0.12*					
	2.02					
d TOT	−0.01					
	−0.67					
ACCU	0.59***				1.49***	
	8.32				*4.37*	
T73	0.014***			0.028***		
	6.70			*7.94*		
R-squared		0.66	0.96	0.47	0.61	0.72
Adjusted R-squared		0.54	0.95	0.31	0.46	0.64
S.E. of regression		0.01	0.01	0.01	0.02	0.01
Durbin-Watson stat		1.73	1.63	2.02	1.95	1.97

Note: The regressions were first estimated with an unrestricted SUR and tested for pooling. Then SUR was performed with the pooling restrictions that we failed to reject. The first column reports the estimate of the parameters that were restricted to be equal for the countries marked 'pooled'.

Adding accumulation to the NAIRU specification does not change the results strongly, whereas adding labour market variables to the Keynesian specification does. Accumulation performs well in the NAIRU specification, and the tax wedge stays significant. But the institutional variables yield very different results in the Keynesian specification. Here it is the replacement ratio that is significant and *TW*, significant once, has the wrong sign. Accumulation has a strong effect on unemployment irrespective of the specification, but institutional variables are sensitive with respect to the specification.[5] Accumulation does seem to do a better job in explaining unemployment than institutional variables.

In terms of the model proposed in Chapter 2, the results imply the following. The wage-push variables that proxy autonomous income distribution have no clear sign (*TW* cannot be interpreted as a variable that affects bargaining power). The wage-led regime would have implied an autoregressive term for unemployment of greater than 1. This is clearly not the case, indicating that the regime is profit-led rather than wage-led. However the conclusion that countries are profit-led is at odds with the stylised facts. As discussed in Chapter 1 unemployment has remained high despite a rising profit share, that is falling wages, which clearly does not suggest a profit-led regime. Given that the estimations have been performed for individual countries our results are consistent with the findings by Bowles and Boyer (1995) who conclude that most developed countries are profit-led due to export component of demand. However, the domestic component of demand is wage-led, which suggests that the world economy as a whole would be wage-led. Stockhammer and Onaran (2004) estimate a similar model with a systems approach and find that the distribution has weak effect on employment, whereas accumulation has strong effects. Further research on the issue is certainly needed.

4.7 CAUSALITY AND SIMULTANEITY

Correlation, of course, is not causation. In particular, the results do not tell us the direction of causation. For both significant variables, we cannot exclude that changes in employment are causing changes in accumulation and the tax wedge respectively. Higher employment may cause investment through an accelerator effect. Higher unemployment may lead to high taxes, since unemployment benefits have to be financed. Granger causality tests could in principle be used to address the question of causality, but in practice they are inconclusive, since we use yearly data. Finer time series data would be needed to distinguish between cause and effect.

One potential problem in the interpretation of the Keynesian regression is the issue of simultaneity and the question of causality. Turning first to simultaneity, accumulation as well as employment growth may be driven by another variable; an obvious candidate for such a variable is capacity utilization. Since we did control for capacity utilization, this problem is taken care of.

It could still be the case that employment growth is causing accumulation rather than the other way. To explore this, a variant of a bivariate Granger causality test was performed (on accumulation and employment growth, controlling for changes in capacity utilization; all variables were entered with two lags) with inconclusive results.[6] This is not inconsistent with the Keynesian argument. Given the high statistical significance of the contemporaneous correlation, the question is which variable is more likely to have an immediate effect. In investment functions usually lags are important, reflecting the time between investment decision and the installment of capital goods. Therefore a contemporaneous causation from employment growth to accumulation is unlikely.

As a more appropriate test, we performed a standard VAR on employment growth, the change of capacity utilization and accumulation, making use of the standard Choleski decomposition.[7] From a Keynesian perspective the above ordering (EPG, $\Delta CAPUT$, $ACCU$) is plausible. As argued above it is more likely that accumulation effects employment contemporaneously rather than vice versa. Further we assume that employment growth reacts immediately on changes in capacity utilization. The results are summarized in Figures 4A.1 and 4A.2 in the Appendix. The results support the Keynesian story. Employment growth and capacity react strongly to innovations in accumulation, but converge to their original values thereafter. Note that a one-time change in employment growth corresponds to a permanent increase in unemployment if labour supply grows at a constant rate. Moreover, employment growth has a negative impact on accumulation in four countries. However, by definition these results depend on the ordering we impose. It has to, since the sensitivity of the results to ordering depends on the contemporaneous correlation (Enders 1995).

Lastly we estimate simple VARs with accumulation, capacity utilization and unemployment. The results are similar to those above, though persistence becomes more obvious. This is unsurprising, since a one-time increase in employment growth corresponds to a permanent increase in unemployment (if labour force growth is constant). Again, an innovation in unemployment has the inverse effect (here: positive) on accumulation than accumulation on unemployment (here: negative). Again, the results support the Keynesian story, but depend on the ordering imposed. However, the negative effect of accumulation on unemployment is present even if ordering is reversed, though the extent decreases. Overall we interpret the VAR results as supportive of the Keynesian story in the sense that imposing a Keynesian ordering does not give counter-intuitive results. This obviously does not rule out that other explanations may be feasible too.

4.8 CONCLUSION

The aim of the chapter was to contrast and test the NAIRU story and the Keynesian theory of unemployment. For the former, wage-push variables are key, for the latter capital accumulation. Moreover, they also suggest different specifications of the dependent variable, the rate of unemployment and the growth of employment respectively. The theories were tested using time series data for Germany, France, Italy, the UK and the USA, using SUR.

Unemployment benefits, union density and the tax wedge were used as wage-push variables. The NAIRU specification performed poorly, with only the tax wedge having a positive effect on unemployment as predicted. As to the Keynesian approach, the role of accumulation was confirmed. Whereas accumulation is robust to the specification and can be pooled across countries, the tax wedge is not. In the Keynesian specification the tax wedge has the incorrect sign and replacement ratios are significant with the predicted sign.

These findings are at odds with parts of the empirical literature on the subject. In particular Nickell's claim that 'in practice, there seems to be no problem in finding wage pressure variables which explain long-run movements in (unemployment)' (Nickell 1998, p. 814) has been decisively rejected. Our evidence does not necessarily mean that labour market institutions play no role. First, our time series measures of labour market institutions may be too crude to measure what they are supposed to measure. Second, we have not studied the interaction between labour market variables and shock variables, here accumulation, that is we have not addressed some of the issues raised by Blanchard and Wolfers (2000). Third, there is multicollinearity between the institutional variables that may make it difficult to assign effects to any specific variable (though this argument does not apply to the employment growth specification, because the collinearity disappears once we move to differences).

However, all these possible and valid objections imply that the simple NAIRU story is too simple. If labour market institutions were really important they should show up with the predicted sign even if imperfectly measured. If important changes occurred in those institutions, they should show up in the variables. If institutions matter mostly because of interactions, then we need to care about the shocks more than about the institutions. Therefore we reiterate that our analysis, while allowing some room for labour market institutions indicates that they do not play the main role in explaining the rise in unemployment.

We conclude that the focus on labour market institutions in combating European unemployment is inappropriate. For example, we found no evidence that reducing unemployment benefits reduces unemployment. Demand variables, that according to the Keynesian theory are key even in the long run, on the other hand, should be taken more seriously. Our evidence indicates that the slowdown in accumulation is at least partially responsible for the insufficient creation of new jobs. This finding raises the question what the causes for the slowdown in accumulation are. This is the subject of the following chapter.

NOTES

1. We say approximated since (2.10) contains autonomous capital accumulation, while (4.4) contains capital accumulation as a whole. Strictly speaking, thus (4.4) does not correspond to (2.10). Note that the autonomous bargaining position is denoted as d_0 in (2.9) but as γ_0 in (4.4).
2. A random walk has no fixed mean, thus it wanders around freely. A time series that stays within given boundaries by definition cannot be a random walk (see Cochrane 1991 for a similar argument with respect to interest rates). However, we do not know what values accumulation will take on in the future. Therefore we cannot prove our case, but common sense certainly confirms that accumulation is not unbounded.
3. Specification (4.2) was estimated first by OLS and a structural break in 1973 was tested for. The break was confirmed for Germany, Italy and the USA at the 1 per cent level and for UK at the 20 per cent level, but not for France. Introducing a shift dummy starting in 1973 and letting it interact with both explanatory variables rendered none of the interacted variables, nor the shift dummy itself significant. Next we estimated for pre- and post-1973 periods separately and found no systematic pattern in the change of the coefficients on explanatory variables. The earlier period gave few significant estimates, which is probably due to the fact that there is little variation in the dependent variable. In the second period the results are highly significant. Thus the overall results are driven by the second period. We settled on including just a shift dummy starting in 1973, which is highly significant in all countries. Moreover, it also cured the autocorrelation problems present in the initial specification.
4. In specifications with differences and levels, levels capture the long-term effect, differences the short-term effect. In our case the short-term effect is the income effect (the income is created only for the year when the investment was undertaken). The long-term effect is the capacity effect (capacity is increased permanently, ignoring depreciation for the sake of the argument). However, there may be a purely technical reason why the capital stock does not seem to affect unemployment. If unemployment and accumulation are $I(0)$, then log capital stock has to be $I(1)$. We are thus regressing an $I(0)$ variable on an $I(1)$ variable, in which case the parameter estimates and the estimated standard errors are bogus.
5. This has been confirmed further by using the employment share (employment/working-age population) instead of the unemployment rate in specification (4.2). The tax wedge is significant twice, but with different signs; *RR* is significant once with the predicted sign; *UD* twice, with different signs.

6. The null that accumulation does not cause unemployment was rejected twice, the null that unemployment does not cause accumulation was rejected once. But the F-value was higher for the unemployment → accumulation in four countries. We failed to reject the null hypothesis that accumulation does not Granger cause employment growth consistently, and rejected the opposite hypothesis twice. However, the F-value was higher in the causation accumulation → private employment growth three times. Thus the results are inconclusive, which might be because of the use of annual data, which may be too crude to distinguish the direction of causation.
7. Vector auto-regression (VAR) models became popular in the 1980s to deal with systems of interrelated equations. Each variable is assumed to depend on the lagged values of all other variables in the system. When first proposed by Sims (1980) it was regarded as an atheoretical approach, because all variables were allegedly treated equally. This is not the case (for example Cooley and LeRoy 1986 as a critique of atheoretical econometrics). To solve a VAR, some assumptions have to be made about the interrelation of the error terms. In standard VARs this problem is dealt with by a procedure called the Choleski decomposition. This procedure does allow one to solve the VAR, but implicitly get the 'degree of exogeneity' of each variable from the ordering of variables in the VAR. In the mid-1980s 'structural VARs' were developed. They allow for an explicit treatment of the contemporaneous relation among variables (Endres 1995). Stockhammer and Onaran (2004) and Onaran and Stockhammer (2004) provide a estimations of a Kaleckian model by means of a structural VAR for some developed and developing countries respectively.

APPENDIX TO CHAPTER 4

4A.1 A Keynesian Model

Table 4A.1 A Keynesian model

investment	$g^I = \frac{I}{K} = \alpha_0 + \alpha_1 r$	1.1
saving	$g^S = \frac{S}{K} = sr$	1.3
prices	$P = \bar{W}a_1 + rPa_0$	1.4
employment function	$g^e = \varphi g^*$	1.2
unemployment	$u_t \equiv (g^n - g^e) + u_{t-1}$	

g^I accumulation
g^S savings/capital stock
g^e employment growth
$\bar{W}$ money wages
g^n natural rate of growth (growth of the labor force)
u unemployment rate
P price level
r profit rate
a_0 capital output ratio
a_1 labour output ratio
s saving ratio of profit income

in equilibrium: $g^* = \frac{s\alpha_0}{s - \alpha_1}$ and $g^e = \varphi \frac{s\alpha_0}{s - \alpha_1}$

4A.2 Unit Root Tests

Table 4A.2 Unit root tests

	France	Germany	Italy	UK	USA
U					
level	1.19	1.02	0.73	1.91	2.53
level + trend	3.48*	2.42	2.72*	3.6*	2.96
differences	3.93***	3.34**	5.09***	5.5***	4.77***
EPG					
period	68–96	63–96	63–94	64–96	64–96
level	3.77***	14.6***	4.22***	4.36***	4.77***
Employment rate (E)					
period	1960–98	1960–98	1960–98	1960–98	1960–98
level	1.09	1.36	2.4	3.2**	0.22
level + trend	2.03	3.36*	3.51**	3.53**	3.17*
differences	2.8	4.36***	3.7***	4.8***	4.9***
diff ADF +	2.7	4.32***	3.8***	4.7***	85***

4A.3 Data Definitions

EPG growth of private employment. Source: OECD Economic Outlook

ACCU growth of private sector gross capital stock. Source: OECD Economic Outlook

CAPUT capital productivity of the private sector. Source: OECD Economic Outlook

RR replacement rate of unemployment benefits. Source: OECD (the Gross Replacement Ratio data set was kindly made available to me). Data is available only for odd years, the rest was interpolated. Since there is little short-term variation in the series, the resulting error is probably small.

UD net union density. Source: Jelle Visser, *Unionisation Trends. The OECD Countries Union Membership File*, Amsterdam: University of Amsterdam, Centre for Research of European Societies and Labour Relations CESAR, 1996.

TW tax wedge. Direct taxes plus social security contributions divided by household income. Source: OECD Economic Outlook data set.

TOT terms of trade (import prices / export prices). Source: OECD Economic Outlook data set.

4A.4 Descriptive Statistics

Table 4A.3 Descriptive statistics

	UNF	D(INFLF)	HRRF	UDF	TWF	TOTF	GKBF	D(ZF)	EPGF
Mean	6.300	0.000	0.300	0.130	0.336	1.113	0.037	−0.001	0.001
Median	6.100	0.002	0.280	0.141	0.343	1.088	0.035	−0.001	0.000
Maximum	10.700	0.033	0.377	0.171	0.405	1.236	0.057	0.009	0.019
Minimum	1.600	−0.024	0.226	0.068	0.255	1.024	0.020	−0.018	−0.016
Std. dev.	3.288	0.014	0.056	0.035	0.057	0.066	0.012	0.006	0.009
Observations	27	27	27	27	27	27	27	27	27
	UD	D(INFLD)	HRRD	UDD	TWD	TOTD	GKBD	D(ZD)	EPGD
Mean	3.990	0.000	0.290	0.272	0.337	1.022	0.044	−0.004	0.007
Median	3.742	−0.001	0.291	0.273	0.369	0.997	0.035	−0.003	0.000
Maximum	8.850	0.038	0.305	0.307	0.406	1.201	0.150	0.012	0.270
Minimum	0.547	−0.022	0.272	0.193	0.219	0.914	0.023	−0.022	−0.039
Std. dev.	2.990	0.013	0.009	0.026	0.068	0.075	0.024	0.009	0.050
Observations	32	32	32	32	32	32	32	32	32
	UI	D(INFLI)	HRRI	UDI	TWI	TOTI	GKBI	D(ZI)	EPGI
Mean	7.794	0.001	0.024	0.243	0.247	1.053	0.038	0.000	−0.002
Median	7.205	−0.005	0.016	0.242	0.228	1.032	0.035	0.002	0.001
Maximum	12.104	0.070	0.167	0.322	0.362	1.289	0.071	0.013	0.021
Minimum	3.921	−0.051	0.003	0.143	0.154	0.887	0.021	−0.024	−0.027
Std. dev.	2.609	0.032	0.031	0.060	0.072	0.135	0.013	0.008	0.012
Observations	31	31	31	31	31	31	31	31	31

	UUK	D(INFLUK)	HRRUK	UDUK	TWUK	TOTUK	GKBUK	D(ZUK)	EPGUK
Mean	5.557	0.000	0.227	0.373	0.233	1.009	0.020	0.002	0.000
Median	4.844	−0.006	0.235	0.364	0.216	0.985	0.019	0.004	−0.001
Maximum	11.026	0.121	0.277	0.449	0.335	1.213	0.037	0.019	0.049
Minimum	1.323	−0.114	0.176	0.275	0.148	0.939	0.010	−0.016	−0.042
Std. dev.	3.447	0.041	0.033	0.047	0.052	0.064	0.007	0.009	0.021
Observations	31	31	31	31	31	31	31	31	31
	UUS	**D(INFLUS)**	**HRRUS**	**UDUS**	**TWUS**	**TOTUS**	**GKBUS**	**D(ZUS)**	**EPGUS**
Mean	6.155	0.001	0.118	0.182	0.256	0.926	0.033	0.000	0.018
Median	5.899	0.003	0.114	0.194	0.268	0.972	0.034	0.005	0.018
Maximum	9.719	0.034	0.155	0.225	0.289	1.145	0.054	0.030	0.047
Minimum	3.507	−0.034	0.091	0.128	0.192	0.762	0.013	−0.038	−0.020
Std. dev.	1.571	0.013	0.018	0.036	0.029	0.122	0.010	0.018	0.016
Observations	32	32	32	32	32	32	32	32	32

4A.5 Testing for Pooling: Specification (4.4)

Table 4A.4 Unemployment regression: testing for pooling, SUR

	France	Germany	Italy	UK	USA
r^2	0.99	0.98	0.98	0.95	0.88
c	−3.13	−1.89	4.41***	13.2**	−4.25**
	−1.16	−0.48	3.95	2.6	−1.95
d infl	−7.21	−19.3***	−1.65	−6.59*	−23.9***
	−1.32	−3.9	−0.67	−1.83	−3.18
RR	4.01	17.1	−8.3***	−18.1	15.8
	0.9	1.32	−3.37	−1.45	1.48
DU	6.05	−21.5***	−0.68	−7.08	15.6**
	1.03	−6.2	−0.37	−1.47	2.44
TW	16.2***	6.74**	15.3***	19.5***	−2.24
	3.02	2.32	3.56	3.43	−0.38
TOT	0.02	3.4***	−2.48***	−4.85*	6.08***
	0.02	3.45	−2.7	−1.82	3.24
u(−1)	0.58***	0.69***	0.53***	0.64***	0.34***
	5.73	14.4	5.06	5.7	4.03
gk	−37.5**	−37.6***	−37.3***	−197***	−43***
	−2.41	−3.4	−3.62	−4.64	−3.72
dw	1.70	1.87	2.00	1.37	1.92

Table 4A.5 Test results for pooling (unemployment regression)

coeff on gk		Chi^2	p
all countries	rejected	21	0
except UK	fail to reject	0.17	0.99
on u(−1)			
all countries	rejected	15	0
except US	fail to reject	2.71	0.44
on *TW*			
all =0		37	
all countries	rejected	11	0.03
except US		6.16	0.1
x US, D		0.36	0.8
on d infl			
all		15.9	0
x Italy		7.5	0.06
x I, US		4.63	0.1
on *RR*			
all		13.83	0.01
all=0		18.7	0
x Italy		5.87	0.12
on *UD*			
all=0		50.3	0
all		44	0
x USA		34	0
on *TOT*			
all=0		32	0
all		32	0
x USA			
c(3)=c(13)=c(33)=c(43), c(8)=c(18)=c(28)=c(38,c(9)=c(19)=c(29)=c(49)			
		12	0.21

4A.6 Testing for Pooling: Specification (4.4′)

Table 4A.6 Testing for pooling: specification (4.2′)

	France	Germany	Italy	UK	USA
const	−0.03	−0.03	−0.03	−0.05	−0.01
	−4.85	*−1.61*	*−2.86*	*−5.03*	*−1.85*
d *CAPUT*	1.20	1.04	0.36	1.74	0.58
	6.73	*5.39*	*1.91*	*5.16*	*8.62*
d *RR*	−0.14	0.74	−0.05	−0.17	−0.24
	−2.09	*1.17*	*−0.54*	*−0.51*	*−2.03*
d *UD*	−0.11	−0.92	0.25	0.21	0.38
	−0.50	*−2.02*	*1.66*	*0.91*	*1.65*
d *TW*	0.07	−0.02	0.04	0.13	0.24
	0.66	*−0.12*	*0.19*	*0.64*	*1.97*
d *TOT*	−0.01	−0.02	−0.01	−0.04	0.09
	−0.61	*−0.56*	*−0.19*	*−0.65*	*2.73*
ACCU	0.57	0.68	0.28	1.59	0.63
	5.15	*1.98*	*1.39*	*4.21*	*4.40*
*T*73	0.012	0.012	0.023	0.017	0.012
	3.64	*1.05*	*4.31*	*2.96*	*4.41*
R-squared	0.687	0.967	0.527	0.620	0.830
Adjusted R-squared	0.572	0.954	0.384	0.482	0.783
S.E. of regression	0.006	0.011	0.009	0.015	0.007
Durbin-Watson stat	1.877	1.700	2.413	2.062	2.088

Table 4A.7 Test results for pooling: specification (4.2′)

Testing restrictions		Chi-2	Prob
const	all =	11.52	0.02
	all = 0	60.25	0
d *CAPUT*	all =	26.14	0
	all exc. C12	24	0
RR	all =	3.5	0.48
	all = 0	10	0.07
	all exc. C13 = 0	1.83	0.06
UD	all =	8.38	0.08
	all = 0	10.83	0.05
	all exc. C14	2.67	0.44
TW	all =	2.21	0.7
	all = 0	4.92	0.42
c6	all =	8.48	0.08
	all = 0	8.64	0.12
	all exc. C46	0.29	0.96
ACCU	all =	9.23	0.06
	all = 0	70.57	0
	all exc. C14	2.23	0.53
*T*73	all =	4.17	0.38
	all = 0	58.59	0
testing restrictions combined			
const	none		
d *CAPUT*	none		
RR	F, I, UK, USA		
UD	F, I, UK, USA		
TW	F, Ger, I, UK, USA		
TOT	F, Ger, I, UK		
ACCU	F, Ger, I, USA		
*T*73	F, Ger, I, UK, USA		
		36.98	0.02
testing restrictions combined			
const	none		
d *CAPUT*	none		
RR	F, I, UK, USA		
UD	F, I, UK, USA		
TW	F, Ger, I, UK, USA		
TOT	F, Ger, I, UK		
ACCU	F, Ger, I, USA		
*T*73	F, Ger, UK, USA		
		14.7	0.79

4A.7 Addressing multicollinearity

Table 4A.8 Correlation among labour market variables

France					
u	d infl	rr	udf	tw	tot
1.00	−0.45	0.94	−0.86	0.99	0.17
	1.00	−0.32	0.37	−0.43	−0.17
		1.00	−0.94	0.92	0.06
			1.00	−0.85	0.11
				1.00	0.17
					1.00
Italy					
u	d infl	rr	udf	tw	tot
1.00	−0.30	0.19	0.36	0.97	0.40
	1.00	−0.10	0.01	−0.31	−0.13
		1.00	−0.21	0.28	−0.35
			1.00	0.41	0.81
				1.00	0.47
					1.00
UK					
u	d infl	rr	udf	tw	tot
1.00	−0.29	−0.79	−0.40	0.46	−0.13
	1.00	0.01	0.09	0.03	0.17
		1.00	0.57	−0.74	−0.06
			1.00	−0.38	0.39
				1.00	0.22
					1.00
Germany					
u	d infl	rr	udf	tw	tot
1.00	−0.17	−0.68	0.29	0.85	0.43
	1.00	0.04	−0.15	−0.06	−0.12
		1.00	−0.04	−0.72	0.06
			1.00	0.63	0.40
				1.00	0.32
					1.00
USA					
u	d infl	rr	udf	tw	tot
1.00	−0.61	0.81	−0.48	0.52	0.71
	1.00	−0.40	0.31	−0.17	−0.21
		1.00	−0.32	0.64	0.75
			1.00	−0.73	−0.74
				1.00	0.86
					1.00

Table 4A.8 summarizes the correlation coefficients between labor market variables. Correlations with *u* are generally very high, but in our view that merely reflects the strong autoregressive component that exists in virtually all series.

Strong correlations, which we take as correlations coefficients greater than .6, between labour market institutions variables exist in all countries:

France: *TW* and *RR*; *TW* and *UD*; *UD* and *RR*

Germany: *TW* and *RR*

Italy: *TW* and *RR*

UK: *TW* and *RR*

USA: *TW* and *RR*; *TW* and *UD*; *TOT* and all other institutional variables

Since *TW* seems to be the variable that causes most correlation problems we decided to drop it as a test for how sensitive the results are to multicollinearity problems.

Table 4A.9 Regression results: specification (4.3) without tax wedge

	France	Germany	Italy	UK	USA
cons	−5.46**	9.36*	0.65	3.58	−4.34
	−2.18	*1.78*	*0.77*	*0.65*	*−1.51*
d Infl	−15.72**	−18.26**	−10.15***	−8.03	−41.03***
	−2.05	*−2.02*	*−3.74*	*−1.49*	*−2.92*
RR	6.02	−41.82**	−6.61**	−8.91	17.43
	0.87	*−2.11*	*−2.06*	*−0.61*	*0.96*
UD	2.31	−8.12	3.25	4.27	7.35
	0.26	*−1.51*	*1.34*	*0.67*	*0.92*
TOT	4.04***	5.67***	−0.84	−2.35	5.83*
	2.59	*3.03*	*−0.71*	*−0.60*	*1.83*
u(−1)	0.89***	0.84***	0.97***	0.91***	0.28**
	9.68	*12.94*	*25.29*	*7.16*	*2.02*
R-squared	0.99	0.96	0.97	0.92	0.83
Adjusted R-squared	0.98	0.96	0.97	0.90	0.80
S.E. of regression	0.44	0.63	0.46	1.08	0.71
Durbin-Watson stat	1.78	1.63	1.97	1.13	1.86

Note: dummy for Germany 1991 (unification) was included.

The regression in Table 4A.9 was performed to test for the sensitivity to multicollinearity. The tax wedge was dropped because correlation analysis found that it was correlated with *RR* and *UD* in many countries. The results of this exercise are interesting and somewhat unexpected. First, the terms of trade variable now turns significant with the predicted sign in three countries, in the other two countries it is the 'wrong' sign and is insignificant. Second, the signs of the remaining two institutional variables are entirely inconsistent with the NAIRU story. *RR* is significant twice (Germany and Italy, both at the 5 per cent level). *UD* is insignificant in all countries. Third, the persistence coefficients get very close to unity in all European countries, suggesting the presence or near presence of a unit root. The first point does encourage some trust in the specification. The second and third point are clearly inconsistent with the NAIRU story. (Autocorrelation does not appear to be a major problem except for the UK, where a standard AR(1) correction did not improve the results.)

4A.8 How Robust are Variables for Labour Market Institutions?

Table 4A.10 Employment regression, specification (4.1′)

	France	Germany	Italy	UK	USA
const	0.23***	0.27***	0.08**	0.08	0.35***
	2.98	*3.54*	*2.24*	*1.15*	*4.35*
d infl	0.11*	0.25***	0.08***	0.09*	0.31**
	1.80	*3.23*	*3.00*	*1.77*	*2.31*
RR	−0.11*	0.01	0.02	0.08	−0.07
	−1.94	*0.03*	*0.46*	*0.55*	*−0.42*
UD	−0.01	0.10*	0.02	−0.05	−0.45***
	−0.08	*1.86*	*0.58*	*−0.74*	*−3.98*
TW	0.00	−0.10***	−0.02	0.02	0.29***
	−0.01	*−2.96*	*−0.97*	*0.35*	*2.95*
TOT	−0.04***	−0.05***	0.00	0.04	−0.03
	−2.86	*−2.87*	*0.37*	*1.02*	*−1.10*
ES(−1)	0.75***	0.68***	0.84***	0.81***	0.54***
	7.05	*8.39*	*13.97*	*6.25*	*5.10*
R-squared	0.99	0.97	0.97	0.83	0.98
Adjusted R-squared	0.99	0.96	0.96	0.79	0.97
S.E. of regression	0.00	0.01	0.00	0.01	0.01
Durbin-Watson stat	1.86	1.58	2.04	1.23	1.77

Note:
Dependent variable: employment share
Sample: 1962 1993

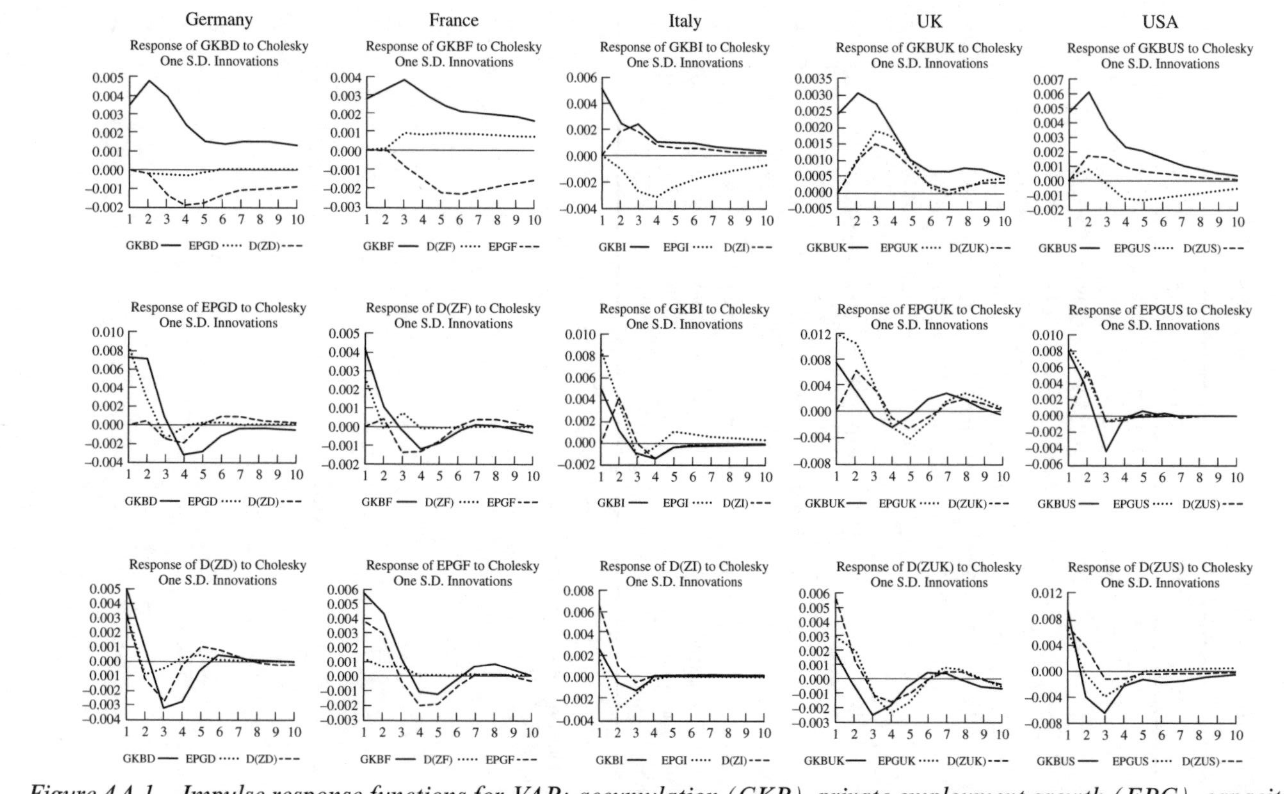

Figure 4A.1 Impulse response functions for VAR: accumulation (GKB), private employment growth (EPG), capacity utilization (Z)

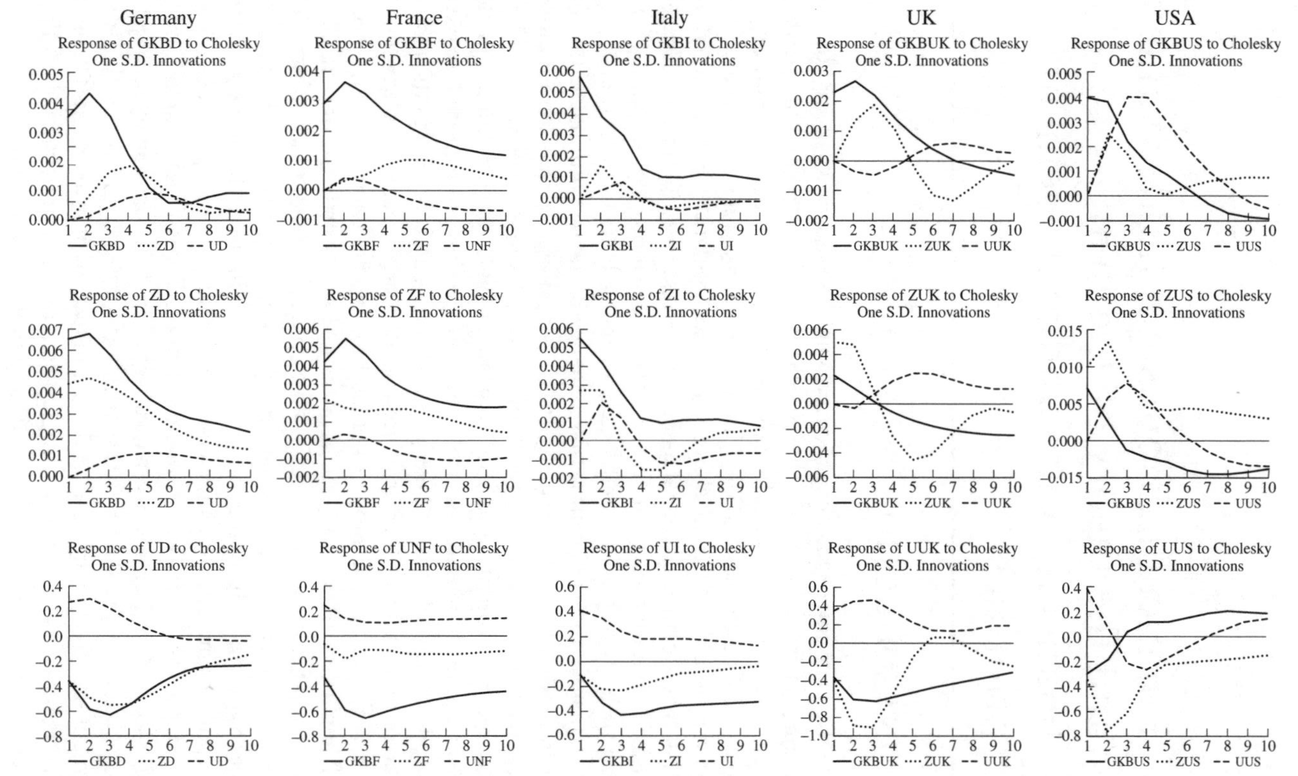

Figure 4A.2 Impulse responses for VAR with accumulation (GKB), capacity utilization (Z) and unemployment (U)

5. Financialization, shareholder value and the theory of the firm: financialization and management priorities

5.1 INTRODUCTION

Most OECD countries have experienced a marked slowdown in growth and accumulation from the 1960s to the 1990s. In this chapter we argue that financialization, that is the adoption of shareholder value orientation by non-financial businesses and their increasing investment in financial assets, is an important factor in the slowdown of accumulation. The argument is not that investment in financial assets itself causes a reduction in physical investment, but that financial investments are a symptom of the changes in management priorities – or preferences of management, if one prefers.

In a nutshell, the argument is that a change in the institutional setting of the firm occurred. The Golden Age was a period of relatively autonomous management that lead to a growth-oriented investment policy, which has been called 'managerial capitalism'. Starting in the 1970s shareholders made stronger claims on management by means of the development of a market of corporate control (hostile takeovers and so on) and changes in the remunerations of managers (performance-oriented pay schemes for example). This led management to adopt, or at least follow, shareholders' preferences, which implies a shift in management priorities from growth to profits. If there is a trade-off between growth and profits, which is a standard assumption in the literature, then this will translate into lower investment (on the firm level).

The chapter introduces the concept of financialization, that is the growing importance of income from financial assets or transactions, provides empirical evidence for the process of financialization, discusses relevant literature on its effects of corporate governance and its impacts on management priorities. Based on the Post-Keynesian theory of the firm, we develop the argument that financialization leads to a reduction in investment. Chapter 6 will set out to test the empirical implications of this argument, namely that financial income is negatively related to capital accumulation.

The 1980s have been different in many respects from the previous decades: lower growth rates and higher unemployment rates have been the topic of the previous chapters; other important issues include the changing role of financial markets, fast-rising incomes from financial investments and high real interest rates. These developments have most likely had an impact on firms' management priorities and consequently on their investment behaviour. This is the topic of the current chapter. We wish to show empirically how rentiers' income has risen over the past decades, review the literature on corporate governance for its implications on the effect of financialization on management priorities, and develop a modern Post-Keynesian theory of the firm that shows how the 'shareholder revolution' has led to a slowdown in desired accumulation rates.

This chapter is structured as follows. The first section reviews the evidence on rising rentiers' income, which we define as dividend and interest income. The aim of this section is to give an overview over the relative importance of rentiers' income for various sectors of the economy. We look at real interest rates as a broad indicator, but focus our analysis on the relative size of rentiers' income relative to overall income for the non-financial business sector. We also provide measures for rentiers' income of the household sector. Section 2 summarizes the literature on the causes and effects of financialization as they are relevant to management priorities and firms' behaviour. The focus of this section is what has become known as the 'shareholder revolution', that is the emergence of a market of corporate governance and a rising orientation of management along the lines of creating shareholder value. The third section of this chapter develops a Post-Keynesian theory of the firm that allows for an analysis of financialization. The standard Post-Keynesian literature on the firm, we argue, is appropriate only for 'managerial capitalism'. Based on a Marxian-inspired class analysis, but keeping the institutional focus, we show how the Post-Keynesian approach can be adapted to analyse the effects on financialization and, more specifically, its effects on investment behaviour.

5.2 THE RISE OF RENTIERS' INCOME

This section illustrates the rising role of financial investment and the income thereof. Note that we are concerned with rentiers' income, not with capital gains. The first variable looked at is real interest rates. Then we will look at the non-financial business sector and finally we investigate profits in the financial sector. The data used on rentiers' income are from the OECD National Accounts Detailed Tables data base.

The Table 5.1 presents data on the real long-term interest rate, here

Table 5.1 Real long-term interests 1950–96

	France	Germany	United States	United Kingdom	Italy	Japan
50–54	−1.32		1.97	−0.71	1.97	
55–59	0.38	4.82	1.81	2.49	4.38	
60–64	1.31	3.73	2.75	2.86	1.75	
65–69	2.14	4.92	1.73	3.45	4.11	2.05
70–74	0.71	3.15	0.68	0.91	−0.71	−3.20
75–79	−0.80	2.99	0.12	−2.27	−2.13	0.35
80–84	2.94	4.16	4.89	2.98	1.92	4.12
85–89	5.80	5.10	5.21	4.51	4.60	3.81
90–94	5.83	3.97	3.63	4.59	6.69	3.24
95/96	5.09	4.39	3.64	5.24	6.20	2.35

Note: CPI used as deflator

Source: IMF

measured as the yield on long-term government bonds minus inflation (CPI). Interest rates are the most basic variable in discussing rates of return on financial investment. Real interest rates were at modest levels (around 2 or 3 per cent) in the 1960s, very low and often negative in the 1970s and increased to almost 5 per cent and more after in the 1980s and 1990s. The major exception to this picture is Germany, where interest was at fairly high levels through the post-war era. In the post-war era the financial sector was heavily regulated, often with ceilings for interest rates, so as to foster growth in the real sector, thus the moderate interest rates back then. The negative interest rates in the 1970s were due to soaring inflation at this time. Ignited by the OPEC oil price increases and heightened distributional conflicts between capital and labour, most countries witnessed double-digit inflation rates that eroded (real) returns on financial investment. In the early 1980s the monetarist revolution changed the priorities of economic policy in general and monetary policy in particular, leading to an anti-inflationist policy that resulted in historically high real interest rates.

5.2.1 Rentier Income by Households

First we look at household income. All countries exhibit a fairly unambiguous rise in interest and dividend income over the entire post-war era. It is interesting to note that the starting level in the Anglo-Saxon countries was much higher than in continental European countries and big differences in

Table 5.2 Rentiers of households' income

	W. Germany	France	UK	US	Italy	Japan
60–64	0.022		0.098	0.086		0.067
65–69	0.029		0.103	0.095		0.074
70–74	0.040	0.044	0.085	0.095		0.082
75–79	0.040	0.049	0.073	0.103		0.083
80–84	0.057	0.058	0.094	0.139	0.090	0.101
85–89	0.059	0.060	0.119	0.148	0.088	0.094
90–94	0.068	0.071	0.119	0.135	0.101	0.090
95/96		0.069	0.117	0.133	0.099	0.061

Note: Rentiers' share is defined as dividend and interest income as a share of total houshold income.

Source: OECD National Accounts.

the rentiers' share still persist. In West Germany and France the share of rentiers' income in household income is around 7 per cent, whereas the UK and US are at 12 and 14 per cent respectively. This is probably related to the differences in the structure of the financial system to be discussed later.

5.2.2 The Non-financial Business Sector

Next we take a look at non-financial enterprises. This is of particular interest, since much of the alleged changes in the relation between finance and enterprises should be reflected here. Three measures of rentiers' income with respect to non-financial enterprises are discussed: interest and dividends received, interest and dividends paid, and the ratio of new liabilities to new financial assets.

First, dividend and interest received (by non-financial enterprises) is compared to the operating surplus of non-financial enterprises. This is a measure that will exhibit an anti-cyclical pattern, since the denominator (operating surplus) has a strong pro-cyclical behaviour. Hence the high rentiers' income ratio in the period 1980–84, a time of recession, may tell more about the low profits than about a structural change in the income composition. In the econometric part we will divide rentiers' income of the non-financial business sector by its value added to avoid this cyclical behaviour (see Appendix 1 for the corresponding data).

Non-financial enterprises now get a significant part of their income from financial transactions. This share is around 50 per cent (interest and dividend income as a percentage of operating surplus) in Anglo-Saxon

Table 5.3 Rentiers' share of non-financial businesses, 1960–94

	W. Germany	Germany	France	USA	UK	Italy	Japan
60–64	0.038			0.171			
65–69	0.048			0.169	0.201		
70–74	0.068		0.092	0.292	0.467		0.181
75–79	0.064		0.164	0.327	0.447		0.201
80–84	0.099		0.300	0.494	0.356	0.269	0.189
85–89	0.092		0.250	0.520	0.325	0.198	0.174
90–94	0.135	0.129	0.415	0.567	0.472	0.197	0.191
95/96		0.105	0.481	0.508	0.399	0.188	0.118

Note: Rentiers' share is defined as dividend an interest income received as a share of operating surplus. Data cover the periods 1960–93 (West Germany), 1980–89 (Italy), and 1968–96 (UK).

Source: OECD National Accounts.

countries and France. A trend to rising financial income is evident in Germany, France and the US. The UK and Japan had high levels in the 1970s.

Next the interest and dividends payments of non-financial firms are discussed. Again we look at the ratio of these payments over the operating surplus. The numbers are surprisingly high. Except for Germany and Japan, interest and dividend payments have exceeded the operating surplus at some point in time. Again we have a strong anti-cyclical pattern. Most countries exhibit the highest values in the early 1980s. Except for the UK and Japan, all countries have rising ratios until the early 1980s, and a stagnation afterwards. However the levels in the late 1980s and early 1990s are significantly above Golden Age levels. In the UK and the USA close to all operating surplus is transformed into dividend and interest payments.

Finally, we turn to the incurrence of liabilities versus acquisition of assets by non-financial firms (a value of less than one indicates that the sector is a net lender). Unfortunately here data availability is much more limited than for the previous measures. Except for the USA and Japan, data start in 1970 only. What is evident nonetheless is that by the early 1990s non-financial businesses moved from a net lenders position towards a net creditor position. But only in France and the USA is the non-financial business sector actually a net creditor in the 1990s.

The evidence presented above does indicate that non-financial businesses do strongly experience the rise of interest and dividend incomes – on the income side as well as on the expenditure side. It is almost tempting to

Table 5.4 Rentiers' payments share of non-financial businesses, 1960–96

	France	W. Germany	UK	USA	Italy	Japan
60–64		0.172		0.488		
65–69		0.218	0.743	0.496		
70–74	0.591	0.309	1.019	0.712		0.691
75–79	0.846	0.324	1.057	0.722		0.816
80–84	1.210	0.452	0.882	1.009	1.077	0.722
85–89	0.829	0.373	0.789	0.958	0.688	0.590
90–94	0.978	0.427	1.145	1.012	0.761	0.698
95/96	1.005		0.981	0.848	0.579	0.564

Note: Rentiers' payments share is defined as dividend and interest payments divided by operating surplus.

Source: OECD National Accounts.

Table 5.5 Incurrence of liabilities vs. acquisition of assets by non-financial businesses, 1960–96

	W. Germany	France	UK	USA	Italy	Japan
60–64				1.906		1.624
65–69				1.840		1.511
70–74	3.129	1.913	2.844	1.829		1.730
75–79	2.330	1.705	1.390	1.232		1.600
80–84	2.569	1.535	0.944	1.403	2.121	1.790
85–89	1.696	1.196	1.088	1.341	1.873	1.512
90–94	1.137	0.956		0.863		3.823
95/96		0.789				1.465

Note: The table gives data for incurrence of liabilities divided by the acquisition of assets by non-financial businesses.

Source: OECD National Accounts.

speak of 'rentieralization' of non-financial businesses. This is likely to affect their investment behaviour.

5.2.3 Profits in the Financial Sector

Lastly we look at profits in the financial sector. In the National Accounts this sector is defined as financial services, insurance and real estate (FIRE). The data show what share of the total operating surplus accrues to the

Table 5.6 Relative profit share of the financial sector, 1960–96

	W. Germany	France	UK	USA	Italy	Japan
60–64	0.027			0.323		0.174
65–69	0.037			0.317		0.199
70–74	0.049		0.339	0.338	0.249	0.219
75–79	0.065	0.264	0.374	0.315	0.247	0.239
80–84	0.096	0.300	0.325	0.391	0.252	0.260
85–89	0.076	0.319	0.336	0.422	0.292	0.287
90–94	0.072	0.325	0.413	0.463	0.339	0.329
95/96			0.425	0.447	0.343	0.387

Note: The relative profit share is calculated as the operating of the financial sector divided by the operating surplus of the entire economy. The data period differs for the following countries: West Germany (1960–93), France (1977–92), and UK (1970–95).

Source: OECD National Accounts.

financial sector. In all countries this share has risen considerably since the 1960s, with interesting differences in levels. While in Germany (West) less than 10 per cent of the total operating surplus go to the financial sector, in all other countries it is more than 30 per cent, in the Anglo-Saxon countries more than 40 per cent.

The overall evidence in this section clearly indicates the rising importance of rentiers' income, that is dividend and interest income, by the private non-financial business sector and the rising ability of the financial sector, once regarded as unproductive, to appropriate profits. What is of particular interest here is that the non-financial business sector is unambiguously part of these developments, which is likely to have an impact on its investment behaviour.

5.3 CAUSES AND EFFECTS OF FINANCIALIZATION

The term 'financialization' is used here to signify the increased importance of income from financial assets, which we will also refer to as rentiers' income, that have been demonstrated above and the hypothesized behavioural impacts that will be elaborated below. Since financialization includes a wide range of phenomena, there is a diverse literature discussing various parts of it, making it impossible to provide a complete coverage. We will focus on the issues relevant to our arguments below, that is the development of a market for corporate control, or the 'shareholder revolution', but provide brief notes on the question of globalization on financial markets and on explanations of real interest rates.

5.3.1 Globalization

The rise in rentiers' income went in parallel with globalization, or more specifically the globalization, or integration, of financial markets. While different methods of measuring the degree of integration of capital market yield different results, there can be little doubt that financial markets are in fact more integrated now than they were some 40 years ago (see Epstein 1996 and Frankel 1992 as surveys). Most of the debate on the effects of capital mobility, the most important effect of the globalization of financial markets, has focused on its impacts on the possibility of national economic policy (for example Baker et al. 1998, Banuri and Schor 1992). This literature is not concerned with investment decisions *per se*, but with the question of mobility of real capital, how sensitive investment is to national policy and whether this sensitivity has increased.

5.3.2 The Rise in Interest Rates

The fact that real interest rates are at historically high rates (Leny and Panetta 1996) has received surprisingly little attention in the mainstream literature. While in political debates it was often argued that high budget deficits and a shortage of savings constitute the major reasons for high real interest rates, empirical research has not provided support to this position. An OECD study summarizes the literature as follows: 'the link between fiscal policy and the real interest rate has been difficult to establish empirically. Most reduced-form studies have found little evidence of a relationship between nominal or real interest rates and fiscal policy' (Tease et al. 1991, p. 126).

While interest rates are a price set by capital markets for neo-classical economists, they are a conventional price set by (or at least influenced greatly by) central banks for heterodox economists. Explaining high interest rates therefore is tantamount to explaining why central banks changed their monetary policy. Smithin (1996) is an extreme example of this viewpoint. He argues that in the post-war era there was a social compromise that allowed for low but positive real interest rates for rentiers. In the 1970s this compromise broke up due to rising inflation, which led to negative interest rates. In parallel, other features of the Golden Age institutional setting had also been eroded. As a consequence rentiers pushed for a policy change:

> The result was ultimately a political revolution around the years 1979 and 1982, the most important feature of which was the 'capture' of central banks by rentier

> interests, and their conversion thereafter to exclusively 'hard money', high interest and anti-inflation policies. . . . In a very real sense, however, the ultimate purpose behind the 'conservative' prescriptions . . . is to maintain and increase the real rate of return to financial capital. (Smithin 1996, p. 5)

Obviously not all Post-Keynesians take such a strong view. More analytically, Epstein and Schor (1990) and Epstein (1994) have argued that the policy of the central bank depends on the institutional settings. In particular, independent central banks will have a bias towards rentier interests. However, whether this translates into restrictive monetary policy also depends on the relation between industrial capital and the financial sector. Whatever the exact argument, most heterodox economists regard high real interest rates, and certainly those of the 1980s, as results of economic policy rather than of market forces.[1]

5.3.3 Shareholder Value and Corporate Governance

Interest rates have a direct effect on investment and the high real interest rates of the 1980s are certainly the most obvious candidate for an effect of financialization on investment. However in practice the interest effect on investment is often rather small (more on this later). But interest rates are not the only channel through which investment may be affected by financialization. Since the 1970s stock markets have played an increasingly important role, especially in the Anglo-Saxon countries. Not only have valuations and stock prices increased, which gives rise to wealth effects in consumption (Potera and Samwick 1995, Boone et al. 1998), but the ascent of shareholder value may have affected business behaviour.

From the early 1970s on, facilitated by deregulation of the financial sector, a series of financial instruments such as tender offers, leveraged buyouts, and junk bonds were developed (or became acceptable) that allowed for hostile takeovers (Baker and Smith 1998). These takeovers against the will of management formed the stick by which shareholders increased their influence over management. Let us quote from an OECD publication[2] to assess the significance of this development:

> One of the most significant structural changes in the economies of OECD countries in the 1980s and 1990s has been the emergence of increasingly efficient markets in corporate control and an attendant rise in shareholders' capability to influence management of publicly held companies. In particular, owing to the expanded possibilities for investors to use the capital market to measure and compare corporate performance of corporations and to discipline corporate management, the commitment of management to producing shareholder value has become perceptibly stronger; this represents a significant change in the behaviour of large corporations. (OECD 1998b, p. 15)

Four questions are worth investigating more closely. First, what is shareholder value? Second, is the claim correct that corporations now pursue a strategy to maximize shareholder value? In particular, the question is whether all countries have participated in this development. Third, has this pursuit of shareholder value in fact resulted in increased efficiency? Or, more broadly, what are the effects of the shareholder revolution on corporate performance? Fourth, what are its effects on investment behaviour?

To address the first question, let us as a consensus definition again quote from the OECD *Financial Trends* that captures the spirit of the literature:

> There is some controversy among specialists as to how shareholder value is best measured. Nevertheless, the concept of shareholder value is broadly used to mean that management is expected to deliver to shareholders in price increases and dividends a competitive return that reflects the cost of capital. . . . Companies that do not pay adequate dividends or that trade at low multiples to book value are judged to be delinquent in terms of duties to shareholders. (OECD 1998b, p. 22)

The second question, to what extent other countries, namely the continental European countries, participate in this development is more contested. A frequent distinction to be found in the literature is between bank-based and market-based finance systems (for example Grabel 1997 as a good overview; Prevezer and Ricketts 1994). Germany and Japan are the most prominent examples of banked finance, where banks and industrial firms have close ties, often expressed in cross-holdings and mutual seats in supervisory boards. In these countries, so the story goes, the primary form of outside finance is bank credit, based on long-run relations. The USA and the UK are the prime examples of market-based financing, where equity supposedly plays a more prominent role in financing and ownership is more dispersed.

The empirical evidence, however, is not as clear cut. While the capitalization ratios are indeed much higher in the USA and UK than in Germany and Japan, and cross-holdings certainly play a much bigger role in the latter group, analyses of the finance of new investment does not conform to the picture. Retained profits are by far the most important source of finance, and credit the most important outside form of finance. Equity is not more important in the capital market-based systems (Mayer 1988, Corbett and Jenkinson 1997). This does not preclude capital markets from playing the disciplinary role since hostile takeovers are still possible, but does cast some doubt on their role in mobilizing finance and savings that the simple dichotomy of bank-based vs. capital market-based finance systems suggests.

Schaberg (1999) is a sophisticated example of this literature, giving a careful empirical analysis of the key countries. Building on H. Minsky's investment theory he proposes a theoretical foundation for analysing the behavioural effects of the different financial systems. This allows him to derive hypotheses about the differences between investment behaviour in bank-based and market-based regimes; however he does not discuss changes within the market-based system in the context of shareholder value orientation.

Accepting, though with qualifications, the bank-based vs. market-based finance distinction, raises the question to what extent the European countries, and Japan, are moving towards the market-based system. The standard answer is that 'the trend began in the English-speaking countries in the 1980s, is now spreading to continental Europe where it is increasingly accepted' (OECD 1998b, p. 21). A recent issue of *Economy and Society* compares various country experiences. Morin (2000) reports a dynamic transformation of the French model towards the market-based model, whereas Jürgens et al. (2000) report great resilience of the Germany model though tendencies to move towards the market-based system exist. Banks as well as management adopt shareholder value even without the pressures by capital markets: 'we have the paradoxical situation that shareholder value orientation in Germany was initiated to a great extent by company management in the industrial sector' (Jürgens et al. 2000, p. 73). This is interesting from a theoretical viewpoint since it suggests that shareholder value as a management strategy need not be linked to market-based financing.

The third question, whether the increasing power of shareholders over management leads to more efficiency, is most difficult to answer and hotly debated in the literature. The financial sector fulfills several functions: it mobilizes and pools savings and provides liquidity; it facilitates risk management and exerts control over management (more complete discussions of the functions of the financial sector can be found in Levine 1997). The discussion often boils down to the question whether market or non-market institutions, that is banks, maybe complemented by government regulation, will allocate resources more efficiently. The agency theory of the firm made a strong case for the superiority of capital markets because management, if not sufficiently controlled, will engage in wasteful behaviour, pursuing their own self-interest, putting prestige and growth before profits. Shareholders, if they have the power, will discipline managment to adopt efficient strategies (for example Ross 1973, Jensen and Meckling 1976). Moreover, bank-based systems often go hand in hand with other stakeholders (for example labour) having influence on business policy, and management may compromise too easily with them. Others, for example Pollin (1995), have made the case that bank-based systems are at least potentially more efficient, since they allow for voice rather than exit as a means of communication (referring to the distinction by Hirschman 1970). Whereas the capital market will withdraw support from inefficient management and replace it, banks will communicate problems in a specific form.

Various intermediate positions are possible (for example Levine 1997 suggests that banks and capital markets may be complements), but as reflected in the first quotation from the OECD the pro-capital market position has gained wider support among economists. We are in no position to resolve the debate but want to draw attention to some empirical and theoretical issues that undermine the case for the superiority of capital markets.

First, and probably most frequently referred to, bank-based systems, that is in Germany and Japan, have fared well in terms of overall economic performance for several decades. Second, in market-based systems very little finance comes from issuing new stocks (Mayer 1988, Schaberg 1999). Capital markets may exert the control functions, but they provide little finance for investment. Moving to theoretical issues now, third, the superiority of shareholder control relies on the assumption that no positive externalities to growth exist. If they do, even a privately suboptimal bias towards growth (as implied in the agency literature) may still be socially optimal. Fourth, with dispersed ownership (as is the case in market-based systems) the individual owner has little incentive to gather detailed information about any particular firm (assuming that acquiring information is costly) and will therefore rely on standardized signals, typically accounting variables (for example Short 1994). Managers therefore have a strong incentive to manipulate these variables. The resulting problems will be particularly strong in areas with information asymmetries, such as innovative sectors. Finally, and possibly a result of the previous point, financial market may exhibit a short-term bias, looking for profits in the near future instead of long-term investment strategies. This last point is a popular criticism of financial markets, though it is weakened by the technological leadership that the USA was able to regain in the 1990s.

On the fourth question, what the impact of the shareholder revolution will be for firms' investment behaviour, there is a fair amount of literature on the question of the quality and composition and quality of the investment, but very little explicit literature on the overall amount. Peck and Temple (1999) and Short (1994) provide surveys of the existing literature. Again short-termism is a major issue here. For example Appelbaum and Berg (1996) and Lazonick and O'Sullivan (2000) argue that in the USA stock markets favoured corporate downsizing rather than expansionary strategies. Empirical findings are mixed, but fail to reject short-termism. Miles (1993) as well as Nickell and Wadhwani (1987) find that the stock market (in the UK) overvalues current dividends relative to future ones. Mayer and Alexander (1990) compare quoted and unquoted firms, finding that the former outperform the latter with respect to investment as well as R&D expenditures (in the UK). McConnell and Muscarella (1985) find that announced investment plans cause higher share prices (in the USA). Farber and Hallock (1999) find that employment reduction announcements increase share prices (in the USA). In any case, methodologically a major shortcoming of these studies is that they compare companies within a country. If there exist positive externalities to investment, these will not be captured.

To summarize, there is a virtual universal agreement that there has been a major change in corporate governance over the past two decades promoting an orientation along the lines of maximizing shareholder value, that is policies that increase stock prices and dividend payments of a company. This shareholder revolution has been stronger in the Anglo-Saxon countries than in continental Europe, but even there we find evidence for its occurrence. No consensus exists on the effects of shareholder value-oriented policy. While the economic mainstream favours the control by shareholders through capital markets, mostly because of the principal–agent problem between management and shareholders, this case has severe shortcomings empirically as well as theoretically. The main criticism has been of a short time horizon in management policy introducing a bias towards cost-cutting measures instead of expansionary policy. Empirical evidence has been consistent, if not fully supportive of this hypothesis, but has failed to take into account growth externalities.

5.4 FINANCIALIZATION AND THE POST-KEYNESIAN FIRM

In this section we will develop a theoretical framework to assess the significance of financialization analytically. The approach adopted here is Post-Keynesian.[3] In this chapter we develop a Post-Keynesian theory of the firm that is applicable to the phenomenon of financialization. Traditional Post-Keynesian theory of the firm, as we will see, has an exclusive focus on managerial capitalism and we will criticize it for its lack of attention to the role of the shareholder.

In order to provide a richer framework, we will base our analysis on a class analysis, distinguishing between workers, management and rentiers (shareholders). Managers do occupy an intermediate class position because they exercise power in the production process, however they will receive at least part of their income as wage income. This ambiguous class position makes management sensitive to institutional changes. The managerial capitalism of the post-war era was characterized by relatively autonomous management that had a certain preference for growth (as opposed to profits). Through the shareholder revolution, their interests got realigned to those of the shareholders, who have a stronger preference for profits, as opposed to growth. If the firm faces a growth–profit trade-off, then such a change will lead to lower investment at the firm level.

This section is structured as follows: we will first discuss the underlying class theory. Then summarize and build critically on the core of the Post-Keynesian theory of the firm. Next we lay out the implications of this theory in the context of financialization. This is crucial since the goal of this section is to provide empirically testable hypothesis for the estimation of investment. Finally the macroeconomic consequences of the argument developed are discussed.

5.4.1 Class Analysis

Classes, or strictly speaking class positions, can be defined with respect to the type of income received, the role in the production process and the political process. We will focus on the first dimension below and merely note the other two dimensions briefly. With respect to types of income, we distinguish three income classes: recipients of wages, recipients of profits and recipients of interest payments, dividends and rents. To these income categories three social categories correspond: workers, (industrial) capitalists and rentiers. In the production process capitalists wield power, control and organize production, whereas workers perform the work. Rentiers, as absentee owners, play no role in the production process, but provide the initial finance to start the business and consume part of the surplus. [4]

The distinction of income classes goes back to the classical economists and can also be found in Keynes (1971), who distinguished between the 'earners', the 'business class' and 'investors' respectively, a distinction that has proven fruitful ever since. Post-Keynesian growth theory is based on class theory, usually ignoring rentiers and focusing on workers and capitalists. Recent examples of applications of these three class models include Epstein (1994) and Dutt (1992).

Note that we have defined class with respect to a type of income received. Therefore, any individual and even groups of individuals will occupy multiple class positions if they receive different types of income, as most people in fact do (this fact is well known and debated among Marxists, for example Resnick and Wolff 1987, Wright 1985). Moreover, the 'industrial capitalist' is an abstract category that, at least in modern capitalism, does not exist as such. The capitalist is defined by virtue of receiving profit income, part of which will be distributed as dividends and paid as interest payments to rentiers. Any real-life capitalist will therefore have a double position as the capitalist during the day, making decisions concerning the firm, and as rentier in the evening and at weekends, living off the income distributed to the owner of the firm.

The classification becomes even more complex for modern-day managers, who take the role of capitalists in terms of exerting power in the firm and making decisions, for example concerning investment expenditures, but typically receive wage income and, more importantly now, receive rentiers' income, often in the form of stock options. Managers therefore have multiple, at times even contradictory, class positions. Their interests and preference are hence likely to depend strongly on the institutional setting of the economy, or more specifically the firm, because the class position is ambiguous.

5.4.2 The Post-Keynesian Theory of the Firm: Basics

What distinguishes the Post-Keynesian approach to the firm from the simple version of the neo-classical approach is that the goal of the firm is not simply taken to be profit maximization. This is a difference that may disappear in more sophisticated neo-classical models. The entire argument presented here can be reformulated in a neo-classical model, that is assuming utility-maximizing individuals. Our presentation will proceed along these lines.

Post-Keynesians are readily willing to accept that there are more goals to a capitalist firm than the maximization of profits: the growth of the firm, the expansion of its market share, exerting power over its workers or suppliers and so on. The specific goal, or the weight of these goals, will depend on the specific institutional setting of the firm and the economy.[5] In contemporary capitalism the pursuit of growth is regarded as the major aim of firms, which stems from the analysis of managerial capitalism. This specific institutional setting is the subject of the next section. In what follows we will discuss two constraints faced by the firm that are considered universal: the finance constraint and the growth–profit trade off.

Inside finance and outside finance are different. This is one of the basic assertions of Post-Keynesian economics that has been slowly and painfully rediscovered by neo-classical economists in the 1980s (more on this in the section on investment). Any owner of a small firm seeking credit will readily confirm. Following the principle of increasing risk, firms are reluctant to accept high leverage rates since a failure will put the existence of the firm at risk. Banks on the other hand will take current profit and wealth as a proxy for a firm's reliability, and give credit only to firms that are already profitable. For simplicity assume that banks give loans as a multiple of the profit earned last year. From this it follows that we can write the amount of investment feasible for a firm as a function of profits:

$$g \leq g(r)$$

where g is investment or growth of the firm and r is profits.

Finance is limited by profits minus dividends paid, that is retained earnings, and outside finance which is a positive function of profits. Note that this constraint need not be binding. It tells how much the firm can possibly invest, not necessarily how much it will invest.

The second fundamental constraint is the growth–profit trade-off. It is assumed that there is some relevant region where an increase in investment does harm future profits (the fact that current distributed profits and current investment expenditures are inversely related is trivial). This can be argued by start-up costs of investment or by increasing managerial costs of fast growth (Penrose effect). Though it may not be obvious that growth harms profits, Post-Keynesians and recent literature on shareholder value agree. For example the already quoted OECD publications reads: 'Among the manifestations of this lack of control over management were the pursuit of market share and growth at the expense of profitability' (OECD 1998, p. 17). To be fair, this is not the only manifestation given, but the existence of such a trade-off is obviously implied.

Accepting the trade-off, we get profits as a function of investment:

$$r = r(g)$$

Again this is a constraint, that need not be binding, but if the only variables that matter to management are growth and profits, as we will assume below, then the firm will choose a point inside the constraint only by mistake.

5.4.3 'Managerial' Capitalism: The Standard Post-Keynesian Theory of the Firm

Developed by Galbraith (1967) and in particular by Eichner (1976), Post-Keynesians have a well-elaborated theory of the firms in the age of managerial capitalism, but have done little to adapt this theory. We will propose a way to do so in the next section. Here we will review the theory of the managerial firms and point out its shortcomings.

The centrepiece of the theory is the separation between ownership and control. Management has objectives distinct from the absentee owners. While the latter are primarily interested in dividends and share prices, the latter aspire to power and prestige, that might be expressed in high market share and fast growth, luxurious offices and many subordinates. Due to various laws and an asymmetry in information about what exactly is going on in the firm and how to run it, management has the upper hand. As a consequence: 'The objective of growth, rather than the consumption of profit, is predominant' (Lavoie 1992, p. 104).

It is important to note that such an institutional arrangement is historically specific to the post-war era. Doing some violence to actual historical complexity, we can say that in the early nineteenth century many firms were owner-controlled, which had changed by the late nineteenth century when a wave of mergers led to a consolidation of industry. In the course of this development two groups of actors emerged as important: financial capitalists and management. Through its crucial position in financial mergers, the financial sector gained an important role at the beginning of the 20th century. Thus this era is sometimes also called 'financial capitalism'. Salaried managers now ran these giant firms, giving rise to what Chandler (1977) called 'managerial capitalism'. After the crises of the 1930s, government severely restricted the influence of the financial sector, even fortifying the position of management:

> Money managers refrained from sitting on boards; and bankers, fearing liabilities, remained aloof from the governance affairs of companies to which they had loaned money. Investment bankers found that they could make plenty of money arranging transactions, while avoiding the liabilities and opprobrium associated with financial control of corporations (Baker and Smith 1998, p. 8)

Students of managerial capitalism (for example Chandler), Post-Keynesians (Galbraith, Eichner) and proponents of shareholder value (Baker and Smith) agree on the broad characteristics of managerial capitalism, though they have different attitudes towards it. While proponents of shareholder value emphasize its wasteful aspects (growth as opposed to efficiency), other are more taken by the administrative abilities of the class of managers (Chandler 1977). However, all agree on the bias towards growth inherent in the arrangement.

Let us now formalize the argument. Assuming that the only two variables that enter management's and the owners' utility functions are growth and profits, we get the following picture. If management only cares about growth and owners only care about profits, the former's utility function will be horizontal (U_M), whereas the latter's will be vertical (U_O). Taking the finance constraint and from above, the growth rate desired by management is not feasible, the finance constraint is thus binding. The actual growth and profit combination chosen will thus be what we designated as r^{MF} and g^{MF} (Figure 5.1).

The Post-Keynesian model has been taken as an ahistoric model of the firm by some. While Eichner and Galbraith emphasize the separation of ownership and control, Lavoie argues that 'that there is no need to emphasize that divorce. Whether the owners are still in control or not is irrelevant: those individuals taking decisions within the firm are in search of power; and their behaviour and motivations will reflect that fundamental fact' (Lavoie 1992, p. 101f). This pursuit of power can only be successful if the firm is big, hence the unambiguous goal of growth.

We disagree with this position, emphasizing the need to regard this model of the firm as the result of specific historic circumstances. The class analysis outlined above indicates that managers occupy a complex position with potentially contradictory interests. Therefore it is impossible to define their interests without reference to institutions. Furthermore, rentiers are underestimated in the managerial model. Rentiers are easily satisfied in this model: 'Managers mitigate the fluctuations of dividends in the attempt to keep the shareholders happy and the stock market quiet. Managers usually keep constant the level of dividends or have them slowly increasing, assuming that

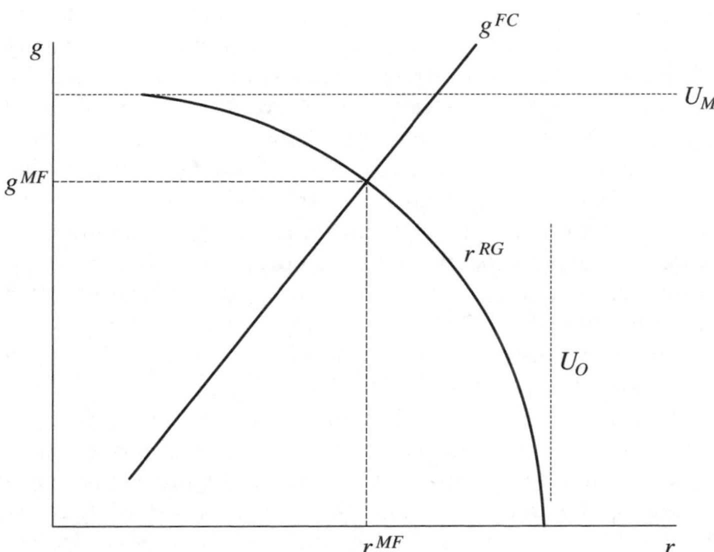

Figure 5.1 Preferences and constraints in a managerial firm (MF)

shareholders do not object to the existing level of dividend payment or dividend ratio' (Lavoie 1992, p. 108). Overall, 'In the Galbraithian and post-Keynesian firm, shareholders play a purely passive role' (Lavoie 1992, p. 107). Again we insist that rentiers are unlikely to content themselves with such a passive role voluntarily. Rather it is specific historic circumstances, namely the Golden Age regime with a big interventionist state, that purposefully restricted the role of finance.

5.4.4 Financialization and Management Priorities

In the course of the 1970s two institutional changes occurred that helped to align management's interest with shareholders' interest: the development of new financial instruments that allowed hostile takeovers, and changes in the pay structure of managers. Among the former were tender offers and junk bonds (Baker and Smith 1998), among the latter were performance-related pay schemes and stock options (Lazonick and O'Sullivan 2000). The former plays the role of the stick, the latter is the carrot. Both have proven fairly effective in making management adopt shareholders' priorities and 'profoundly altered patterns of managerial power and behavior' (Baker and Smith 1998, p. 3).

The effects of this development of course are viewed differently, unsurprisingly, since it represents a shift in the power structure within the firm. Baker and Smith emphatically welcome the fact that after the deregulation and changes of the 1970s and 1980s 'the pendulum could swing back toward financial capitalism, which would limit managerial discretion in favor of more rigorous exploitation of corporate resources' (Baker and Smith 1998, p. 22). Marxists would probably agree but be more specific in saying: 'the exploitation of workers'. Lazonick and O'Sullivan on the other hand write: 'In the name of creating "shareholder value", the past two decades have witnessed a marked shift in the strategic orientation of top corporate managers in the allocation of corporate resources and returns away from "retain and reinvest" and towards "downsize and distribute"' (Lazonick and O'Sullivan 2000, p. 18).

Both arguments are consistent with our Post-Keynesian theory of the firm. Management has an ambiguous class position and its interests are therefore sensitive to institutional changes. Changes in the pay structure as well as the threat of hostile takeovers will make it adopt shareholders' preferences. Compared to the situation depicted in Figure 5.1, management's utility function will thus rotate. This change is analysed in Figure 5.2.

The new chosen growth–profit combination will exhibit higher profits and lower growth. In the extreme case of perfect assimilation of managers by shareholders, they will adopt a vertical indifference curve and choose the

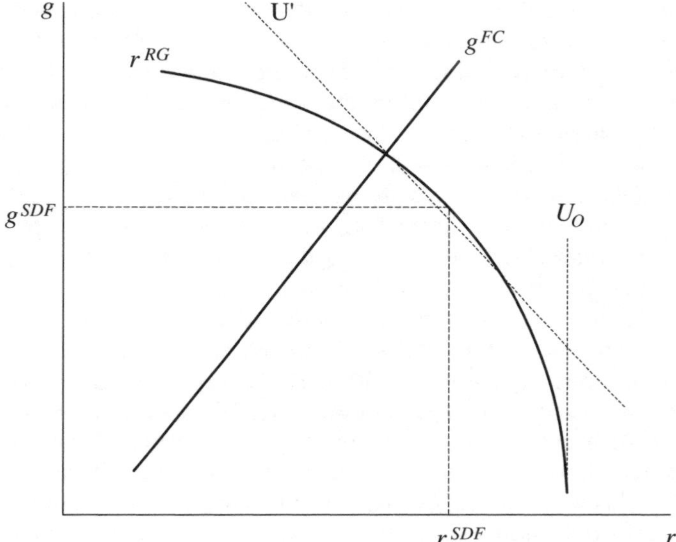

Figure 5.2 Preferences and constraints in the shareholder dominated firm (SDF)

profit-maximizing point. In the new optimal point the finance constraint is not binding. Firms could grow faster, given their access to finance, but they choose not to because that would reduce profits.

If our story were true we would expect that managers and consequently non-financial businesses identify increasingly as rentiers and consequently will also behave as such. We would expect higher dividend payout, lower growth and more financial investment of non-financial businesses. Note that our story also avoids assigning the active role exclusively to rentiers and financial markets. Given the ambiguous class positions of management they may, after initial changes, actively promote and further the shareholder value orientation, as noticed by Lazonick and O'Sullivan (2000) and Jürgens et al. (2000).

5.4.5 Macroeconomic Consequences: Profits, Growth and Efficiency

So far our analysis has remained on the microeconomic level, explaining the adoption of shareholder value orientation by management. Neither the finance constraint nor the simple growth–profits trade-off will exist in a macroeconomic framework. Moreover, it is not clear whether a reduction of investment expenditure that increases profits in an individual firm assuming a given behaviour (including the investment behaviour) of other firms, will yield similar outcomes if all firms adopt such a strategy. Especially in a Post-Keynesian macro economy, where capitalists earn what they spend, it is counter-intuitive that reducing investment will increase profits. We will briefly outline a macroeconomic argument why this can be the case and we will also address the question whether this leads to increased efficiency from a Post-Keynesian viewpoint.

Reducing investment will, in fact, in a Post-Keynesian model, as discussed in Chapter 2, reduce profits, if other income unrelated expenditures of capitalists remain constant. (In an open economy with a state sector, of course, foreign trade surpluses and budget deficits could be a source of profits.) In the case of financialization there are strong reasons to assume that autonomous expenditures will increase. The two features of shareholder value-oriented management were high dividend payments and policies that increase share prices. Increases in share prices in turn induce a wealth affect that leads to increased consumption expenditures. Empirical studies of this wealth effect estimate it to be around .05, that is $100 more wealth leads to $5 more expenditures (Potera and Samwick 1995, Boone et al. 1998). This may not sound much, but given that in the USA stockmarket valuations exceed GDP significantly, this constitutes a significant source of aggregate demand. The argument that autonomous consumption demand has increased, and thereby stabilized profits, is also confirmed by the historically low private savings rate.

Finally, did efficiency increase? We have already discussed problems with the argument of efficient capital markets. From a Keynesian point of view, we want to emphasize the externalities that stem from investment. In the Post-Keynesian view excess capacity and unemployment are the rule rather than the exception in a capitalist economy. Under these circumstances increasing growth will, through the multiplier effect, lead to pecuniary externalities: higher effective demand. (It may also lead to non-pecuniary externalities like faster technological growth.) However these effects will not be distributed equally. In particular, higher growth rates will, so we have argued in the previous chapters, reduce unemployment and thereby squeeze the profit share.

From our viewpoint, the shareholder revolution is more about distribution than it is about efficiency. The new management regime leads to lower growth, but higher profits. Investment policy is oriented towards the interests of the owners of capital. Non-market-based forms of finance are, at least potentially, oriented towards a larger group of the population than shareholders. This is explicitly recognized, and condemned by the OECD: non-market-based finance systems 'usually posited a wider group of "stakeholders" (for example workers, local communities, closely allied companies, banks, etc) who had claims which may have been seen to be as valid as the shareholders' and whose interests were sometimes recognized by law' (OECD 1998b, p. 19).

5.5 CONCLUSION

To summarize, our starting point was the dual definition of class with respect to income types and in relation to production process. Managers have an ambiguous class position in that they assume the role of the industrial capitalist with respect to the production process, but as to their income they either receive wages or rentiers' income. Since their class position is ambiguous, thus their preferences will be sensitive to the institutional setting. Managers do not have the maximization of profits as their sole goal, as rentiers will more likely do. Rather managers have an interest in the growth of the firm, in prestige and so on. We focused on the trade-off between profits and growth, arguing that the Post-Keynesian theory of the firm may be appropriate for managerial capitalism, where rentiers as absentee owners play a minor role. However after the shareholder revolution a new theory of the firm is needed. By means of establishing a market for corporate control and changing managers' pay schemes, managers' interests were realigned with those of rentiers. Assuming a trade-off between growth and profits this change in management priorities will lead to lower autonomous investment expenditures. This hypothesis will be examined empirically in the following chapter.

NOTES

1. This view presupposes that the money supply is endogenous and interest rates are set exogenously. Pollin (1991) develops a different view of money endogeneity based on institutional innovations. Such a view would not be compatible with the argument presented above.
2. We quote from an OECD publication because the OECD, though somewhat conservative in its political orientation, is one of the major mainstream organizations and as such is more sober than parts of the euphoric management literature on the same subject (for example Rappaport 1986).
3. We use Post-Keynesian theory in an inclusive sense, implying that it can potentially integrate various streams of heterodox economics. In this sense we are closer to Lavoie (1992) than to Davidson (1994). Davidson bases his Post-Keynesian approach on fundamental uncertainty and non-ergodicity, whereas Lavoie integrates a rich variety of heterodox economics. Such an attempt of integration raises the issue of consistency and Lavoie attempts to provide a consistent framework. While we applaud his seminal presentation that is successful in combining Post-Keynesian micro- and macroeconomics, we are not fully satisfied with the degree of theoretical consistency he offers. In particular, there is a strong asymmetry in that Lavoie borrows heavily from institutional economics in his theory of

the firm and from Marxists in the theory of accumulation. If we are serious about the integration of different approaches, classes have to matter in the firm and institutions for accumulation.

4. Dividends and interest payment, of course, are paid out of profits. Therefore capitalists and rentiers may be considered part of the same class. However, they occupy different positions within the production process and, as we will argue, they have different interests. Hence we regard the distinction between (industrial) capitalists and rentiers as important – even if it is an intra-class distinction.
5. However, the urge to grow and the quest for survival are often equated and take a somewhat more fundamental place in the literature (for example Robinson 1962).

6. Financialization and the slowdown of capital accumulation

6.1 INTRODUCTION

We established in the previous chapter our hypothesis that financialization will lead to a change in management priorities that translates into less investment. In this chapter we will carry out empirical tests of this hypothesis. Before we can do so, we review the literature on investment functions and their empirical estimation. This is necessary to establish variables that need to be controlled for in our estimations. Throughout this chapter we will use the terms 'investment' and 'accumulation' almost synonymously: accumulation is investment normalized by the capital stock.

We test the hypothesis by means of aggregate annual investment data for the business sector for Germany, France, the UK and the USA. We find our argument that financialization is negatively related to accumulation clearly confirmed for France and the USA and, at less satisfactory levels of statistical significance, for the UK. Only in Germany do the estimations indicate the opposite sign from what we predicted. This may however be reconciled with our argument by the fact that shareholder value orientation is much less advanced in Germany than in other countries. As to the economic significance of our results, calculation confirms that financialization may in fact have been a major force in the slowdown in accumulation.

The chapter is structured as follows. The first section contains the literature review on investment. We will discuss the rationales behind the most frequently found variables: output, profits and the cost of capital. The debate has long focused on the rivalry between Keynesian investment functions (including output and profits) and neo-classical investment functions (including output and the cost of capital). We do not think such a confrontation is very useful and argue for an integrative approach, including all three variables. Other recent developments and Post-Keynesian contributions are also discussed. Section 2 describes the econometric methods used, but offers a somewhat more general discussion of the problem of unit roots, their measurement and strategies to deal with them. Section 3 presents the results of our empirical research, discussing data sources, regression results, their interpretation and robustness.

6.2 INVESTMENT: A LITERATURE REVIEW

In this section we will review the literature on investment expenditures with a focus on studies on aggregate investment. The aim of this section is to set the stage for our own empirical work and to determine which variables need to be controlled for in our estimations.

From a pragmatic applied point of view one is tempted to say that not much progress was made in our understanding of investment since the 1940s. The first generation of empirical research on investment, which we will refer to as 'old Keynesian', did assume that investment depends on output, the availability of internal finance and the cost of capital. The recent debate basically posits the same. In between, that is from the mid-1960s to the mid-1980s, neo-classical theory assumed perfect capital markets and, proven by the Modigliani-Miller (1958) theorem, the equivalence of internal and external finance and Tobin's q emphasized the role of stock markets. Neither of these propositions is supported by the empirical literature.

From a theoretical point of view, of course, things look different. While early investment functions lacked rigorous theoretical foundations, that is microeconomic foundations based on well-informed maximizing individuals and firms, neo-classical investment theory (in the 1960s) provided a sound grounding for further development that allowed (in the 1980s) for the incorporations of phenomena like imperfect capital market and uncertainty. Given that little of substance was added, however, it seems that what happened in the 1960s was a paradigmatic shift from Keynesian economics to neo-classical economics, and by the 1980s neo-classical economists started to incorporate Keynesian ideas.

After decades of investigations, the explanation of investment still poses a major challenge to economists. But by now we do have a fairly good idea about what models and factors are robust (in short: the accelerator is, q models are not, cost of capital and profits sometimes are). Most progress however was probably made in learning about econometric pitfalls. Lags are of paramount importance. Investment is highly autocorrelated, therefore its own lags have to be included. Simultaneity is a major problem, therefore we have to test how robust the findings are when changing the explanatory variables from current values to lagged values.

This part is organized as follows. Section 1 reviews the old Keynesian investment theory; section 2, the neo-classical theory of investment; section 3 discusses recent developments. In section 5 we bring together the conclusions from various studies and propose an investment function that Keynesian as well as neo-classicists could agree on. In section 6 we present the specification that will be tested later on.

6.2.1 Old Keynesian Investment Theory

The first generation of studies on investment were carried out by the pioneers of econometrics, who mostly considered themselves Keynesians; Jan Tinbergen and Lawrence Klein are prominent examples (see Meyer and Kuh 1957 for a survey of the early literature, with a strong focus on American studies). As a representative example we will present Klein's (1966) discussion of investment.

After pointing out Keynes's break from classical economics, Klein establishes 'the following fundamental Keynesian relationship: The demand for capital goods depends upon the real value of national income, the interest rate and the stock of accumulated capital' (Klein 1966, p. 63). But he goes on to say that interest empirically does not play a major role, because firms have too short a time horizon (investment projects have to be profitable within five years) and internal finance plays an important role:

> Business men appear to have psychological preferences for financing their investment operations from surplus funds which have been accumulated through undisturbed profits, depreciations and other reserves. Theoretically, the rational entrepreneur should charge himself imputed interest costs when he uses his internal funds for investment, but he does not behave that way, as a matter of fact. (Klein 1966, p. 65).

The view that the priority of internal finance is irrational is not shared by other Keynesians. For example Meyer and Kuh write: 'Where imperfect capital markets are the rule, market interest rates should not be key variable' (Meyer and Kuh 1957, p. 8). In a chapter to the second edition of his book, Klein presents estimations of investment functions for Japan, UK, Israel and India, all with different specifications. The explanatory variables include output, profits, lagged investment, the capital stock and the interest rate.

We can therefore establish that the 'old Keynesians' regarded the accelerator effect as the most important variable, accepted a theoretical role for the interest rate but doubted its empirical importance, and also assumed a practical role for internal finance. They did not offer a systematical theoretical foundation for these factors. For the neo-classical critics who would take over the scene in the 1960s, this lack of theoretical foundation was a lack of microfoundations assuming optimizing behaviour of firms. From our point of view, the old Keynesians remained undecided as to whether they wanted to stay within the neo-classical framework of optimizing behaviour (for example Haavelmo 1960) or whether they wanted to establish a genuinely Keynesian theory of investment. This ambivalence in Keynesian investment theory is of course symptomatic of post-war

Keynesianism as incarnated in the Keynesian–neo-classical synthesis that tried to be Keynesian in the short run, but neo-classical in the long run. Samuelson, who was the dissertation supervisor of the quoted Klein book, was not only the main popularizer of neo-classical synthesis (IS-LM) Keynesianism, but also one of the founding fathers of neo-classical growth theory.

6.2.2 Neo-Classical Investment Theory

During the 1950s and 1960s the said compromise between Keynesians and neo-classicists was slowly undermined (see Minsky 1986, Palley 1996 for discussions); this also found its expression in investment theory. This occurred in two steps. First, an influential paper by Modigliani and Miller (1958) proved that under the assumption of perfect capital markets, internal and external finance are equivalent. Implicitly, a role for profits in determining investment was denied. This finding was embraced by neo-classical economists and led to the neo-classical investment theory, as developed in a series of papers by Dale Jorgenson (Jorgenson 1963). In this theory, the optimal capital stock is derived from profit maximization and investment is regarded as the adjustment to optimal capital stock. This raises the question why the capital stock is not instantaneously adjusted to capital stock. Jorgenson assumed delivery lags, an assumption that would later come under criticism. This question of why capital stock adjusts so slowly has been the focus of the neo-classical debate on investment, some of which is discussed below.

The neo-classical theory of investment indicates output and the cost of capital as the variables determining the optimal capital stock and thus investment. The term 'investment theory' is therefore somewhat of a misnomer, since it really is a theory of the optimal capital stock, and investment is merely the adjustment to optimal capital stock.

The user cost of capital, that is the shadow price of capital, is at the core of neo-classical theory. In neo-classical theory the optimal capital stock is derived from the profit maximization given a production function. The user cost of capital consists of the interest rate, the price of capital goods and taxes. In theory, this term plays a central role, because substitution is the crucial mechanism in neo-classical theory, whereas Keynesian have always regarded it as a side issue. However, in practice, the cost of capital has only a small effect. Chirinko, for example, concludes: 'output (or sales) is clearly the dominant determinant of investment spending with user cost having a modest effect' (Chirinko 1993, p. 1881). Similar findings can be found in many other studies, such as Ford and Poret (1991).

6.2.3 Recent Developments in Investment Theory

Several topics have become prominent in the recent discussion of investment: first, Tobin's q, which is actually not that recent, but still discussed here; second, the revival of internal funds; third, the explicit treatment of adjustment costs; and fourth, uncertainty and irreversibilities (see Driver and Temple 1999 for an overview of various recent developments).

6.2.3.1 Tobin's q

Tobin (1969) regards investment as a portfolio decision that is related to financial markets. If the demand price of a firms is the market value (roughly speaking the value of its shares) and its supply price the cost of additional capital goods, then investment should be a function of the ratio of the two, which is called Tobin's q. Expectations about future sales and profits should be captured in share prices. Note that in this theory no other variables are needed to explain investment because all expectations, for example concluding future sales, ought to be captured in share prices.

Tobin's financial theory is appealing because it offers a genuine theory of investment (as opposed to a theory of capital stock) and elegantly combines real and financial aspects. However, empirically it has fared rather dismally, which is the conclusion of many empirical studies. For example Tease (1993) concludes: 'When other determinants of investment are controlled for, share prices do not seem to explain much of the variation in investment in any of the G7 countries' (Tease 1993, p. 58; see Blanchard et al. 1993, Morck et al. 1990 for similar results). While this may be surprising theoretically, it is fully consistent with the empirical fact that equity is not an important source for financing investment (Mayer 1988, Corbett and Jenkinson 1997).

6.2.3.2 Profits and imperfect capital markets

In the 1980s information asymmetries took a prominent place in economic theory. In particular, it has been shown that banks will rationally ration credit in order to be able to screen firms, if the latter know more about the risks associated with an investment project (Stiglitz and Weiss 1981). Interest in internal finance rose again, pushed forward by panel data studies by Fazzari with various coauthors (for example Fazzari and Mott 1986) and Hubbard (for example Hubbard et al. 1995; Hubbard 1998 as a survey). Fazzari's work has a more Kaleckian flavour, whereas Hubbard is rooted in neo-classical economics. The tension between the Keynesian and neo-classical interpretation of internal finance give rise to an interesting exchange between Fazzari and Variato (1994) and Crotty (1996) in the *JPKE*. The mainstream has become much friendlier towards internal finance. For example Chirinko (1993), while emphasizing that further research is needed, unambiguously acknowledges its relevance.

6.2.3.3 Adjustment costs

The question of how adjustment takes place had long bothered neo-classical economists, not least because they have a theory of the optimal capital stock, but none about investment itself – other than through slow adjustment. Moreover, in empirical work lags have proven of pivotal importance in the estimation of investment functions. The progress in the 1980s meant that adjustment is now regarded as costly and, assuming an adjustment cost function, has become part of the optimization problem. This approach, originating from Abel (1980), has become known as the 'Euler equation', named after the first order condition of the Hamiltonian to be solved. Intuitively it is just maximizing expected cash flow minus the adjustment cost function subject to the identity that investment equals the change in capital stock (see Chirinko 1993). While this approach is obviously appealing to neo-classical economists, for empirical research it runs into immediate problems because it requires assumptions about the adjustment cost function and the formation of expectation (usually 'rational expectations' are assumed).

6.2.3.4 Irreversibilities and neo-classical uncertainty

Uncertainty becomes important in the face of irreversibilities and sunk costs. Uncertainty is one of the constituent parts of Post-Keynesian economics, where uncertainty refers to a situation where we cannot give a probability distribution. However, mainstream economists use uncertainty in the sense of what Post-Keynesians call risk, that is future events are known with a certain probability distribution. To be consistent with the literature we still use the term 'uncertainty'. Various papers have shown that uncertainty in the presence of irreversibilities can reduce investment (see Pindyck 1991 for a survey). Few empirical studies exist so far (Guiso and Parigi 1999 combine survey information with firm-level data).

6.2.4 The Post-Keynesian Approach

The theoretical foundations of the Keynesian independent investment function were discussed in Chapter 2, where it was argued that the Marglin-Bhaduri approach is the most general Post-Keynesian growth model. We will here only refer to the empirical literature on the subject. The Marglin-Bhaduri investment function consists of an accelerator and a profit term. While this investment function was a breakthrough for Post-Keynesian macroeconomic modelling because it allowed for various regimes and the combination of Keynesian and Marxian arguments, it is hardly a grand innovation for a specification for empirical research on investment. Putting it in the terminology of investment research, it is an accelerator–cash-flow model. Moreover, empirically it is sometimes complemented by a measure for the cost of capital, which brings it back to a general model of the three most important determinants of investment.

While there is no big difference between the Keynesian approach and the neo-classical approach in the variables that explain investment, there is a difference in units. Since neo-classical theory is one of optimal capital stock and capital stock is a function of income, investment is determined by the change in output. In the Post-Keynesian model, derived from investment being a function of expected profits, investment is a function of the level of income, or: accumulation is a function of capacity utilization. This difference in units may seem trivial, and in fact is hardly of practical relevance for empirical research, but it does reflect underlying theoretical differences. As has been elaborated earlier (Chapter 2), Post-Keynesian economics is not anchored in the idea of an optimal capital stock, but regards investment as a genuine (as opposed to derived) decision variable. Neo-classical economics regards investment merely as the adjustment to optimal capital stock.[1] However, in empirical work usually various lags are included (see below), which erodes the distinction of levels vs. differences.

Bhaskar and Glyn (1995), Bowles and Boyer (1995), Glyn (1998) and Stockhammer and Onaran (2004) provide empirical tests of the Marglin-Bhaduri investment function and find confirmation for its explanatory power. We will discuss the details of their test later, when we compare them to our own work.

6.2.5 What Have we Learnt?

6.2.5.1 Horse races

Much of the empirical literature from the mid-1960s to the mid-1980s was set up as horse races between the competing theories of investment. Typically the horses were a 'Keynesian' accelerator–cash-flow model (with output and profits as explanatory variables), a neo-classical model (with output and the cost of capital) and a q model (with Tobin's q), or some variation on these models. The terrain of the race was usually quarterly data for the US business sector (Clark 1979, Kopcke 1985) or the US manufacturing sector (Jorgensen et al. 1970). The conclusion was that both the accelerator–cash-flow model as well as the neo-classical model performed quite well, with output being the single most important determinant, whereas the q models performed worse.

While these findings are consistent with the rest of the literature, we think that the horse race literature really misses the point. As we have argued above, the difference between the theories is not in the variables. It is certainly true that most Keynesians think the cost of capital effect is small, maybe even practically irrelevant, but there are no reasons from a Keynesian viewpoint to exclude it from the specification of an investment function. Similarly, while neo-classical economists would have doubts about the empirical significance of internal finance, there is little reason to a priori exclude it from the estimation. Therefore the dichotomy between Keynesian accelerator–cash-flow models vs. neo-classical output cost of capital models is misleading.

6.2.5.2 Comparative aggregate investment studies

Since we will use annual data for the business sector in our own empirical work and use identical specifications for all countries, it is worth discussing the findings of similar comparative work in some more depth to show methodological differences. Ford and Poret (1991) provide a similar comparative time series study from a neo-classical perspective, and Bhaskar and Glyn (1995) and Bowles and Boyer (1995) from a Post-Keynesian perspective. Here we are interested in their key findings and their time series specification.

Ford and Poret (1991), already referred to earlier, offer a careful empirical investigation with a great emphasis on time series properties. They use semi-annual data for the business sector for the USA, Germany, France, the UK, Italy, Japan and Canada. They use the standard explanatory variables discussed above: output growth and the cost of capital in their core models, and profits in an elaboration. Their dependent variable is accumulation. The strength of the paper is the discussion of the importance of lags. They successively include lags of accumulation to show how sensitive the coefficient estimates on the explanatory variables are (they are) and show that lagged explanatory variables are generally less significant (see below). They also test for cointegration, finding no evidence for cointegration of capital stock, output and the cost of capital. (We will argue in the next section that cointegration may be too restrictive a concept.) Since the work is largely about the robustness of results, it is hard to summarize stylized findings for countries. Their overall conclusion is that output is the most robust explanatory variable, with both the cost of capital and profits having a more elusive effect (profits' performance in the regression deteriorates once output is controlled for). Overall they come to the sobering conclusion: 'for most of the OECD economies examined, the best explanation of current investment growth may be its own past' (Ford and Poret 1991, p. 116).

Bhaskar and Glyn (1995) test the role of profitability in investment function. They adopt a partial adjustment model (the econometric method is discussed below) and use lagged explanatory variables to avoid simultaneity problems as well to allow for lags from investment decision to investment expenditures. The countries investigated are the USA, the UK, France, Germany, Japan, Italy and Canada; they present separate estimations for the business and the manufacturing sector. The explanatory variables include the profit rate, output growth and the cost of capital. They conclude:

> The basic conclusion from this analysis is support for the long-held belief that profitability affects the rate of accumulation. The impact varies in strength and statistical robustness from country to country and sector to sector but so does that of other variables. Thus profitability should take its place in investment models, alongside both demand and relative costs. (Bhaskar and Glyn 1995, p. 191)

Bowles and Boyer (1995) wish to investigate the effect of an increase in wages and trace it through a Marglin-Bhaduri type of model by means of single equation estimation. In the course of doing so, they also have to estimate an investment function. The countries investigated are the USA, the UK, France, Germany and Japan. Their time series specification is similar to that of Bhaskar and Glyn, with the only difference being that Bowles and Boyer include a time trend. To be consistent with the rest of their estimations Bowles and Boyer use the unemployment rate as their indicator for capacity utilization and include no cost of capital variable. Their results confirm the model, but we will raise criticisms of their specification later.

6.2.5.3 Stylized findings

The conclusions of both the horse race literature and the comparative country studies are confirmed by various other studies, that is sectoral and panel studies. The summaries of various surveys bear a strong resemblance, and we will summarize these findings in a stylized way:

- The accelerator effect is strong and robust. For example Jorgenson in his 1971 survey concludes that 'real output emerges as the most important single determinant of investment expenditures' (Jorgensen 1971, p. 1141).
- The cost of capital effect is neither strong nor robust. For example Chirinko in his 1993 survey concludes: 'output (or sales) is clearly the dominant determinant of investment spending with user cost having a modest effect' (Chirinko 1993, p. 1881). Or: 'a robust empirical relationship between the cost of capital and investment has proved very elusive' (Ford and Poret 1991, p. 89).
- The evidence on profits as a determinant of investment is similarly mixed. For example while Ford and Poret acknowledge that 'profit,

or cash flow, models have been found to perform no worse than, and sometimes better than, standard investment equations' (Ford and Poret 1991, p. 102), they find only weak effects for it. Joregenson (1971) is dismissive of the effects of profits, whereas Bhaskar and Glyn (1995) make a strong case in favour.

- The evidence on q models has almost unanimously been negative. For example: 'the usefulness of q theory is called into question by its generally disappointing empirical performance' (Chirinko 1993, p. 1889).

The other models (neo-classical uncertainty, Euler equations) have not or have hardly been tested in the aggregate time series context of this chapter. We therefore conclude that the following investment function captures the general sentiment on the most important factor determining investment:

$$INV = f(Y, CC, R)$$

with the expected signs being: $f_Y > 0, f_{CC} < 0, f_R > 0$

where	INV	investment
	Y	output
	CC	cost of capital
	R	profits

Note that in the above equation we are not yet concerned with the units or lag structure of the model, but merely with the variables that are regarded as important. The above general investment function is acceptable to neo-classical economists as well as to Keynesians. The former would expect the variables to enter in differences, the latter in levels. Next we will consider the some econometric conclusions from time series investigations of investment.

6.2.5.4 Econometric issues

Ford and Poret (1991) provide the most detailed recent test of the neo-classical investment theory by means of aggregate investment data. As far as the econometric issues involved, they confirm previous studies. It is thus instructive to summarize their conclusions:

- Investment expenditures (or log investment) is a variable that needs to be normalized, because it is integrated at least of order one, if not higher. Either accumulation (investment over capital stock) or the investment share (investment over output) are the standard candidates for such a normalization.

- Investment, even if normalized by the capital stock, is highly autocorrelated. Including lagged values is therefore important. In particular, including lagged investment affects the significance of other explanatory variables. To disentangle the genuine effect of explanatory variables, generous lags of investment are important.
- Current output (growth) and interest rates do perform better than their respective lagged variables. Given the time lag between investment decisions and investment expenditures and that current macroeconomic variables will be influenced by investment expenditure, this suggests that current variables may be unreliable because of simultaneity bias.

6.2.6 The Specification to be Tested

The hypothesis of this chapter is that financialization has contributed to the slowdown in accumulation since the Golden Age. As we have argued above, management has adopted an ambiguous class position, the preferences of rentiers in the process of institutional changes of financialization. The consequence of this is that management, among other things, has less growth-oriented priorities.

As an indicator for financialization we will use the interest and dividend income of the non-financial business sector divided by its value added, or, as we will henceforth say, the 'rentiers' share of non-financial businesses' (RSNF). The numerator of this expression captures the rentiers' income. The denominator consists of the value added rather than operating surplus to avoid the anti-cyclical behaviour that such a ratio would exhibit. Since we defined classes by income types this is the proper indicator for our purposes.

It is of course difficult to operationalize the concept of financialization for quantitative research. The interest and dividend income – rentiers' income – of non-financial businesses will be used as a proxy for financialization. This measure corresponds to the income-related definition of class. It measures to what extent non-financial businesses have acquired rentier status, and, as has been argued, the hypothesis is that this corresponds to a change in management priorities. This measure obviously also has shortcomings. First, it is an indirect measure, a proxy, because we cannot measure the changes in management priorities directly, instead we look at a measure that in our hypothesis is itself a result of the change in attitude. Second, rentiers' income may rise because interest rates or dividend payout ratios have risen or because more financial investment has been undertaken. Thus we cannot distinguish between additional income due to changes in management priorities or due to changes in rates of return. In the econometric analysis this problem is countered by including interest rates in the regression, thus controlling for one important measure of financial rates of return.

We wish to control for the standard variables in the literature. Thus we include an accelerator term, a profit term and a term for the relative cost of capital. As we have shown, the Post-Keynesian and a consensus model of investment converge towards the same variables. Our investment equation thus becomes (the choice of units and lag structure are discussed in the next section):

$$ACCU = f(CAPUT, PS, CC, RSNF)$$

with the expected signs being: $f_{CAPUT} > 0, f_{PS} > 0, f_{CC} < 0, f_{RSNF} < 0$

where		
	ACCU	accumulation
	CAPUT	capacity utilization
	PS	profit share
	CC	cost of capital
	RSNF	rentiers' share of non-financial businesses

The signs of the first three derivatives should be clear from the discussion above. We expect higher rentiers' income of non-financial businesses to have a negative effect on their autonomous, that is output unrelated, accumulation. Note that this is in contrast to the idea of firms being finance constrained. Rentiers' income is still income, after all. However, we argue that this type of income is an expression of the financialization and thus has a negative effect on their preference for growth.

6.3 TIME SERIES ANALYSIS AND UNIT ROOTS

Ignited by Newbold and Granger (1974) and Nelson and Plosser (1982), one of the major debates in econometrics took place in the 1980s, setting new standards in the treatment of time series data. But despite a decade or more of debate, there is no agreement as to the consequences and relevance of unit roots (this is nicely and informatively illustrated by Campbell and Perron 1991 and in the replies by Cochrane 1991 and Miron 1991).

Regressing a time series that has a unit root[2] onto another time series with a unit root may give rise to spurious regression results, that is, inflated significance levels because the standard inference procedures do not apply. Typically such spurious regressions exhibit high t-values and a high R^2, but very low Durbin-Watson (DW) statistics.[3] Inconveniently for macroeconomists, many economic time series seem to exhibit unit roots (Nelson and Plosser 1982). Since then it has become fashionable to test for unit roots and cointegration,[4] and if the null hypothesis of cointegration is rejected, to perform regressions in differences rather than in levels.

However, it has been pointed out that the hopes invested into unit roots have not been realized. First, there cannot be a conclusive test of unit roots with finite samples: any time series with a unit root can be approximated arbitrarily close by a trend stationary process and vice versa (this has become known as the 'near observational equivalence of trend-and-difference stationary processes' (Christiano and Eichenbaum 1990); summarized as rules 7 and 9 in Campbell and Perron 1991). This of course also applies to cointegration tests. Second, while it was originally hoped that unit root tests would allow discrimination between competing economic theories, it has been shown that various economic theories are consistent with the existence of unit roots in economic time series (Cochrane 1991, Miron 1991).

What do we learn from the debate? First, to worry about the time series properties of the variables without throwing the baby out with the bath water. Defining variables in a regression in differences loses crucial long-run information, whereas having variables in levels may give rise to the spurious regression results. Second, that unit root tests by themselves cannot solve the question of whether to run a regression in differences or levels. Thus economic theory or even intuition have to be taken seriously. Overall, 'since we can never know whether the data are trend stationary or difference stationary, any result that relies on the distinction is inherently uninteresting' (Miron 1991, p. 212). Thus we want to adopt a general procedure that allows for autocorrelation of the dependent variable without either imposing or ruling out a unit root restriction, but at the same time prevents spurious regression results. For this, autoregressive distributed lag models (ADL)[5] or Cochrane-Orcutt correction for first-order autocorrelation in the residuals are appropriate candidates (Hamilton 1994).

We will adopt an autoregressive distributed lag (ADL) model (a row of a VAR, if you prefer) and then we will test restrictions on the ADL, in order to simplify the specification. This is desirable since the ADL specification will lead to multicollinearity problems because the independent variables enter the regression twice and are usually autocorrelated.

We proceed in the spirit of the 'general to specific modelling' (Hendry et al. 1984), but use a much simpler version since we are mostly interested in the role of differences versus levels of the variables. Consider a simple ADL specification:

$$\text{ADL} \qquad y_t = \alpha_0 + \alpha_1 y_{t-1} + \alpha_2 x_t + \alpha_3 x_{t-1} \tag{6.1}$$

Since we are interested in the role of differences versus levels, the ADL tested is reparameterized to

$$y_t = \alpha_0 + \alpha_1 y_{t-1} + \beta_2 x_t + \beta_3 \Delta x_t$$
$$\text{where } \beta_2 = \alpha_2 + \alpha_3 \text{ and } \beta_3 = -\alpha_3 \qquad (6.2)$$

In this formulation the variables appear in differences as well as levels, which is convenient in our search for the appropriate time series specification. Hence the ADL will be estimated in this form. It is worth noting that we can also rewrite the above formulation to get Δy, an $I(0)$ variable in any case, on the LHS:

$$\Delta y_t = \alpha_0 + \beta_1 y_{t-1} + \beta_2 x_t + \beta_3 \Delta x_t$$
$$\text{where } \beta_1 = (\alpha_1 - 1) \qquad (6.3)$$

the first part of which is the standard Dickey-Fuller unit root test. This transformation of y affects neither the parameter estimates nor the estimated standard error of α_0, β_2 and β_3.

Returning to equation (6.2), if the 'true' underlying relation between the variables were in differences, the estimates for α_1 should be close to unity and for β_2 close to zero. If, on the other hand, the underlying relation is in levels, β_3 should converge to zero. For the coefficient a_1 there are several possibilities. First it could be unity, which means a unit root and the regression should be run in differences. Second it could be zero and the regression should be run in levels. Third, the coefficient is between zero and one, in which case we have a partial adjustment model (PAM).

Since it will be important later on, let us briefly consider this third case. If $0 < \alpha_1 < 1$ and $\beta_3 = 0$, the equation becomes:

$$\text{PAM} \qquad y_t = \alpha_0 + \alpha_1 y_{t-1} + \beta_2 x_t \qquad (6.4)$$

This specification is called a partial-adjustment model because one way to generate this type of model is via assuming that x_0 does determine the desired level of y, (y^*), and the actual y results from a partial adjustment to this desired level. $(1-\alpha_1)$ then is the speed of adjustment and $\bar{\beta}_2 = \beta_2/(1-\alpha_1)$ is the long-run effect of x_0 on y (see Hendry 1995, Chapter 7 for an in-depth treatment of partial adjustment models and their relation to the general ADL):

$$\text{long-run effect:} \qquad \bar{\beta}_2 = \frac{\beta_2}{1-\alpha_1}$$

In time series analysis autocorrelation of the error term is a frequent problem. So it is here. Since we will be exclusively dealing with ADL models where lagged dependent variables are used as explanatory variables, the Durbin-Watson statistics is invalid. We will therefore use the more general Godfrey Breusch test for serial correlation. This test is regarded as preferable to Durbin's h test (Kennedy 1992, p. 128), which is often employed when lagged dependent variables are used. Next to more desirable statistical properties, the Godfrey Breusch test has the advantage that is not restricted to first-order autocorrelation (if it is used to test for first-degree autocorrelation it is also known as Durbin's m test). The test belongs to the class of asymptotic (large-sample) tests known as Lagrange multiplier (LM) tests. Its null hypothesis is 'no serial correlation'. (We will as a standard test for first and second-order autocorrelation. We still report the DW statistics because, even though its critical value do not apply, its value usually gives a good idea of how serious autocorrelation problems are.)

6.4 EXPLAINING ACCUMULATION

This section presents the empirical results of the econometric tests of our hypothesis that financialization leads to a slowdown of accumulation. We first discuss data issues and the construction of variables. Second, we present regression results of the ADL specification and some narrowed down versions. Third, we modify some variables to test the robustness of our results. Fourth, we interpret the findings carefully, comparing them with previous findings in the mainstream as well as in the Post-Keynesian tradition. Finally, we offer some calculations to assess the contribution of financialization to the slowdown of accumulation.

6.4.1 Data

The rate of growth of the capital stock (*ACCU*) is the growth rate of gross business capital stock. The profit share (*PS*) is gross profit share in the business sector and capacity utilization (*CAPUT*) is the capital productivity in the business sector. The data are from the OECD Economic Outlook data set. The cost of capital measure is the (short-term) interest rate times the price index of investment goods divided by the wage costs per worker (all from the OECD Economic Outlook data set). The 'rentiers' share of the non-financial business sector' (*RSNF*) is the interest and dividend income received by non-financial businesses divided by their value added. The data were extracted from the Detailed Tables of the OECD National Accounts. Unfortunately the calculation of these series is possible only for a few countries. Furthermore, the time periods for which we were able to compile the data, differ across countries.

Plots of all relevant variables can be found in Figure 6.1. Descriptive statistics are in Appendix Table 6A.4.

The 'rentiers' share of the non-financial business sectors' measures the receipts from financial investment rather than financial investment itself. A measure for the latter was presented above, but is available for even shorter time periods only.

We know from theory that unit root tests cannot help us distinguish sharply between difference stationarity and trend stationarity. However, we still performed unit root tests (reported in Appendix 6A) to get an idea of how big the problem could be. For accumulation the ADF test without trend fails to reject the null hypothesis of a unit root in four out of six countries, the ADF with trend in three out of six. For *PS* the null is rejected in three countries, for CAPUT in only one. For RSNF the null was rejected in none of the four countries. Theoretically, it is implausible that growth rates of capital stock exhibit a unit root, that is that they are free to wander around, given that the interval −5 to +10 per cent probably captures the entire range of values that growth rates of capital stock have ever taken on.[6] Thus we interpret the results as a high degree of autocorrelation rather than as unit roots.

6.4.2 Regression Results

Given the strong a priori presumption that the growth rate of capital stock is stationary over long time periods and the prima facie evidence of the existence of a unit root in many of the time series cannot be rejected, we will adopt a flexible procedure, allowing for autocorrelation and influences in levels as well as in differences and adopt an ADL model that will be tested down afterwards.

$$\begin{aligned} ACCU_t = {} & \beta_0 + \beta_1 ACCU_{t-1} + \beta_{11} ACCU_{t-2} + \beta_2 CAPUT_{t-1} \\ & + \beta_3 \Delta CAPUT_{t-1} + \beta_4 PS_{t-1} + \beta_5 \Delta PS_{t-1} + \beta_6 CC_{t-1} \\ & + \beta_7 \Delta CC_{t-1} + \beta_8 RSNF_{t-1} + \beta_9 \Delta RSNF_{t-1} + \varepsilon_t \end{aligned} \tag{I}$$

This specification differs from the ADL model discussed in the above section in two ways that do not affect its time series properties or interpretation. First, all explanatory variables are lagged. In the case of accumulation this is also sensible because of the time lag between investment decision and investment expenditure. Furthermore it prevents problems of simultaneity and inverse causation. For example since we use last year's

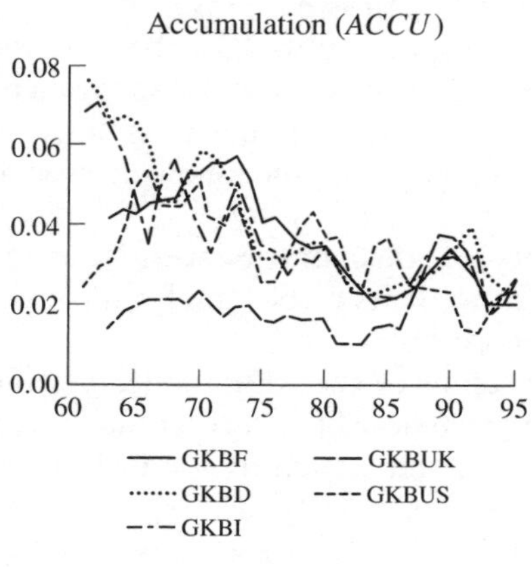

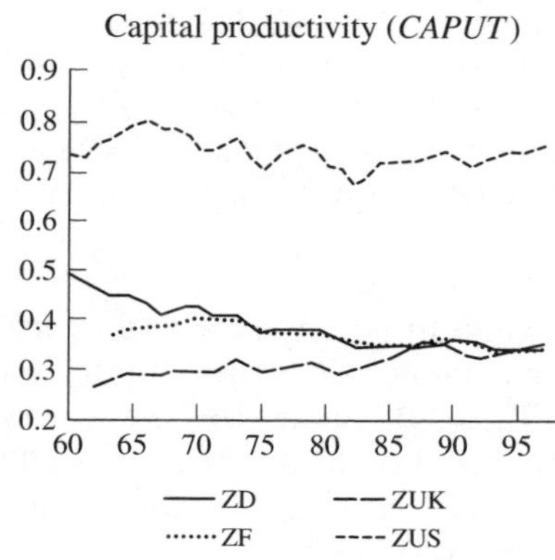

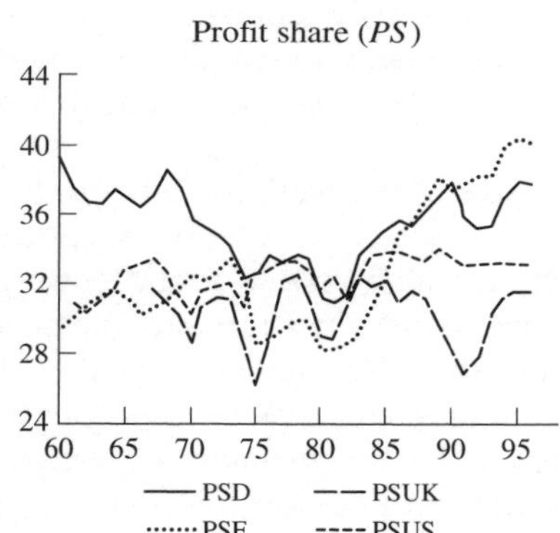

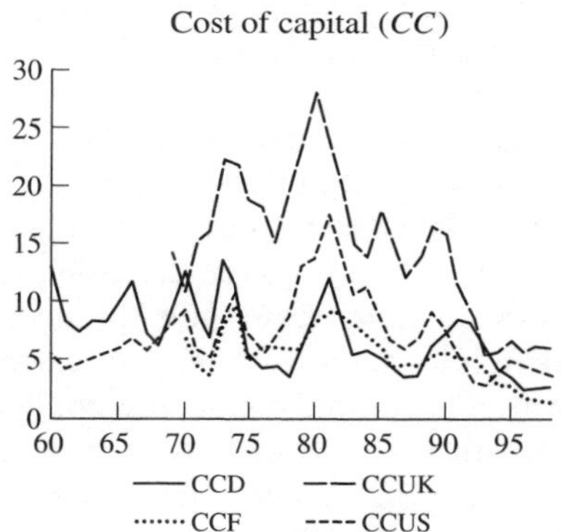

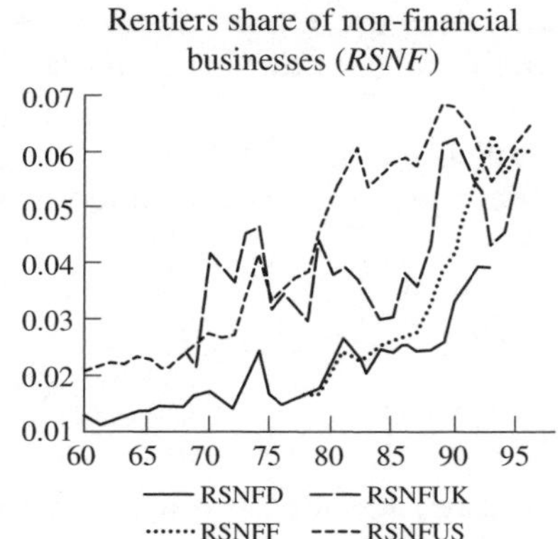

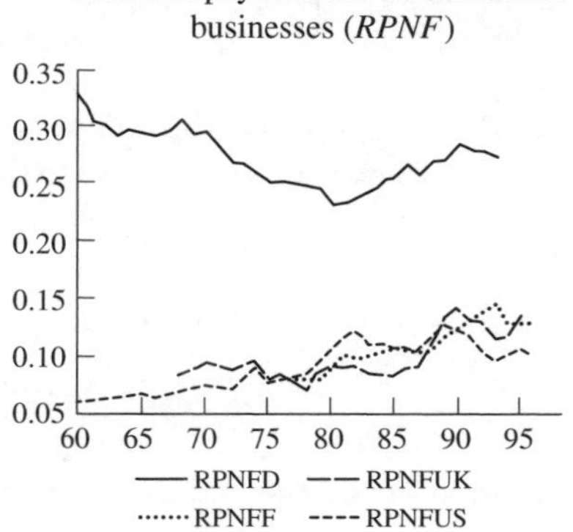

Figure 6.1 Plots of variables

capacity utilization, it cannot be influenced by this year's investment. Nor can this year's investment cause last year's capacity utilization. Second, the dependent variable is used twice, once with one and once with two lags. The second lag was included because the test indicated the possibility of second-order autocorrelation. We use two lags in all the following specifications.

We aim at testing one specification for all countries without much attempt to optimize the fit for each country. Thus we abstain from including dummies or further country-specific variables.

Table 6.1 summarizes the regression results of the ADL model. Overall the model performs modestly well, but given how little success the profession has had with explaining investment, the standards for investment regressions are low.

Since the regression is in levels and an autoregressive term is included, the R^2 are very high with only the USA below 90 per cent. Autocorrelation is a problem in France and the USA even though we included two lagged variables. This may reflect missing variables. However, it is not obvious what these variables would be.

As laid out in the previous section we regard the ADL model as a starting point to narrow down the number of parameters. The t-values reported are free of spurious correlation problems arising from unit roots. However, they do suffer from multicollinearity since we have ten variables included. The information we wish to extract from the ADL model is whether the variables should be included in levels or in differences. With respect to this question, the results are somewhat ambiguous, but strongly suggestive, if we take the higher t-value as the indicator: t-values are higher for levels rather than differences for all countries for *RSNF*, and three times for *CAPUT* and *PS*. Only for *CC* do we have an indication that differences may be the more appropriate specification, t-values are higher than for the coefficient estimate on the differenced variable then for the one on the level in three cases.

Table 6.2 reports the regression results imposing the same time series specification on all countries. The regression specification then becomes:

$$\begin{aligned} ACCU_t = \beta_0 + \beta_1 ACCU_{t-1} + \beta_{11} ACCU_{t-2} + \beta_2 CAPUT_{t-1} \\ + \beta_4 PS_{t-1} + \beta_7 \Delta CC_{t-1} + \beta_8 RSNF_{t-1} + \varepsilon_t \end{aligned} \tag{II}$$

Compared to the ADL model, the adjusted R^2 improved a little and autocorrelation is a problem only in the USA. With this specification we get results where half of the coefficients are statistically significant at the 5 per

Table 6.1 Regression results: ADL model

	Germany	France	UK	USA
period	63–90	79–97	71–96	63–97
Const	−0.13	0.01	−0.03	−0.04
	−2.79	*0.04*	*−1.33*	*−0.61*
$ACCU_{-1}$	0.85***	0.33	0.96***	0.71***
	2.50	*0.49*	*4.30*	*2.65*
$ACCU_{-2}$	−0.60*	0.31	−0.09	−0.37
	−1.89	*0.64*	*−0.38*	*−1.42*
$CAPUT_{-1}$	0.31**	−0.01	0.14**	0.07
	2.36	*−0.02*	*2.32*	*0.72*
$\Delta CAPUT_{-1}$	−0.153	0.195	0.182	0.039
	−0.82	*0.56*	*1.36*	*0.39*
PS_{-1}	0.001*	0.001	0.000	0.001
	1.84	*0.91*	*−0.37*	*0.48*
ΔPS_{-1}	0.00	0.00	0.00	0.00
	0.33	*−0.44*	*0.26*	*0.99*
$RSNFD_{-1}$	0.36	−0.31	−0.16	−0.30*
	0.77	*−1.57*	*−1.09*	*−1.91*
$\Delta\ RSNF_{-1}$	−0.13	0.19	0.03	0.39
	−0.27	*0.83*	*0.23*	*1.06*
CCD_{-1}	0.000	−0.001	0.000	0.001
	−0.62	*−1.20*	*0.79*	*0.89*
$\Delta\ CCD_{-1}$	0.000	0.000	0.000	−0.001*
	−0.78	*0.41*	*−1.25*	*−1.72*
R-squared	0.97	0.94	0.93	0.86
Adjusted R-squared	0.95	0.86	0.88	0.79
Durbin-Watson stat	2.00	2.38	1.91	1.68
GB Obs. R^2	2.45	6.63**	.61	6.72**

Note:
Calculations performed with Eviews. Italic numbers are t-values.
*, ** and *** denote significance at 10, 5 and 1 per cent respectively.

cent level or better, all of them with the predicted signs: capacity utilization is statistically significant in Germany and the UK; *PS* is also statistically significant twice, again with the predicted sign, in Germany and France. The change in *CC* is statistically significant only once, in Germany. *RSNF* is statistically significant twice, in France and the USA. *ACCU* lagged once is statistically significant in three countries, lagged two periods, it is statistically significant twice. Note that *ACCU* lagged once has rather high

Table 6.2 Regression results: specification II

	Germany	France	UK	USA
period	63–90	79–97	71–96	63–97
const	−0.11***	−0.02	−0.05***	0.01
	−3.12	*−0.23*	*−3.27*	*0.19*
CAPUT(−1)	0.24***	0.00	0.16***	−0.02
	2.50	*−0.00*	*3.70*	*−0.49*
PS(−1)	0.001***	0.001**	0.000	0.001
	3.08	*2.52*	*0.41*	*1.09*
RSNF(−1)	0.17	−0.33**	−0.15	−0.31***
	0.64	*−2.46*	*−1.46*	*−3.05*
Δ CCD(−1)	−0.001**	0.000	0.000	−0.001
	−2.35	*0.56*	*−1.14*	*−1.19*
ACCU(−1)	0.83***	0.56	0.91**	0.96***
	3.67	*1.03*	*4.95*	*4.88*
ACCU(−2)	−0.48***	0.14	−0.18	−0.45**
	−2.99	*0.42*	*−1.05*	*−2.98*
R-squared	0.97	0.93	0.91	0.83
Adjusted R-squared	0.96	0.90	0.89	0.80
Durbin-Watson stat	2.05	2.29	1.75	1.79
GB Obs. R^2	1.08	1.7	.89	6.93**

positive values (0.8 and higher where it is significant), but lower negative values with two lags (close to −0.5 where it is significant). This suggests that *ACCU* has very high initial autocorrelation that is counteracted in the following period, a finding consistent with the literature. Further lags are not significant.

Since including part of the variables in levels and other in differences may make us feel uncomfortable, we also estimated the same equation with *CC* in lags. This has the advantage of consistency and facilitates interpretation since we move to a partial adjustment model.

Table 6.3 present the results of this regression. All variables have the expected signs, with two out of the three being significant for each country. Only for the USA is only one variable, *RSNF*, significant.

Customizing a best-fit regression based on the ADL results above gives different specifications for France and the USA. For France *CAPUT* would be in differended form (the other variables in level) and, for the USA *PS* would be in differended form (other variables in levels). However none of these modifications gives different results, thus they are not reported.

Table 6.3 Regression results: partial adjustment model

	Germany	France	UK	USA
period	63–90	78–97	70–96	63–97
C	−0.09**	−0.03	−0.03	0.01
	−2.44	*−0.40*	*−1.96*	*0.14*
CAPUT(−1)	0.19**	0.09	0.16***	−0.04
	1.98	*0.37*	*3.43*	*−0.67*
PS(−1)	0.001**	0.001	0.000	0.002
	2.00	*1.13*	*−0.08*	*1.63*
RSNF(−1)	0.13	−0.21**	−0.22**	−0.37***
	0.40	*−1.71*	*−2.38*	*−3.67*
CC(−1)	−0.001	−0.001	0.000	0.000
	−1.43	−1.25	−0.70	0.04
ACCU(−1)	0.72***	0.68	0.93***	0.84***
	3.07	*1.52*	*5.19*	*3.48*
ACCU(−2)	−0.25*	−0.05	−0.17	−0.40**
	−1.69	*−0.19*	*−0.90*	*−2.69*
R-squared	0.96	0.94	0.90	0.82
Adjusted R-squared	0.95	0.91	0.88	0.79
Durbin-Watson stat	1.81	2.44	1.93	1.78
GB Obs. R^2	1.08	6.02*	.89	6.55**

6.4.3 Testing Robustness

We also tested whether the results were due to our somewhat unconventional measure of capacity utilization. This is clearly not the case. We used the output gap and the rate of growth of business sector output, both of which confirmed the results that we got with capital productivity.

Table 6.4 reports the results of this regression with output growth of the business sector (*GROWTH*) instead of *CAPUT*. Few changes compared to the earlier regression can be reported. Autocorrelation problems decrease, but are still present in the USA. Note that output growth performs worse than capacity utilization. Its significance is very sensitive to the lags in accumulation. It is significant only in the UK. Other parameter estimates are hardly affected. *CC* ceases to be significant in Germany but turns significant in the UK. *RSNF* remains highly significant in France and the USA. Therefore the significance of financialization does not rest on the specification of capacity utilization.

While we reject second-order autocorrelation in this specification for both France and the USA, we do so by a very thin margin. Since autocorrelation

Table 6.4 Regression specification with output growth

	Germany	France	UK	USA
period	63–90	78–97	70–96	63–97
const	−0.03*	−0.02	0.00	0.01
	−1.85	*−1.67*	*−0.03*	*0.40*
GROWTH	−0.01	0.02	0.08**	0.08
	−0.11	*0.31*	*2.52*	*1.24*
PS	0.0012**	0.0011**	7.E-05	0.000
	2.42	*2.38*	*0.10*	*0.24*
RSNF	−0.22	−0.32***	−0.04	−0.22
	−0.83	*−2.66*	*−0.34*	*−2.45*
ΔCC	−0.0004	0.0004	−0.0003**	−0.001
	−1.12	*0.61*	*−1.71*	*−1.47*
ACCU	1.13***	0.49	1.18***	0.75
	4.26	*1.13*	*6.63*	*3.09*
ACCU	−0.36	0.18	−0.28	−0.22
	−1.60	*0.52*	*−1.45*	*−0.99*
R^2	0.96	0.93	0.89	0.84
adj R^2	0.94	0.90	0.85	0.80
DW	1.80	2.41	1.81	1.68
BG Obs. R^2	2.16	4.11	1.1	4.45

was a persistent problem for these countries in earlier specifications, we want to test whether our findings are related to second-order autocorrelation. First-order autocorrelation does not seem to be a serious problem: regressing the estimated error term on its own lag (with or without controlling for the various explanatory variables) shows significant t-values only for the second lag. A first suspicion is of course that this indicates missing variables. We therefore experimented with adding more lagged variables, but this did not cure autocorrelation. Finally we resorted to the rather crude method of including the second lag of the error of the OLS estimate. The results are summarized in Table 6.5.

The results clearly indicate that the significance of the coefficient on *RSNF* does not depend on the presence of (second-degree) autocorrelation. However, we wish to add that from a theoretical point of view we are not satisfied with this correction. While it certainly shows that the findings regarding *RSNF* are sound, the *AR*(2) term is really a measure of our ignorance. It is a rather crude ad hoc remedy for a problem that we are unable to pin down more precisely. The only apparent effect of the *AR*(2) correction is that the profit term turns significant in the specification for France.

Table 6.5 Regression with AR(2) correction

	France	USA	France	USA
period	79–97	63–97	79–97	63–97
C	−0.02	0.03	−0.02	0.04
	−0.17	*0.83*	*−1.35*	*1.12*
CAPUT	0.00	−0.04		
	0.00	*−0.93*		
GROWTH			0.00	0.09
			0.07	*1.48*
PS(−1)	0.001**	0.001	0.001**	0.000
	2.05	*0.85*	*2.06*	*−0.44*
RSNF(−1)	−0.32*	−0.30***	−0.32**	−0.21**
	−1.86	*−2.82*	*−2.31*	*−2.37*
D(*CC*(−1))	0.000	−0.001	0.000	−0.001
	0.54	*−1.18*	*0.54*	*−1.31*
ACCU(−1)	0.57	1.06***	0.55	0.77***
	0.89	*5.38*	*1.06*	*2.78*
ACCU(−2)	0.11	−0.51***	0.12	−0.25
	0.27	*−3.35*	*0.27*	*−1.20*
AR(2)	−0.09	−0.39*	−0.09	−0.28
	−0.26	*−1.74*	*−0.23*	*−1.12*
R-squared	0.90	0.87	0.90	0.87
Adjusted R-squared	0.84	0.83	0.84	0.84
Durbin-Watson stat	2.35	1.97	2.38	1.80

Note: AR(2) is the error of the OLS estimation with two lags.

From an internal finance point of view it may be surprising that rentiers' income should affect accumulation in a negative way. If firms were finance constrained, it should rather increase accumulation. This concerns the core of our argument that implies that firms (on average) are not constrained by finance (profits are high), but their priorities make them choose not to invest. However, it might be that our measure of financialization, *RSNF*, is picking up increased rentiers' payments that rose in parallel with rentiers' income, as they in fact did. To control for this we included rentiers' payments as well as rentiers' income. If the significance of *RSNF* were due to its correlation with payments, we would expect payments to have a negative sign and *RSNF* to switch to a positive sign.

The results are interesting. *RPNF*, the rentiers' payments (divided by the

Table 6.6 Regression including rentiers' payments

	Germany	France	UK	USA
period	63–90	78–97	70–96	63–97
const	−0.11***	−0.02	−0.06***	0.00
	−2.71	*−0.31*	*−3.66*	*−0.05*
CAPUT	0.25**	0.03	0.20***	−0.01
	2.26	*0.14*	*4.01*	*−0.23*
PS	0.0013	0.0012**	0.0003	0.0012
	1.21	*2.88*	*0.60*	*1.04*
RPNF	−0.03	−0.11	−0.14	0.08
	−0.22	*−1.47*	*−1.44*	*0.35*
RSNF	0.20	−0.23	0.04	−0.41
	0.65	*−1.62*	*0.21*	*−1.40*
Δ *CC*	−0.0007**	0.0007	−0.0003	−0.0006
	−2.22	*0.94*	*−1.67*	*−1.20*
ACCU	0.82***	0.32	0.85***	0.95***
	3.55	*0.59*	*4.64*	*4.60*
ACCU	−0.47***	0.26	−0.06	−0.46***
	−2.81	*0.82*	*−0.29*	*−2.95*
R^2	0.97	0.94	0.92	0.83
Adj R^2	0.95	0.91	0.89	0.79
DW	2.06	2.72	1.67	1.77
GB Obs R^2	1.32	8.25**	2.57	6.69**

value added) of the business sector are not significant, but close to the 10 per cent level in France and the UK, both with a negative sign, as expected. *RSNF* does lose significance but keeps its sign in France and the USA, in both countries being close to the 10 per cent level. It is not overly surprising that none of the two variables are significant because they are correlated. Note that for both France and the USA the t-value is greater for *RSNF* than for *RPNF*. From this we conclude that *RSNF* does play an independent role. As in previous specifications autocorrelation problems exist in France and the USA.

6.4.4 Interpretation

Leaving aside the question of financialization for a moment, how do these overall results compare to the existing literature on investment functions? In short, they mostly confirm it. First, and unfortunately, we confirm that standard variables have problems in explaining investment and that lagged investment itself may in fact explain most of current investment. Second, and more encouraging, the standard variables do play a role: roughly half of the time they are significant with the expected sign. Third, and most surprising, the accelerator term does not perform better than other variables. This at first sight contradicts previous findings, but it actually need not be such a big difference. It may be due to the generous lags with which we include lagged investment. This is consistent with findings by Ford and Poret (1991). Furthermore, changes in capacity utilization still by far explain most of the short-run changes in accumulation. Multiplying the standard deviation of *CAPUT* with the parameter estimate gives by far the highest value. Fourth, the importance of past profits is confirmed, even though the second lag in accumulation also decreases their significance. Fifth, the cost of capital has only a limited influence. Only in one country, Germany, is it consistently significant, in all others it is not.

We note the following pattern regarding countries: Germany conforms to what we labelled the consensus model of investment: capacity, profits and the cost of capital are statistically significant, our variable of financialization is not. In France the profit share and the rentiers' share of non-financial businesses are consistently significant. In the UK capacity utilization is significant and, depending on the specification, the *RSNF* is too. In the USA, *RSNF* is the only consistently significant variable, the profit share is sometimes. Are these finding consistent with our story on financialization? The lack of significance for Germany certainly is, since the literature regards Germany as a latecomer in the development of shareholder value and our time series for Germany ends in 1990.

Correlation among explanatory variables, unsurprisingly given the number of variables we employ, is a problem. Bivariate correlation tests are reported in Appendix Correlations. Defining high correlation somewhat arbitrarily as a correlation coefficient higher than 0.8 (Kennedy 1992, p. 180), *PS* is correlated with *RSNF* and *CC* in France. *CAPUT* and *RSNF* are correlated in Germany. *CAPUT* is highly correlated with past *ACCU* in both Germany and France.

Our tests can hardly be conclusive of our hypothesis that financialization has caused a reduction in accumulation rates, but they certainly provide strong initial support. Our variable for financialization, *RSNF*, fares as well as any standard variable in investment regressions. It is robust to changes in the specification, especially with respect to how we measure capacity utilization. However, some caveats apply. There are technical problems like multicollinearity and some degree of autocorrelation for some countries. However, *RSNF* remains significant once autocorrelation is controlled for. But probably more important, the general results of our investment function are not overwhelming, though certainly not worse than many other studies. While we may have made some contribution to explaining the recent slowdown in accumulation, investment remains the bane of empirical macroeconomics. Further empirical research is needed to examine the effect of financialization. On a macroeconomic level, a systems approach would be desirable to endogenize capacity utilization and on a microeconomic level one could attempt to test our underlying model, for example one could control for factors like the pay scheme of managers.

6.5 COMPARISON WITH OTHER RECENT POST-KEYNESIAN INVESTMENT ESTIMATIONS

Bhaskar and Glyn (1995) and Bowles and Boyer (1995) provide empirical tests of the Marglin-Bhaduri investment function. All of them adopt a partial adjustment model (the econometric method is discussed above) and use lagged explanatory variables to avoid simultaneity problems as well to allow for lags from investment decision to investment expenditures. Thus there is little difference in the time series specification.[7] Unlike the previous literature, we derive the specification from a more general ADL model. Bhaskar and Glyn (1995) also test for cointegration, but this is inappropriate in the context of a partial adjustment model.[8]

Bowles and Boyer use the employment rate as the measure of capacity utilization, which is motivated by their purpose to estimate the effects of redistribution. Unemployment thus captures the disciplinary effect of capacity utilization on wages. For our purpose and context, that is European unemployment, this is unacceptable. Since the slowdown in accumulation changes the link between unemployment and capacity utilization. Unemployment is therefore a bad measure of capacity.

Bhaskar and Glyn (1995) do control for the cost of capital, even though they use a somewhat different measure (they adjust for technical progress via a Solow residual). The only substantial difference is that we include a variable for the rentiers' income.

6.5.1 Financialization and the Slowdown in Accumulation

So far we have been concerned with the statistical significance of our measure of financialization. Next we wish to investigate its economic significance, or in other words: to what extent can we explain the slowdown in accumulation from the late 1960s to the early 1990s as the result of financialization? To answer this question Table 6.7 summarizes the coefficient estimates for the autoregression of *ACCU* and the coefficient estimates for *RSNF*.

Table 6.7 Summary of the coefficients on the lagged dependent variable and RSNF from various specifications

	France	Germany	UK	USA
autoregressive terms of ACCU				
ADL	.64	.25	.85	.34
quasi PAM	.7	.35	.73	.41
with growth	.67	.77	.9	.53
mean	*0.67*	*0.46*	*0.83*	*0.44*
coefficient on RSNF				
ADL	−.31	.36	−.16	−.3
quasi PAM	−.33	.13	−.15	−.31
with growth	−.32	−.22	−.04	−.22
mean	*−0.32*	*0.09*	*−0.12*	*−0.27*

Taking the mean from the values in Table 6.7, we can calculate the long-run effect of the change in the rentiers' share of non-financial businesses on capital accumulation. This is done in Table 6.8. The long-run effect of a change in the rentiers' share is the regression coefficient divided by one minus the autoregressive coefficient (see the section on the econometric issues). Multiplying this by the change in the rentiers' share (column '$\Delta RSNF$'), we get the explained change in accumulation (column 'explained $\Delta ACCU$'), which we contrast with the actual change in accumulation (column 'actual $\Delta ACCU$'). The changes refer to the differences between the average of the period 1964–74 and of the period 1985–94 (or the closest value we had).

Unsurprisingly, this value varies greatly between countries. For Germany, where most coefficient estimates for *RSNF* were positive, we

Table 6.8 Explaining the slowdown in accumulation

	reg coeff β_{RSNF}	autoreg coeff β_{ACCU}	ΔRSNF	long-run effect $\bar{\beta}_{RSNF}$	explained $\Delta ACCU$	actual $\Delta ACCU$
Germany	0.09	0.46	0.015	0.17	0.002	−0.021
France	−0.32	0.67	0.026	−0.97	−0.025	−0.027
UK	−0.12	0.83	0.034	−0.71	−0.024	0.005
USA	−0.28	0.43	0.015	−0.49	−0.007	−0.023
mean	−0.24	0.64	0.025	−0.67	−0.017	−0.015

Note: $\Delta RSNF$ and $\Delta ACCU$ are the difference between average rates 65–74 and 85–94.

calculate a positive contribution to accumulation. For France we explain almost the entire slowdown in accumulation. The UK is the only country where there was no slowdown in accumulation. Note that our 'explained $\Delta ACCU$' for the UK is about as high as for France. Thus even though the coefficient estimates for UK were not statistically significant, they are economically significant, that is if the point estimates were correct, *RSNF* would have a strong impact on accumulation. In the USA we roughly explain a third of the reduction in accumulation. Taking the mean of the various coefficients, we explain the entire slowdown of accumulation from the late 1960s to the late 1980s.

Thus while on average the story that increased financial investment caused the slowdown in accumulation can be substantiated, our calculations for individual countries vary in plausibility. The calculations certainly do confirm that financialization potentially played an important role in reducing investment.

6.6 CONCLUSION

The chapter developed and tested a theory arguing that financialization leads to a slowdown in accumulation. By means of an elaboration on earlier Post-Keynesian theories of the firms, we showed how the 'shareholder revolution', that is the development of a market for corporate control and the reorientation of management priorities along the lines of creating shareholder value, leads to a reduction in the growth rate desired by firms. Managers have various goals in running a firm, in particular growth is an intrinsic goal and maximizing profits is not the exclusive goal, whereas shareholders will exclusively be interested in profits. Bodies of literature as diverse as business history (Chandler), Post-Keynesians (Galbraith, Eichner) and recent management literature (Baker and Smith) agree on these stylized facts, implying that the firm faces a trade-off between growth and profits. The shareholder revolution included a market for corporate control, that is the possibility of firing managers, and performance-related pay schemes. These institutional changes will lead managers to adopt management policy closer to shareholders' preferences, that is profitability will gain in weight relative to growth. If the firm in fact faces a trade-off between profits and growth, this translates into lower investment activity.

The empirical tests were performed with annual data for the business sector for Germany, France, the UK and the USA. The choice of countries was determined by the interest in European unemployment and data availability. The findings show some support for the hypothesis that financialization caused a slowdown in accumulation. For the USA and France the rentiers' share of non-financial business, our financialization variable, is consistently statistically significant with the predicted sign; for the UK it has the correct sign in most specifications, but usually not at conventional significance levels. In Germany, the variable is neither significant nor does it have the predicted sign. We therefore found full support for our hypothesis for the USA and France, but not for the UK. Financialization occurred in the UK, but there is no general slowdown in accumulation because the UK had very low accumulation rates in the Golden Age. The insignificant findings for Germany are consistent with our story, since the literature indicates that shareholder value orientation is a very new phenomenon in Germany. We did perform tests for robustness and experimented with the lag structure. The results are robust.

We conclude that financialization is likely to have the effects implied by our theory but further research is needed to confirm our findings. If our parameter estimates come close to the actual effects this has strong implications. For France, financialization explains the entire slowdown in accumulation; for the USA about one-third of the slowdown. Financialization therefore can potentially explain an economically significant part of the slowdown in accumulation.

NOTES

1. Note that this distinction has an important effect for growth theory. In a world with a constant labour force and fixed technology, neo-classical theory predicts a stationary state once the optimal level of output and optimal factor combination are reached. Post-Keynesian theory, on the other hand, predicts growth according to expected profitability.
2. If a series exhibits a unit root its current value can be written as its past value plus a random variable, this is also called a random walk. Such a series is called non-stationary, and has no fixed mean and an infinite variance, contrary to a stationary variable. If a non-stationary variable can be transformed into a stationary series by differencing once, it is called integrated of order one ($I(1)$).
3. A frequently found rule of thumb to determine whether a regression is spurious is to look whether its R^2 exceeds its DW.
4. Regressing two non-stationary variables onto each will generally result in a non-stationary residuals, thus the DW statistic converges to zero. However, if the two variables share a common stochastic trend, intuitively if there exists a long-term relation, the residuals will be stationary. Then the two variables are said to be cointegrated. Most cointegration tests are analog to unit root tests on the residual, though with different critical values. (The seminal paper on cointegration is Engle and Granger 1987; a comprehensive introduction is offered in Charemza and Deadman 1997.)
5. ADL models have been shown to have desirable properties even in the face of unit roots (Sims et al. 1990, Hamilton 1994), they 'solve many of the problems associated with spurious regressions, although tests of some hypotheses will still involve non-standard distributions.' (Hamilton 1994, p. 562).
6. 'The unit roots question amounts to the specification of units: should we use levels or first differences (etc.). For most series we know the answer. GNP, consumption, investment,

etc. belong in growth rates. Variables that are already rates, such as interest rates, inflation, and unemployment belong in levels' (Cochrane 1991, p. 207).

7. Bowles and Boyer (1995) do add a time trend, which we do not. Their approach may be appropriate if one is interested in short-run effect; in a more long-run analysis, it is hard to interpret the time trend. Unsurprisingly, Bowles and Boyer do encounter high autocorrelation problems. In most of our specifications a time trend is not statistically significant and does not effect the significance of *RSNF*.
8. First we have argued that there are theoretical reasons to assume that accumulation is *I*(0) rather than *I*(1). Second, even if accumulation were *I*(1) testing for cointegration in a partial adjustment model is meaningless: since an *I*(1) variable by definition is, technically speaking, cointegrated with its lagged value, that is there exists a linear combination that is *I*(0), and the partial adjustment model includes a lagged value of the dependent variable, the resulting error term has to be *I*(0). Finally they use incorrect critical values (ADF critical values differ for a unit root test and cointegration tests).

APPENDIX TO CHAPTER 6

Table 6A.1 Data on RSNF

	Dividend and interest received / value added of the private non-financial sector			
	W. Germany	France	USA	UK
60–64	0.012			0.022
65–69	0.015		0.023	0.023
70–74	0.018		0.042	0.032
75–79	0.016	0.016	0.034	0.038
80–84	0.023	0.023	0.036	0.056
85–89	0.025	0.030	0.042	0.062
90–94	0.037	0.054	0.053	0.061
95/96		0.061	0.057	0.064

Source: OECD National Accounts Database.

Table 6A.2 Data on ACCU

	Growth rate of business gross capital stock					
	Italy	Germany	France	UK	USA	Japan
60–64	6.5%	7.0%			3.0%	12.4%
65–69	4.7%	5.1%	4.8%	2.1%	4.7%	12.8%
70–74	4.4%	4.8%	5.5%	1.9%	4.0%	11.2%
75–79	3.1%	3.4%	3.8%	1.7%	3.5%	6.5%
80–84	2.4%	2.6%	2.5%	1.1%	3.0%	5.3%
85–89	2.8%	2.7%	2.6%	2.5%	2.6%	5.6%
90–95	2.5%	3.0%	2.4%	2.5%	1.6%	5.0%

Note: Germany is adjusted for unification.

Source: OECD Economic Outlook Database.

Table 6A.3 Unit root tests

	Germany	France	UK	USA
ACCU				
period	1961–98	1963–98	1963–98	1961–98
levels	2.3	1.07	2.24	2.65*
levels + trend	3.52***	2.21	2.8	3.59**
differences	4.02***	2.8*	3.67***	5.3***
differences + trend	4.1**	2.7	3.5**	5.2***
PS				
period	1962–96	1969–96	1963–96	1962–96
levels	1.58	1.46	5.15***	3.53**
differences	4.48***	3**		
CAPUT				
period	1962–97	1965–97	1964–97	1962–97
levels	2.45	2.8	4.01**	2.86
differences	4.85***	3.27**		4.74***
RSNF				
period	1962–93	1979–96	1971–95	1963–96
levels + time	2.44	1.65	2.9	2.6
differences + trend	5.4***	2.26	4.6***	4.5***

Source: OECD.

Table 6A.4 Descriptive statistics

Germany	GKBD_90	ZD(−1)	PSD(−1)	RSNFD(−1)	CCD(−1)
Mean	0.040	0.393	34.916	0.019	7.509
Median	0.034	0.385	35.126	0.017	7.136
Maximum	0.067	0.465	38.560	0.027	13.739
Minimum	0.023	0.347	30.922	0.012	3.518
Std. Dev.	0.015	0.036	2.094	0.005	2.908
Observations	28	28	28	28	28
France	**GKBF**	**ZF(−1)**	**PSF(−1)**	**RSNFF(−1)**	**CCF(−1)**
Mean	0.026	0.358	34.223	0.035	5.643
Median	0.025	0.356	35.225	0.027	5.559
Maximum	0.036	0.376	40.467	0.064	9.235
Minimum	0.019	0.339	28.215	0.016	1.829
Std. Dev.	0.006	0.011	4.581	0.017	1.988
Observations	20	20	20	20	20
UK	**GKBUK**	**ZUK(−1)**	**PSUK(−1)**	**RSNFUK(−1)**	**CCUK(−1)**
Mean	0.020	0.319	30.212	0.041	15.779
Median	0.019	0.313	30.838	0.039	15.077
Maximum	0.037	0.359	32.472	0.063	28.098
Minimum	0.010	0.295	26.124	0.022	5.676
Std. Dev.	0.007	0.021	1.728	0.010	5.568
Observations	27	27	27	27	27
USA	**GKBUS**	**ZUS(−1)**	**PSUS(−1)**	**RSNFUS(−1)**	**CCUS(−1)**
Mean	0.033	0.743	32.595	0.044	7.630
Median	0.032	0.744	32.790	0.046	6.821
Maximum	0.054	0.804	34.085	0.069	17.532
Minimum	0.013	0.674	30.253	0.021	2.867
Std. Dev.	0.010	0.029	0.999	0.017	3.277
Observations	35	35	35	35	35

Table 6A.5 Correlation among variables

Germany	GKBD_90	ZD(−1)	PSD(−1)	RSNFD(−1)	CCD(−1)	GKBD(−1)	GKBD(−2)
GKBD_90	1.00	0.95	0.68	−0.80	0.33	0.95	0.88
ZD(−1)	0.95	1.00	0.53	−0.83	0.48	0.98	0.95
PSD(−1)	0.68	0.53	1.00	−0.43	−0.09	0.56	0.46
RSNFD(−1)	−0.80	−0.83	−0.43	1.00	−0.10	−0.79	−0.76
CCD(−1)	0.33	0.48	−0.09	−0.10	1.00	0.50	0.55
GKBD(−1)	0.95	0.98	0.56	−0.79	0.50	1.00	0.96
GKBD(−2)	0.88	0.95	0.46	−0.76	0.55	0.96	1.00
France	**GKBF**	**ZF(−1)**	**PSF(−1)**	**RSNFF(−1)**	**CCF(−1)**	**GKBF(−1)**	**GKBF(−2)**
GKBF	1.00	0.90	−0.37	−0.60	0.24	0.89	0.70
ZF(−1)	0.90	1.00	−0.63	−0.75	0.55	0.94	0.82
PSF(−1)	−0.37	−0.63	1.00	0.89	−0.87	−0.46	−0.57
RSNFF(−1)	−0.60	−0.75	0.89	1.00	−0.71	−0.54	−0.48
CCF(−1)	0.24	0.55	−0.87	−0.71	1.00	0.42	0.53
GKBF(−1)	0.89	0.94	−0.46	−0.54	0.42	1.00	0.91
GKBF(−2)	0.70	0.82	−0.57	−0.48	0.53	0.91	1.00
UK	**GKBUK**	**ZUK(−1)**	**PSUK(−1)**	**RSNFUK(−1)**	**CCUK(−1)**	**GKBUK(−1)**	**GKBUK(−2)**
GKBUK	1.00	0.82	−0.06	0.57	−0.47	0.85	0.58
ZUK(−1)	0.82	1.00	0.16	0.60	−0.47	0.64	0.37
PSUK(−1)	−0.06	0.16	1.00	−0.38	−0.08	−0.38	−0.61
RSNFUK(−1)	0.57	0.60	−0.38	1.00	−0.24	0.77	0.74
CCUK(−1)	−0.47	−0.47	−0.08	−0.24	1.00	−0.36	−0.35
GKBUK(−1)	0.85	0.64	−0.38	0.77	−0.36	1.00	0.85
GKBUK(−2)	0.58	0.37	−0.61	0.74	−0.35	0.85	1.00

USA	GKBUS	ZUS(−1)	PSUS(−1)	RSNFUS(−1)	CCUS(−1)	GKBUS(−1)	GKBUS(−2)
GKBUS	1.00	0.67	−0.22	−0.77	−0.02	0.80	0.51
ZUS(−1)	0.67	1.00	−0.05	−0.66	−0.44	0.64	0.33
PSUS(−1)	−0.22	−0.05	1.00	0.53	−0.18	−0.27	−0.37
RSNFUS(−1)	−0.77	−0.66	0.53	1.00	0.20	−0.67	−0.56
CCUS(−1)	−0.02	−0.44	−0.18	0.20	1.00	0.27	0.40
GKBUS(−1)	0.80	0.64	−0.27	−0.67	0.27	1.00	0.80
GKBUS(−2)	0.51	0.33	−0.37	−0.56	0.40	0.80	1.00

7. Policy conclusions

7.1 INTRODUCTION

This book developed a Keynesian explanation of the rise of European unemployment from the 1960s to the 1990s. The work is motivated by the dissatisfaction with the mainstream NAIRU explanation of European unemployment. Chapter 2 proposed a theoretical model that incorporates a negative effect of unemployment on the wage share (reserve army effect) into a flexible Post-Keynesian growth model. Chapter 4 tested the employment function that this model implied and contrasted it with the NAIRU story of European unemployment. In the Keynesian explanation, the slowdown of accumulation is the major cause of the rise of European unemployment. Therefore the reasons for the slowdown of accumulation are of interest. Chapter 5 argued that financialization, that is the changing relation between the financial and the industrial sector, may have played an important role. The shareholder revolution aligned management's interests with those of shareholders, causing a shift of management priorities from growth to profits. Finally, the argument that financialization has a negative effect on investment was tested econometrically in Chapter 6. In the remainder of this conclusion we will summarize the key findings of each chapter, and then draw some policy conclusions.

7.2 A SUMMARY

Traditionally Keynesians, arguably Keynes himself, but certainly Kaldor and Robinson, regarded income distribution as an outcome of variables on the goods market, such as investment decisions and savings propensities. The model presented in Chapter 2 differs from other Post-Keynesian growth models in that a reserve army effect, that is a negative effect of unemployment on wages, is allowed for. As a starting point we took the Marglin-Bhaduri (1990) model that, by virtue of assuming flexible capacity utilization, is subsumed as a Kaleckian growth model. This model is particularly flexible in that it allows for wage-led as well as for profit-led growth regimes. The goods market side of this model was complemented with an employment function in the fashion of Okun's law and a distribution function that has profits being a positive function of unemployment (reserve army effect). Equilibrium values and stability conditions were carefully analysed for the short run and the long run.

Profit-led and wage-led growth regimes exhibit very different properties in the long run. Profit-led regimes do have a stable long-run equilibrium rate of unemployment, which serves as an anchor for the economic system and will determine actual unemployment. The long-run equilibrium rate of unemployment is thus similar to the NAIRU. However, one crucial difference exists: the equilibrium rate of unemployment in our model does depend on demand, that is autonomous growth. The wage-led regime, if it is stable in the short run, does not exhibit a stable equilibrium rate of unemployment in the long run. The long run is thus a succession of (well-defined) short-run equilibria. Conventional labour market policies like increasing wage flexibility and decreasing workers' wage demands will not cure unemployment under these circumstances, but demand policy, that is increasing autonomous growth, will.

Chapter 3 gives a thorough literature review on the NAIRU literature and Keynesian analyses of European unemployment. The NAIRU story of European unemployment asserts that labour market institutions are the major explanatory factor to explain the rise in unemployment. In the Keynesian story derived from the model developed in Chapter 2, the slowdown in accumulation plays this role. Thus, both models were tested econometrically for the four large EU economies – Germany, France, Italy and the UK – and, as a benchmark case, for the USA in Chapter 4. We focused on the large European countries, because they are the ones where the rise in unemployment was most pronounced. Particular attention was paid to the robustness of results. The key finding is that variables of labour market institutions – unemployment benefits, union density and the tax wedge– do perform poorly. While the tax wedge and unemployment benefits are statistically significant in some specifications, they are not in others, and often take on the 'wrong' sign. They are not robust. Accumulation, on the other hand, does perform consistently well. It is statistically significant in all specifications, that is the finding is not sensitive to other variables being included or the specification of the dependent variable. Accumulation and unemployment therefore are negatively correlated – at least for the countries and the period under investigation. With respect to the model proposed in Chapter 2, the fact that the autoregressive coefficients of unemployment added up to less than one implies that the regime must have been profit-led.

Chapter 5 proposed a novel theory of the slowdown of accumulation. Evidence was given for a tremendous rise of income from financial assets, that is rentiers' income, in most countries over the post-war era. This process reflects a changing relation between the financial and the industrial sectors of the economy. Building critically on the Post-Keynesian theory of the firm as well as on literature on financial markets, we argued that managers and rentiers (shareholders) do have different preferences with respect to the goals of the firm. Managers do care more about growth, whereas rentiers care more about profits. Moreover management's preferences will be sensitive to institutional changes because it has an intermediate class position by assuming the role of the industrial capitalist in the production process while receiving wage income as well as rentiers' income. The institutional changes that occurred since the early 1970s are often summarized as the shareholder revolution: the establishment of a market for corporate control by means of hostile takeovers as well as changes in the pay schemes of managers have led to an adoption of increasing shareholder value as the top management priority. In other words management priorities have become aligned with shareholders' preferences. If the firm faces a growth–profit trade-off, which is the standard assumption, this will lead to lower investment.

The argument that financialization has a negative effect on investment is tested econometrically for Germany, France, the UK and the USA in Chapter 6. The measure used for financialization is the rentiers' income by non-financial businesses as a share of their value added. Note that this is a form of income for the firm, thus if firms were finance constrained, one would expect the opposite effect on investment. Derived from the literature on investment estimation, the control variables were capacity utilization (an accelerator term), profits and the cost of capital. Further, lags of investment itself were included to allow for autocorrelation of the dependent variable. Extensive tests were performed to evaluate the robustness of the results and attention was paid to the time series properties of the data. The measure of financialization performs at least as well as other variables, in many cases better. For France and the USA financialization is consistently statistically significant, and robust with respect to the specification. For Germany it is almost consistently insignificant. In the UK the estimated coefficient on financialization is not robust, but consistently has the predicted negative sign. Finally, we calculated how strong an impact the actual increase in the financialization variable from the 1960s to the 1990s has had on accumulation, according to our parameter estimates. Financialization does potentially explain an economically significant part of the slowdown in accumulation, though the results vary by country.

The book provided a Keynesian alternative to the dominant NAIRU story of European unemployment. It was shown that, at least in a time series context, the NAIRU story has little explanatory power, whereas the

Keynesian story does a much better job in explaining the actual development of unemployment. Finally we have offered an explanation for the slowdown of accumulation based on the institutional changes in the relation between management and shareholders in the post-war era. Again, the empirical evidence is consistent with the story. We therefore think that we have outlined a viable alternative to the standard explanation of European unemployment.

We hasten to stress the word 'outlined' since much remains to be done, in terms of the theoretical modelling as well as in terms of its empirical implementation. The model presented in Chapter 2 is a real private closed economy model that is in obvious need of incorporating a financial sector, a foreign sector and a government sector. With respect to the empirical work, again there are obvious ways to go, such as applying our estimations to more countries. More substantially, future research will have to operate both on a more macroeconomic level as well as on a more microeconomic level. In the present version, we have mostly estimated single equations (some system estimations are presented in an appendix, but only briefly), which while a necessary first step, is against the spirit of the theoretical model. Therefore the estimation of the employment function and the accumulation in a full system, endogenizing capacity utilization and income distribution, remains a challenge for future empirical Keynesian research.[1] The argument developed in Chapter 5 is a microeconomic argument. As such it deserves investigation on the microeconomic level, that is on the firm level. This would allow the modelling of the relation between management and shareholder in a richer and more precise way.

7.2.1 Immediate Policy Conclusions

This study was not about policy prescriptions. Indeed, it was largely critical by going to great lengths to show that policy prescriptions derived from the NAIRU theory will not work, because the NAIRU variables do not play the role assigned by the NAIRU theory. However, there is one basic and important policy conclusion, which is that unemployment has to be fought on the goods market and not on the labour market. Labour market reforms alone are unlikely to reduce unemployment. However, there is a notable asymmetry in our estimation results on employment and on accumulation. While accumulation does have a very strong impact on employment that is, in fact, very similar across countries, none of the variables in the accumulation function estimated has an overwhelming impact that would be similar across countries. Thus while our results suggest that higher accumulation will reduce unemployment, it is not obvious how to increase accumulation. The relation between the financial sector and the industrial sector was identified as an important determinant of investment behaviour. But economic policies to reverse the shareholder revolution are difficult to design and unlikely to have an effect in the short run since they relate to social institutions and the mindset as well as the power of managers and shareholders.

7.3 A POST-KEYNESIAN PERSPECTIVE ON ECONOMIC POLICY

As the empirical work presented in this book only allows for a narrow set of immediate policy conclusions, the final section will outline some broader policy suggestions in the spirit of the Post-Keynesian approach. In doing so for the most part pragmatic measures are discussed that operate within the setting of an economy where allocation is governed by market mechanisms.

Given our stress on capital accumulation, what is called for in general terms is a policy that recognizes the pivotal role of capital investment in the employment creation process and the complex determinants of private capital investment. Capital investment not only has an effect on the firm that invests but, through the multiplier effect, a demand effect on the rest of the economy. Through increasing the productive capacity it affects the supply side of the economy. This not only increases potential employment but *ceteris paribus* decreases inflationary pressures. Moreover technological progress is usually incorporated in capital goods. The determinants of investment expenditures, however, have proven elusive to economic research. Standard investment models are only modestly successful in explaining investment.

From a Keynesian perspective this is hardly surprising because of the specificities of investment expenditures. These are expenditures with a time horizon long into the future. Since history is an open, not a deterministic process, the magnitude of the future income streams of an investment project cannot be determined objectively. Subjective judgements must enter the decision process. Potential investors do not form these judgements in isolation. They discuss them within their circles, they consult the business press and so on. Thus, firms rely on conventional judgement when forming what Keynes called 'the state of long-term expections', expectations which are largely results of mass psychology. In mediating the uncertainty of an open future firms will engage in long-term contracts and develop conventions that make their own behaviour and that of their business partners predictable (Crotty 1992). Thus the formation of expectations about the future is based on the institutional setting of the economy and its stability.

Consequently Keynesian policy recommendations centre around two major issues. First, the need to complement private investment expenditures by public investment, in particular in times of recession. Keynes famously went further than this calling for the 'socialization of investment'. He did so based on the presumption that private investment would fall short of full-employment investment not only at some points during the course of the business cycle but on average in its growth trend. The evidence presented in Chapter 4 indicates that this has been the case in Europe. Thus major public investment projects would be one way to fight unemployment.

Second, to enhance private investment an institutional setting that is conducive to a stable 'state of long-term expectations'. Fordism, the accumulation regime that underlay the high growth and low unemployment of the post-war era, provided such an institutional setting that enabled firms to predict the future and reduced uncertainty through various institutional arrangements. It was based on three pillars:

- a state committed to growth and full employment;
- an institutionalized balance of power between capital and labour;
- a financial sector subordinated to the real sectors of the economy.

All three of these foundations were successfully attacked by the neoliberal revolution of the early 1980s. However the promises of the neoliberal market fundamentalists failed to materialize. Growth rates generally were lower in the Neo-Liberal Era than in the Fordist Era (see Chapter 1), unemployment rates increased substantially (in Europe more so than in the USA) and so did income inequality (in the USA more so than in Europe). A series of financial crises shook the world, though most of the pain has so far been borne by developing economies. Finally, the boom of the late 1990s in the USA came to a bitter end with one of history's worst stock market crashes.

Clearly, a new social compromise is necessary to provide the institutional foundations of a new phase of growth and full employment, to guarantee a stable macroeconomic environment for investment as well as the participation of a large part of society. We will first summarize the changes that occurred in the Neo-Liberal Era and then outline the contours of a possible Keynesian alternative.

7.3.1 The Neo-Liberal Era

Neo-liberals redefined the goals of economic policy. Instead of full employment and growth, price stability and sound fiscal policies became the objectives.[2] Combined with reducing taxes and cutting 'overgenerous' welfare benefits this amounted to a redefinition of the role of the state in the economy society. The state would henceforth play a minimal role and not interfere with the working of the market mechanism. Consequently restrictive fiscal and monetary policy was complemented by deregulation and liberalization of various markets.

In Europe this redefinition of the role of the state is closely related to the development of the European Union and was codified in its various treaties. This is instructive for two reasons. First, the Maastricht Treaty and the Pact for Stability and Growth are clear about the priorities of economic policy: price stability and fiscal conservatism have a clear priority over stabilization and full employment. Moreover the ECB has no obligation to take labour markets into consideration and, by virtue of its independence, is not obliged to cooperate with democratically elected governments. In Europe the zeal to write neo-liberal economic policies in stone has resulted in an institutional setting that led to 'extraordinarily incompetent macroeconomic policies' which have 'exacerbated the recent economic downturn' as the conservative *Economist* magazine writes (*Economist*, 20 September 2003, 'A survey of the world economy', p. 4).

Second, it is interesting to consider the decision-making bodies that drafted these treaties. Recent developments illustrate a shift away from institutions that are democratically elected, to commissions and institutions that are neither responsible to the electorate nor transparent. Unlike national parliaments, the European Commission meetings are not in public. The ECB president, who – given the restrictions placed on fiscal policies of national governments and their problems in coordinating them – holds arguably the most powerful position in European economic policy, has neither been elected nor is he accountable to Europe's people.

An important reason for shifting decisions away from democratically elected parliaments, of course, is simply that electorates often would not have supported the policies eventually pursued by EU bodies. Consequently whenever EU treaties are voted upon in referenda the results are anxiously awaited in Brussels and usually are tight (such as the 1992 referendum on the Maastricht Treaty), often rejecting the proposals as happened in Denmark 1992. The discontent with the much bemoaned 'democratic deficit' of the EU is not the least expressed by the thousands of protesters who now regularly gather at EU summits.

Redefining the role of the state went hand in hand with the weakening of civil society. In the early 1980s, when organized labour was the strongest and most important part of civil society, neo-liberals were at the forefront of attacking labour unions. The air controller strike in the USA and the miners' strike in the UK, both ending with bitter defeats for labour, set the tone for two decades of union decline and concession bargaining. On the Continent the decline was probably more due to sustained high unemployment. The result and expression of the decline of labour is its falling share of income (see Chapter 1). Moreover, corporatist arrangements where employers' organizations, labour unions and governments would meet and compromise have been abandoned. Wage negotiations are being decentralized.

A reaction to this has been that labour unions have become replaced or complemented as the leading organizations of civil society. Discontent has become organized differently – it had to, since with the end of corporatist agreements the traditional voice of workers has lost much of its strength.

The third area that was transformed by neo-liberals is the role of finance. Financial liberalization has been one of the most important developments and proceeded externally as well as internally. Externally, the post-war regime of fixed exchange rates and capital controls had been liberalized gradually. The early 1970s witnessed the switch to a flexible exchange rate system. Since this was unworkable for the relatively open and integrated economies of Europe, various ways of stabilizing exchange rates were tried leading to the ERM with periodical readjustments of exchange rates that otherwise remained fixed (within bands) and finally the introduction of the euro. The ERM crisis in 1992 had demonstrated that stable exchange rates were inconsistent with free capital movements.

The European economies irrevocably froze their exchange rates, protecting themselves from the violent exchange rate swings that often come as the result of free capital movement and that shook developing economies throughout the 1990s. Speculative short-term investments left a trace of economic and social scars around the world, hitting Mexico and Latin America in 1994, East Asia in 1997, Russia in 1998, and Argentina and Turkey in 2001. Each time, painful recessions and unemployment were the immediate consequences; the longer-term effects remain to be seen. But the protection from unstable exchange rates came at a price: European countries have given up on the exchange rate as a policy instrument that could be used to compensate for differential developments with what is now the euro-zone.

Internally, the liberalization of financial markets meant the lifting of interest rate ceilings and a reduction of state influence on credit allocation, permitting new financial instruments and new financial institutions (most famously hedge funds). The most important macroeconomic consequence was the rise of interest rates. Since 1980, interest rates have hardly dropped below GDP growth. In part this was due to the restrictive monetary policies pursued by the FED and the Bundesbank, which dominated European monetary policy until the introduction of the euro; in part due to financial deregulation. The effects of the rise in world interest rates can hardly be overrated. This was an important factor in precipitating the debt crises of the early 1980s; it created a structural problem for government finances since their tax income would henceforth grow below the rate of interest rates. Equally, this situation made financial investment more attractive compared to physical investment.

7.3.2 A Keynesian Alternative

Neo-conservativism is an ongoing political project that has already resulted in increased social polarization. It has brought mass unemployment and declining real wages (relative to productivity) for some social groups, and rising profits and financial incomes for others (see Chapter 1; Dumenil and Levy 2001). While in the 1990s a shift to the moderate centre-left brought B. Clinton, T. Blair and G. Schroeder to power, the hope this would mark the end of the neo-liberal revolution was premature. First, the new generation of social democrats themselves adopted many of the neo-liberal policies and embraced a minimal state. Second, with G.W. Bush and S. Berlusconi another generation of even more aggressive neo-liberals came to power in the late 1990s and after. The following policy proposals would mark a clear break with the current policies. While the dominance of neo-liberals might make the implementation of the following policy proposals appear unlikely, it also makes the discussion of alternative policies all the more urgent.

The envisioned policies rest on three pillars. First, the state has to be enabled to play an active role. This presupposes that economic policies are freed from the shackles the current treaties of the EU impose. States also have to be empowered fiscally in order to play a more proactive role. Thus a reform of the tax system is called for. Second, a broad participation in the political process is needed. Given the frustration with conventional political parties in most countries, this implies including non-conventional political organizations, such as NGOs, in the processes of policy-making as well as developing institutions for the mediation of the conflict between capital and labour. Mediation presupposes that the parties in the conflict are recognized as equals. After two decades of neo-liberal policies this, unsurprisingly, is not the case. Under the current state of affairs, mediation requires an empowerment of workers and their organizations. Third, the role of finance has to be reconsidered. While the financial system fulfils essential functions in a modern economy such as the provision of credit and instruments for hedging against risks, in its present state the financial system often has turned into a source of instability and impediment for growth.

7.3.2.1 A state committed to full employment and growth

In order for European states to pursue an active and growth-oriented role in the economy, key treaties of the EU have to be revised. In the 2001 recession, this was best illustrated by the trap economic policy-makers have found themselves in. When countries face a recession they have three macroeconomic areas to respond: fiscal policy, monetary policy and exchange rate policy. Since the Maastricht Treaty national fiscal policies have been severely restricted. Moreover, given the fact that the EU's budget is limited and dominated by agricultural expenditures, no fiscal stimulus can be expected from the EU. Monetary policy is subordinated to the goal of price stability and therefore unlikely to play an expansionary role as has become painfully clear in the course of the recent recession. Finally, exchange rate policy is not an option since internally the exchange rates have been locked into the euro and externally, exchange rates are freely floating. In short, European economic policy has blocked all its means to respond to a situation of crisis.

To enable policy-makers to pursue policies aiming at full employment or even to fight a recession, a complete comprehensive redesign of the Growth and Stability Pact is necessary. The spirit of the Pact has to include the aim of sustainable growth and full employment as the primary goals and has to materialize through institutional changes. Arestis et al. (2001) have made a proposal for a Full Employment, Growth and Stability Pact. This proposal includes removing the 3 per cent budget deficit limitation and making the ECB responsible to the European Parliament. A strict separation of fiscal and monetary authorities is counterproductive, in particular in the setting of the EU, where fiscal policies are overwhelmingly carried out by national governments and are thus extremely hard to coordinate.

Removing fixed rules on budget deficits is not to be misunderstood as an invitation to increase government debt, but is necessary to give governments the flexibility to react to economic crises. Structural budget deficits however are neither part of a Keynesian programme nor desirable.[3] If the state is to play an active role it has to make available the necessary income. Thus financial empowerment is important. The question is what the state's role is and whether it should shrink. From a Keynesian perspective there is little hope for the state's role in the economy to decrease. The government's role would not only increase in the efforts to fight unemployment, but also because the public sector is increasingly important to counteract the instability emanating from the financial sector. Financial crises have hit developed economies as well as developing economies increasingly hard in the 1990s and thereafter. Since such crises can hardly be ruled out in the future, the economy needs a sector that is independent of the financial sector in a way the private sector cannot be (Minsky 1985).

How can the income base for the state be secured and the chronic deficits in most developed countries be overcome? It is important to note that a part of fiscal consolidation would be accomplished automatically if interest rates fell below growth rates of income and thus tax revenues. However, there should be no illusion that the crisis of government balances has to be addressed on the income side as well. The tax system has to be modernized. Most tax systems rely on income taxes and social security contributions mostly paid by wage earners. However, the income segments that have grown most dynamically in recent decades, profits and incomes from financial transactions, are notorious for contributing little to tax revenues. The share of profits in total tax income has declined since 1965 (Devereux et al. 2002). Three remarks are in place to address some well-known problems in the taxation of profits. First, there is the issue of tax evasion. Enron famously reported zero taxable profits while reporting $2.3 billion to shareholders. While in the case of Enron much of the reported profits turned out to be a fraud, this is merely the tip of the iceberg of tax evasion. Taxable profits have drifted from accounting profits (*Economist*, 10 May 2003). Tightening accounting regulations alone will thus improve the tax base. Second, part of the deterioration in the taxation of profits is due to tax competition between countries. Increasing taxes on profits in one country does risk capital flight. However, if coordinated at the EU level, this problem arises to a much smaller extent. Third, high taxes on profits may have a negative impact on investment. This problem can be addressed in designing a tax reform that broadens the tax base while not, or hardly, affecting marginal tax rates that are influencing investment decisions.

Similarly, states need to be empowered politically. The decades since 1980 have witnessed a loss of economic and legal sovereignty that has led to a severe democratic deficit. Bodies that lack democratic legitimization and control now make important decisions. Not least, this has been the case in the course of European monetary unification. More blatantly, the IMF is dictating economic policies in developing economies in the interest of investors, and overruling national governments that in many cases at least have more democratic legitimation than the IMF. Whatever the role of governments in the future is to be, this role has to be decided on by the electorate and not by supranational institutions that are themselves not controlled democratically and are thus open to special-interest lobbying.

7.3.2.2 A new balance between capital and civil society

The Neo-Liberal Era was marked by a retreat of organized labour and the establishment (or expansion of the scope) of institutions that are remote from democratic control such as the IMF or the WTO. Post-Keynesian policies insist on a participatory structure of the state and in the inclusion of civil society and organized labour. Within a Keynesian approach this is important not only to ensure a wide dispersion of the gains of growth but also to mitigate distributional struggles through institutions. Distributional struggle is identified as a key source of inflation by Post-Keynesian theory and also underlies the NAIRU theory. It is also well established in the empirical literature that centralized collective bargaining reduces inflation and the NAIRU. The reason for this being that the more centralized the bargaining process, the closer unions and employers come to negotiating real wages rather than nominal wages. Consequently distributional conflicts can be dealt as such and do not have to be expressed as inflation.

Participation can take place in the form of the inclusion of these groups in core policy advising bodies, but in the case of labour also needs to be reflected in firm-level labour policies. The wave of accounting frauds and exorbitant pay packages for managers that have shaken the corporate world since the year 2000 have repeatedly led to calls for reforms of corporate governance structures. Curiously, enduing debates have focused on the role of various bodies within the firms (in particular, supervisory boards) and on the rights of shareholders. However, those most directly affected by bankruptcies, the employees, are rarely considered as worthy of playing any role in corporate governance and control. The German model of codetermination and works councils may be a starting point for a firm-level participation. As elaborated in Chapter 5 a greater say of such growth and employment-oriented groups in management may also cause positive growth externalities through changes in corporate governance.

7.3.2.3 Subordinating the financial sector

The structure and growth of the financial sector has to be regulated and directed such that it serves the need of the real sectors of the economy and such that financial development (and reaping profits thereof) does not become an end in itself. Needless to say, such a redesign is a challenging task for which no ready-made blueprints exist. The goals of such a restructuring are to create a financial system that provides finance for long-term expenditures, that is mostly investment. Tobin called this the 'functional efficiency' of the financial sector. Second, it is important to create a financial sector that is in itself stable and does not, as has happened throughout the 1990s cause disruptive crises. Third, all this has to be accomplished without negatively effecting the vital services of risk pooling provided by the financial sector.

Such policies will require a broad range of measures that include transparency of financial accounts and tighter supervision of hitherto unregulated financial actors to a restructuring of the tax system. The former demand has become a commonplace after the series of scandals of which

Enron and Worldcom are the most famous. Notably these firms were supported in their criminal activities by well-respected financial consultancies and rating agencies. For one of them, Arthur Andersen, the affair proved lethal.

Several proposals exist for restructuring the tax system to adapt to the rising importance of financial transactions and the incomes thereof. Most fundamentally, the proper taxation of interest incomes has long been discussed. Theoretically there exists no reason why interest income should be taxed at a lower rate than other kinds of income since this violates the principle of horizontal tax equality. However in many countries interest incomes are in fact taxed at lower rates because of successful lobbying attempts by financial groups. A proposal for a European interest tax has been put on hold by the European Commission after a veto from Luxembourg.

The most widely discussed proposal is that of Tobin (1978) who proposed a minor tax on foreign exchange transactions that would translate into a sizeable tax for speculative short-term transactions. This proposal has been updated by Eichengreen et al. (1995) and extended by Pollin et al. (2002) who propose a security transactions tax that would apply to all financial transactions. These proposals, technical difficulties not withstanding, would have positive effects on the economy. First, they would contribute to financial stability by making speculation more expensive (they could, however, not be expected to guarantee financial stability by themselves). Second, they would divert resources from financial investment to physical investment, which under the current conditions would be socially desirable. Third, they would provide an income source for the state that would allow the state sector to resume an active role in pursuing full employment and stabilization policies.

From the perspective taken here the current pressure to shift pension systems toward capital-based private systems is misguided. Financial markets are inherently unstable. Shifting the provision of pensions to financial markets will be macroeconomically dangerous because it will strengthen the real effects of large swings in asset prices. Distributionally it is questionable as it will increase income dispersion for the retired. Moreover it creates serious moral hazard problems. It is hard to believe that the state would not support a big pension fund that faces bankruptcy, since hundreds of thousands of people (and voters) might lose their old-age income. Thus prudent behaviour on part of the pension funds could only be ensured by stringent regulation.

These policy proposals are certainly a long way from today's political mainstream as well as the preaching of organizations such as the OECD or the IMF. While some of the proposals, like improving the coordination of economic policy institutions or probably even modifying the goals of the ECB to give more consideration to growth, are almost common sense, they may still meet fierce resistance. This should not come as a surprise. While the overall macroeconomic performance of the Neo-Liberal Era is dismal, some social groups have unambiguously benefited. While growth rates have been worse since 1980 than before and unemployment has been higher, profits have recovered to levels above the Fordist Era and financial profits have grown even faster (see Chapter 1). Thus the controversy between Keynesian and neo-liberal policy recommendations is not only a debate around macroeconomic priorities and instruments most appropriate for social welfare, it is also a controversy about whose interests economic policy should serve. This is more obvious in the case of emerging economies on which the IMF imposes deflationary policies, which benefit the creditors to the indebted countries, but not necessarily its population. However, macroeconomic policies do of course also have distributional effects in advanced economies. This is what makes macroeconomic theorizing so contested. It is also what gives hope, even in times of an entrenched economic orthodoxy, that Keynesian policy proposals will be adopted: they benefit a greater part of society than neo-liberal ones, and in a democratic society the majority ought to prevail over special interests.

NOTES

1. Stockhammer and Onaran (2004) and Onaran and Stockhammer (2004) offer an econometric systems approach to a similar Kaleckian macro model.
2. The neo-liberals did not always live up to their declared objectives: under Reagan the US government debt reached its historically highest level.
3. One qualification to this is that capital expenditures can be credit financed.

References

Abel, A (1980), 'Empirical investment equations: an integrative framework', in K. Brunner and A. Meltzer, *On the State of Macro-Economics*, Carnegie-Rochester Conference on Public Policy vol. 12, Amsterdam: North Holland.

Aglietta, Michel (1979), *A Theory of Capitalist Regulation. The US Experience*, London: Verso.

Aglietta, Michel (2000), 'Shareholder value and corporate governance: some tricky questions', *Economy and Society*, **29** (1) 146–59.

Alesina, A. and Perotti (1996), 'Income distribution, political instability, and investment', *European Economic Review*, **40** (6) 1203–28.

Alogoskoufis, G. and A. Manning (1988), 'Wage setting and unemployment persistence in Europe, Japan and the USA', *European Economic Review*, **32** (2–3), 698–706.

Amisano, G. and C. Giannini (1997), *Topics in Structural VAR Econometrics*, 2nd edition, Berlin: Springer Verlag.

Appelbaum, E. and P. Berg (1996), 'Financial market constraints and business strategy in the USA', in J. Michie and J. Smith (eds), *Creating Industrial Capacity. Towards Full Employment*, Oxford: Oxford University Press.

Appelbaum, E. and R. Schettkat (1995), 'Employment and productivity in industrialized economies', *International Labour Review*, **134** (4–5), 605–23.

Arestis, P. and I. Biefang-Frisancho Mariscal (1998), 'Capital shortages and asymmetries in UK unemployment', *Structural Change and Economic Dynamics*, **9**, 189–204.

Arestis, P., C. McCauley and M. Sawyer (2001), 'An alternative stability pact for the European Union', *Cambridge Journal of Economics*, **25**, 113–30.

Arestis, P. and M. Sawyer (1998), 'Keynesian economic policies for the new millennium', *Economic Journal*, **108**, 181–95.

Baker, D., G. Epstein and R. Pollin (1998), *Globalization and Progressive Economic Policy*, Cambridge, MA: Cambridge University Press.

Baker, D., A. Glyn, D. Howell and J. Schmitt (2002), 'Labor market institutions and unemployment: a critical assessment of the cross-country evidence', CEPA Working Paper 2002–17.

Baker, G. and G. Smith (1998), *The New Financial Capitalists: Kohlberg Kravis Roberts and the Creation of Corporate Value*, New York: Cambridge University Press.

Ball, Lawrence (1994), 'Disinflation and the NAIRU', in C. Romer and D. Romer (eds), *Reducing Inflation. Motivation and Strategy*, Chicago, IL: University of Chicago Press.

Ball, Lawrence (1999), 'Aggregate demand and long-run unemployment', *Brookings Papers on Economic Activity 2/1999*, 189–236.

Banuri, T. and J. Schor (1992), *Financial Openness and National Autonomy Opportunities and Constraints*, Oxford: Clarendon Press.

Barro, R. (1988), 'The persistence of unemployment', *American Economic Review*, **78**, 32–7.

Bean, Charles (1994a), 'European unemployment: a retrospective', *European Economic Review*, **38**, 523–34.

Bean, C. (1994b), 'European unemployment: a survey', *Journal of Economic Literature*, **32**, 573–619.

Bean, C., P. Layard and S. Nickell (1986), 'The rise of unemployment: A multi-country study', *Economica*, **53**, S1–S22.

Bentolina, Samuel (1997), 'Discussion', in D. Snower and G. de la Dehesa (eds), *Unemployment Policy: Government Options for the Labor Market*, Cambridge: Cambridge University Press.

Bernanke, B. (1986), 'Alternative explanation of the money income correlations', Carnegie Rochester Conference Series on Public Policy 25.

Bernanke, B. and M. Gertler (1990), 'Financial fragility and economic performance', *Quarterly Journal of Economics*, **105** (1), 87–114.

Berndt, Ernst (1991), *The Practice of Econometrics: Classic and Contemporary*, Reading, MA: Addison Wesley Publishing Company.

Bhaduri, A. and S. Marglin (1990), 'Unemployment and the real wage: the economic basis for contesting political ideologies', *Cambridge Journal of Economics*, **14**, 375–93.

Bhaskar, V. and A. Glyn (1995), 'Investment and profitability: the evidence from the advanced countries', in G. Epstein and H. Gintis (eds), *Macroeconomic Policy after the Conservative Era. Studies in Investment, Saving and Finance*, Cambridge: Cambridge University Press.

Blanchard, Olivier (1989), 'A traditional interpretation of macroeconomic fluctuations', *American Economic Review*, **79** (5), 1146–64.

Blanchard, Olivier (1990), 'Unemployment: getting the questions right – and some of the answers', in J. Dreze and C. Bean (eds), *Europe's Unemployment Problem*, Cambridge, MA: MIT Press.

Blanchard, Olivier (1994), 'Comment', in C. Romer and D. Romer (eds), *Reducing Inflation. Motivation and Strategy*, Chicago, IL: University of Chicago Press.

Blanchard, Olivier (1997), 'The medium run', *Brookings Papers on Economic Activity*, **2**, 89–141.

Blanchard, O. and L. Katz (1997), 'What we know and do not know about the natural rate of unemployment', *Journal of Economic Perspectives*, **11** (1), 51–72.

Blanchard, O., C. Rhee and L. Summers (1993), 'The stock market, profit, and investment', *Quarterly Journal of Economics*, **108**, 115–36.

Blanchard, O. and L. Summers (1986), 'Hysteresis and European unemployment problem', in S. Fischer (ed.), *NBER Macroeconomics Annual 1986*, Cambridge, MA: MIT Press.

Blanchard, O. and L. Summers (1987), 'Hysteresis in unemployment', *European Economic Review*, **31**, 288–95.

Blanchard, O. and L. Summers (1988), 'Beyond the natural rate hypothesis', *American Economic Review*, **78** (2), 182–7.

Blanchard, O. and J. Wolfers (2000), 'The role of shocks and institutions in the rise of European unemployment: the aggregate evidence', *Economic Journal*, **110**, 1–33.

Blanchflower, D. and A. Oswald (1994), *The Wage Curve*, Cambridge, MA: MIT Press.

Blank, Rebecca (1994), 'Does a larger social safety net mean less economic flexibility?' in R. Freeman (ed.), *Working Under Different Rules*, New York: Russell Sage Foundation.

Blecker, R. (1989), 'International competition, income distribution and economic growth', *Cambridge Journal of Economics*, **13**, 395–412.

Blecker, R. (1999), 'Kaleckian macromodels for open economies', in J. Deprez and J.T. Harvey (eds), *Foundations of International Economics: Post Keynesian Perspectives*, London, New York: Routledge.

Blecker, Robert (2002), 'Distribution, demand and growth in neo-Kaleckian macro-models', in Setterfield (ed.), *The Economics of Demand-led Growth,* Cheltenham: Edward Elgar.

Boone, L., C. Giorno and P. Richardson (1998), 'Stock market fluctuations and consumption behaviour: some recent evidence', OECD Economics department working papers No. 208.

Bowles S., D. Gordon and T. Weisskopf (1986), 'Power and profits: the social structure of accumulation and the profitability of the Postwar US economy', *Review of Radical Political Economics*, **18** (1,2), 132–67.

Bowles, S. and R. Boyer (1995), 'Wages, aggregate demand, and employment in an open economy: an empirical investigation', in G. Epstein and H. Gintis (eds), *Macroeconomic Policy after the Conservative Era. Studies in Investment, Saving and Finance*, Cambridge: Cambridge University Press.

Boyer, R. and P. Petit (1981), 'Progrès technique, croissance et emploi: Un modèle d'inspiration kaldorienne pour six industries européennes', *Revue Economique*, **32** (6) 1113–54.

Boyer, Robert (1988), 'Formalizing growth regimes', in G. Dosi, C. Freeman and R. Nelson (eds), *Technical Change and Economic Theory*, London: Pinter.

Boyer, Robert (1990), *The Regulation School: A Critical Introduction*, New York: Columbia University Press.

Boyer, Robert (1993), 'Labour institutions and economic growth: a survey and a "régulationist" approach', *Labour*, **7** (1), 25–72.

Boyer, Robert (2000), 'Is a finance-led growth regime a viable alternative to Fordism? A preliminary analysis', *Economy and Society*, **29** (1), 111–45.

Bruno, M. and W. Easterly (1998), 'Inflation crises and long run growth', *Journal of Monetary Economics*, **41** (1), 3–26.

Buchele, R. and J. Christiansen (1992), 'Industrial relations and productivity growth', *International Contributions to Labour Studies*, **2**, 77–97.

Buchele, R. and J. Christiansen (1993), 'Industrial relations and relative income shares in the US', *Industrial Relations*, **32** (1), 49–71.

Buchele, R. and J. Christiansen (1995), 'Productivity, real wages, and worker rights: a cross-national comparison', *Labour*, **9** (3), 405–22.

Buchele, R. and J. Christiansen (1999a), 'Employment and productivity growth in Europe and North America: the impact of labor market institutions', *International Review of Applied Economics*, **13** (3), 313–32.

Buchele, R. and J. Christiansen (1999b), 'Labor relations and productivity growth in advanced capitalist economies', *Review of Radical Political Economics*, **31** (1), 87–110.

Campbell, J. and P. Perron (1991), 'What macroeconomists should know about unit roots', *NBER Macroeconomics Annual*, 121–201.

Card, D. and A. Krueger (1994), *Myth and Measurement. The New Economics of the Minimum Wage*, Princeton, NJ: Princeton University Press.

Carlin, W. and D. Soskice (1990), *Macroeconomics and the Wage Bargain. A Modern Approach to Employment, Inflation and the Exchange Rate*, Oxford: Oxford University Press.

Case, K., R. Shiller and J. Quigley (2001), 'Comparing wealth effects: the stock market versus the housing market', NBER Working Paper No. w8606 November.

Cassetti, Mario (2002), 'Conflict, inflation, distribution and terms of trade in the Kaleckian model', Mark Setterfield, (ed.), *The Economics of Demand-led Growth*. Cheltenham, UK: Edward Elgar.

Chandler, Alfred (1977), *The Visible Hand: The Managerial Revolution in American Business*, Cambridge, MA: Harvard University Press.

Charemza, W. and D. Deadman (1997), *New Directions in Econometric Practice. General to Specific Modelling, Cointegration and Vector Autoregression*, Aldershot: Edward Elgar.

Chechi, D. and C. Lucifora (2002), 'Unions and labor market institutions in Europe', *Economic Policy*, **35**, 362–408.

Chirinko, Robert (1993), 'Business fixed investment spending: modeling strategies, empirical results and policy implications', *Journal of Economic Literature*, **31**, 1875–911.

Christiano, L. and M. Eichenbaum (1990), 'Unit roots in GNP: do we know and do we care?', Carnegie-Rochester Conference Series on Public Policy 32, 7–62.

Clark, Peter (1979), 'Investment in the 1970s: theory, performance, and prediction', *Brookings Papers on Economic Activity* 1/1979, 73–113.

Cochrane, J. (1991a), 'Critique of application of unit root tests', *Journal of Economic Dynamics and Control*, **15** (2), 275–83.

Cochrane, John (1991b), 'Comment', *NBER Macroeconomics Annual*, 201–10.

Coddington, A. (1976), 'Keynesian economics: the search for first principles', *Journal of Economic Literature*, **14**, 1258–73.

Cooley, T. and S. LeRoy (1986), 'Atheoretical macroeconometrics: a critique', *Journal of Monetary Economics*, **16**, 283–308.

Corbett, J. and T. Jenkinson (1997), 'How is investment financed? A study of Germany, Japan and the United Kingdom and the United States', *Manchester School*, Supplement, 69–93.

Cross, Rod (ed.) (1988), *Unemployment, Hysteresis and the Natural Rate Hypothesis*, Oxford: Blackwell.

Cross, Rod (ed.) (1995), *The Natural Rate of Unemployment: Reflections on 25 Years of the Hypothesis*, Cambridge: Cambridge University Press.

Crotty, James (1990), 'Keynes on the stages of development of the capitalist economy: the institutionalist foundation of Keynes's methodology', *Journal of Economic Issues*, **24** (3), 761–80.

Crotty, James (1992), 'Neoclassical and Keynesian approaches to the theory of investment', *Journal of Post Keynesian Economics*, **14** (4), 483–97.

Crotty, James (1993), 'Rethinking Marxian investment theory: Keynes-Minsky instability, competitive regime shifts and coerced investment', *Review of Radical Political Economics*, **25** (1), 1–26.

Crotty, James (1994), 'Are Keynesian uncertainty and macrotheory compatible? Conventional decision making, institutional structures, and conditional stability in Keynesian macromodels', in G. Dymski and R. Pollin (eds), *New Perspectives in Monetary Macroeconomics: Explorations in the Tradition of Hyman P. Minsky*, Ann Arbor: University of Michigan Press.

Crotty, James (1996), 'Is New Keynesian investment theory really "Keynesian"? Reflections on Fazzari and Variato', *Journal of Post Keynesian Economics*, **18** (3), 333–68.

Crotty, J. and J. Goldstein (1992), 'A Marxian-Keynesian theory of investment demand: empirical evidence', in F. Moseley and E. Wolff (eds), *International Perspectives on Profitability and Accumulation*, Aldershot: Edward Elgar.

Davidson, Paul (ed.) (1993), *Can the Free Market Pick Winners? What Determines Investment*, Armonk, NY: Sharpe.

Davidson, Paul (1994), *Post Keynesian Macoreconomic Theory. A Foundation for Successful Economic Policies for the Twenty-first Century*, Aldershot: Edward Elgar.

Davidson, Paul (1998), 'Post Keynesian employment analysis and the macroeconomics of OECD unemployment', *Economic Journal*, **108**, 817–31.

De Long, J. and L. Summers (1991), 'Equipment investment and economic growth', *Quarterly Journal of Economics*, **106** (2), 445–502.

Demirgüc-Kunt, A. and R. Levine (2001), 'Bank-based and market based financial systems: cross country comparisons', in A. Demirgüc-Kunt and R. Levine (eds), *Financial Structure and Economic Growth*, Cambridge, MA: MIT Press.

Devereux, M., R. Griffith and A. Klemm (2002), 'Corporate income tax reforms and international tax competition', *Economic Policy*, **35**, 450–95.

Dreze, J, and C. Bean (1990), *Europe's Unemployment Problem*, Cambridge, MA: MIT Press.

Driver, C. and P. Temple (1999), 'Overview: a survey of recent issues in investment theory', in C. Driver and P. Temple (eds), *Investment, Growth and Employment: Perspectives for Policy*, New York: Routledge.

Dumenil, G. and D. Levy (2001), 'Costs and benefits of neoliberalism: a class analysis', *Review of International Political Economy*, **8** (4), 578–607.

Dutt, Amitava (1984), 'Stagnation, income distribution and monopoly power', *Cambridge Journal of Economics*, **8**, 25–40.

Dutt, Amitava (1987), 'Alternative closures again: a comment on growth, distribution and inflation', *Cambridge Journal of Economics*, **11** (1), 75–82.

Dutt, Amitava (1989), 'Accumulation, distribution and inflation in a Marxian/Post-Keynesian model with a rentier class', *Review of Radical Political Economics*, **21** (3), 18–26.

Dutt, Amitava (1992), 'Rentiers in Post-Keynesian models', in P. Arestis and V. Chick (eds), *Recent Developments in Post-Keynesian Economics*, Aldershot: Edward Elgar.

Eatwell, John (1997), 'Effective demand and disguised unemployment', in J. Michie and J. Smith (eds), *Employment and Economic Performance*, Oxford and New York: Oxford University Press.

Eichengreen, Barry (1993), 'European Monetary Unification', *Journal of Economic Literature*, **31** (3), 132–58.

Eichengreen, Barry (1998), *Globalizing Capital. A History of the International Monetary System*, Princeton University Press.

Eichengreen, B., J. Tobin and C. Wyplosz (1995), 'Two cases for sand in the wheels of international finance', *Economic Journal*, **105**, 162–72.

Eichner, A. (1976), *Megacorp and Oligopoly: Micro Foundations of Macro Dynamics*, Cambridge: Cambridge University Press.

Eisner, R. and R. Strotz (1963), 'Determinants of business investment', in *Commission on Money and Credit: Impacts of monetary policy*, Englewood Cliffs, NJ: Prentice-Hall.

Endres, Walter (1995), *Applied Econometric Time Series*, New York: John Wiley & Sons.

Engle, R. and C. Granger (1987), 'Co-integration and error correction: representation, estimation and testing', *Econometrica*, **55** (2), 251–76.

Epstein, Gerald (1994), 'A political economy model of comparative central banking', in Gary Dymski and Robert Pollin (eds), *New Perspectives in Monetary Macroeconomics*, Ann Arbor, MI: Michigan University Press.

Epstein, Gerald (1996), 'International capital mobility and the scope for national economic management', in R. Boyer and D. Drache (eds), *States Against Markets: The Limits of Globalization*, New York: Routledge.

Epstein, G. and D. Power (2003), 'Rentier income and financial crisis. An empirical examination of trends and cycles in some OECD countries', PERI Working Paper 57.

Epstein, G. and J. Schor (1990), 'Macropolicy in the rise and fall of the Golden Age', in S. Marglin and J. Schor (eds), *The Golden Age of Capitalism*, Oxford: Clarendon Press.

Epstein, G. and J. Schor (1992), 'Structural determinants and economic effects of capital controls in OECD countries', in T. Banuri and J. Schor (eds), *Financial Openness and National Autonomy. Opportunities and Constraints*, Oxford: Clarendon Press.

Farber, H. and K. Hallock (1999), 'Have employment reductions become good news for shareholders? The effect of job loss announcements on stock prices 1970–97', NBER Working Paper No. W7295.

Fazzari, Steven (1993), 'Monetary policy, financial structure, and investment', in G. Dymski, G. Epstein and R. Pollin (eds), *Transforming the US Financial System: Equity and Efficiency for the 21st Century*, Armonk, NY: Sharpe.

Fazzari, S. and T. Mott (1986), 'The investment theories of Kalecki and Keynes: an empirical study of firm data, 1970–1982', *Journal of Post Keynesian Economics*, **9** (2), 171–87.

Fazzari, S. and A. Variato (1994), 'Asymmetric information and Keynesian theories of investment', *Journal of Post Keynesian Economics*, **26** (3), 351–69.

Feldstein, M. and C. Horioka (1980), 'Domestic saving and international capital flows', *Economic Journal*, **90**, 314–29.

Ford, R. and P. Poret (1991), 'Business investment: recent performance and some implications for policy', *OECD Economic Studies*, **16**, 79–131.

Frankel, Jeffrey (1992), 'Measuring international capital mobility: a review', *American Economic Review*, **82** (2), 197–202.

Franz, W. and R. Gordon (1993), 'German and American wage and price dynamics. Differences and common themes', *European Economic Review*, **37**, 719–62.

Friedman, Milton (1968), 'The role of monetary policy', *American Economic Review*, **58**, 1–117.

Fritsche, U. and C. Logeay (2002), 'Structural unemployment and the output gap in Germany: evidence from an SVAR analysis within a hysteresis framework', DIW Discussion Papers 312.

Froud, J., C. Haslam, S. Johal and K. Williams (2000), 'Shareholder value and financialization: consultancy promises, management moves', *Economy and Society*, **29** (1), 80–110.

Galbraith, John (1967), *The New Industrial State*, New York: New American Library.

Glyn, Andrew (1997), 'Does aggregate profitability really matter?', *Cambridge Journal of Economics*, **21**, 593–619.

Glyn, Andrew (1998), 'Employment growth, structural change and capital accumulation', ESRC Centre for Business Research, University of Cambridge, Working Paper No. 97.

Glyn, A., A. Hughes, A. Lipietz and A. Singh (1990), 'The rise and fall of the Golden Age', in S. Marglin and J. Schor (eds), *The Golden Age of Capitalism*, Oxford: Clarendon Press.

Godfrey, L. (1988), *Specification Tests in Econometrics*, Cambridge University Press.

Gordon, David (1993), 'Putting heterodox macro to the test: comparing Post-Keynesian, Marxian and Social Structuralist macroeconometric models for the postwar US economy', Working Paper No. 43 New School for Social Research; published in M. Glick (ed) (1994), *Competition, Technology and Money*, Cheltenham, UK: Edward Elgar.

Gordon, David (1995a), 'Growth distribution, and the rules of the game: social structuralist macro foundations for a democratic economic policy', in G. Epstein and H. Gintis (eds), *Macroeconomic Policy after the Conservative Era. Studies in Investment, Saving and Finance*, Cambridge: Cambridge University Press.

Gordon, David (1995b), 'Putting the horse (back) before the cart: disentangeling the macro relationship between investment and saving', in G. Epstein and H. Gintis (eds), *Macroeconomic Policy after the Conservative Era. Studies in Investment, Saving and Finance*, Cambridge: Cambridge University Press.

Gordon, David (1996), *Fat and Mean. The Corporate Squeeze of Working Americans and the Myth of Managerial 'Downsizing'*, New York: Simon & Schuster.

Gordon, M. (1992), 'The Neoclassical and a Post Keynesian theory of investment', *Journal of Post Keynesian Economics*, **14** (4), 425–44.

Gordon, Robert (1990), 'What is new-Keynesian economics?' *Journal of Economic Literature*, **28**, 1115–71.

Grabel, Ilene (1997), 'Savings, investment, and functional efficiency: a comparative examination of national financial complexes', in R. Pollin (ed.), *The Macroeconomics of Savings, Finance and Investment*, Ann Arbor, MI: University of Michigan Press.

Greene, William (1997), *Econometric Analysis*, 3rd edition, Upper Saddle River, New Jersey: Prentice-Hall.

Grubb, D., R. Jackman and R. Layard (1983), 'Wage rigidity and unemployment in OECD countries', *European Economic Review*, **21** (1–2), 11–39.

Guiso, L. and G. Parigi (1999), 'Investment and demand uncertainty', *Quarterly Journal of Economics*, **114** (1), 185–228.

Haavelmo, T. (1960), *A Study in the Theory of Investment*, Chicago, IL: University of Chicago Press.

Hahn, F. and R. Solow (1995), *A Critical Essay on Modern Macroeconomic Theory*, Cambridge, MA: MIT Press.

Hall, Robert E. and Dale Jorgenson (1969), 'Tax policy and investment behavior: reply and further results', *American Economic Review*, June 1969, **59** (3), 388–401.

Hamilton, James (1994), *Time Series Analysis*, Princeton, NJ: Princeton University Press.

Harcourt, G. (1969), 'Some Cambridge controversies in the theory of capital', *Journal of Economic Literature*, **7** (2), 369–405.

Harris, Donald (1978), *Capital Accumulation and Income Distribution*, London: Routledge.

Harrod, R. (1948), *Towards a Dynamic Economics*, London: Macmillan.

Hein, E. and H. Krämer (1997), 'Income shares and capital formation: patterns of recent developments', *Journal of Income Distribution*, **7** (1), 5–28.

Hendry, David (1995), *Dynamic Econometrics*, Oxford: Oxford University Press.

Hendry, D., A. Pagan and J. Sargan (1984), 'Dynamic specification', in Z. Griliches and M. Intriligator (eds), *Handbook of Econometrics*, Volume II, Amsterdam, New York: North-Holland Pub. Co.

Henley, A. and E. Tsakalotos (1991), 'Corporatism, profit squeeze and investment', *Cambridge Journal of Economics*, **15**, 425–50.

Heye, Christopher (1995), 'Expectations and investment: an econometric defense of animal spirits', in G. Epstein and H. Gintis (eds), *Macroeconomic Policy after the Conservative Era. Studies in Investment, Saving and Finance*, Cambridge: Cambridge University Press.

Heylen, F. and A. Van Pock (1995), 'National labour market institutions and the European economic and monetary integration process', *Journal of Common Market Studies*, **33** (4), 573–95.

Hicks, John (1937), 'Mr Keynes and the Classics: a suggested interpretation', *Econometrica*, **5**, 147–59.

Hirschman, Albert (1970), *Exit, Voice, and Loyalty*, Cambridge, MA: Harvard University Press.

Hubbard, Glenn (ed.) (1990), *Asymmetric Information, Corporate Finance, and Investment*, Chicago, IL: University of Chicago Press.

Hubbard, R. (1998), 'Capital market imperfections and investment', *Journal of Economic Literature*, **36**, 193–225.

Hubbard, R., A. Kashyap and T. Whited (1995), 'Internal finance and firm investment', *Journal of Money, Credit and Banking*, **27** (3), 683–701.

IMF (2003), 'Unemployment and labor market institutions: why reforms pay off', Chapter 4 of *World Economic Outlook*, April.

Jensen, M. and W. Meckling (1976), 'Theory of the firm: managerial behavior, agency costs, and ownership structure', *Journal of Financial Economics*, **3**, 305–60.

Jorgenson, Dale (1963), 'Capital theory and investment behaviour', *American Economic Review*, **53** (2), 247–59.

Jorgenson, D. (1971), 'Econometric studies of investment behaviour: a survey', *Journal of Economic Literature*, **9** (4), 1111–47.

Jorgenson, D., J. Hunter and M. Nadiri (1970), 'A comparison of alternative econometric models of quarterly investment behavior', *Econometrica*, **38** (2), 187–212.

Jürgens, U., K. Naumann and J. Rupp (2000), 'Shareholder value in an adverse environment: the German case', *Economy and Society*, **29** (1), 54–79.

Kaldor, Nicholas (1956), 'Alternative theories of distribution', *Review of Economic Studies*, **23** (2), 83–100.

Kaldor, Nicholas (1957), 'A model of economic growth', *Economic Journal*, LXVII, 591–624.

Kalecki, Michal (1936), 'Some remarks on Keynes's Theory', *Ekonomista*. Reprinted in J. Osiatynski (ed.), *Collected Works of Michal Kalecki*, Vol. 2, Oxford: Clarendon Press.

Kalecki, Michal (1943), 'Political aspects of full employment', *Political Quarterly*, **14** (4), 322–31. Reprinted in Michal Kalecki (1971), *Selected Essays on the Dynamics of the Capitalist Economy*, Cambridge: Cambridge University Press.

Kalecki, Michal (1954), *Theory of Economic Dynamics*, in J. Osiatynski (ed.), *Collected Works of Michal Kalecki*, Vol. 1, Oxford: Clarendon Press.

Kalecki, Michal (1968), 'Trend and business cycle', *Economic Journal*. Reprinted in J. Osiatynski (ed.), *Collected Works of Michal Kalecki*, Oxford: Clarendon Press.

Kalecki, Michal (1969), *Theory of Economic Dynamics*, New York: A.M. Kelley.

Kalecki, Michal (1971), *Selected Essays on the Dynamics of the Capitalist Economy*, Cambridge: Cambridge University Press.

Kalecki, Michal (1987), *Krise und Prosperität im Kapitalismus. Ausgewählte Essays 1933–1971*, Marburg: Metropolis.

Kennedy, Peter (1992), *A Guide to Econometrics*, Cambridge, MA: MIT Press.

Keynes, John (1971), *A Tract on Monetary Reform, The Collected Writings of John Maynard Keynes. Vol. 4*, London: Macmillan.

Kindleberger, Charles (1989), *Manias, Panics and Crashes. A History of Financial Crises*, revised edition, Basingstoke: MacMillan.

Klein, L. (1950), 'Economic fluctuations in the United States, 1921–41', Cowles Commission for Research in Economics, Monograph No. 11.

Klein, Lawrence (1966), *The Keynesian Revolution*, 2nd edition, New York: Macmillan.

Kopcke, Richard (1985), 'The determinants of investment spending', *New England Economic Review*, July/August, 19–35.

Krugman, P. (1994), 'Past and prospective causes of high unemployment', in Federal Reserve Bank of Kansas City (ed.), *Reducing Unemployment: Current Issues and Policy Options*, Kansas City: Author.

Kurz, Heinz (1990), 'Effective demand, employment and capacity utilization in the short run', *Cambridge Journal of Economics*, **14** (2), 205–17.

Lavoie, Marc (1992), *Foundations of Post-Keynesian Economic Analysis*, Aldershot: Edward Elgar.

Lavoie, Marc (1995), 'The Kaleckian model of growth and distribution and its neo-Ricardian and neo-Marxian critiques', *Cambridge Journal of Economics*, **19**, 789–818.

Lavoie, Marc (1996), 'Traverse, hysteresis, and normal rates of capacity utilization in Kaleckian models of growth and distribution', *Review of Radical Political Economy*, **28** (4), 113–47.

Lavoie, Marc, (2002), 'The Kaleckian growth model with target return pricing and conflict inflation', Mark Setterfield (ed.), *The Economics of Demand-led Growth*, Cheltenham, UK: Edward Elgar.

Layard, R. and S. Nickell (1986), 'Unemployment in Britain', *Economica*, **53**, S121–69.

Layard, R., S. Nickell and R. Jackman (1991), *Unemployment. Macroeconomic Performance and the Labour Market*, Oxford: Oxford University Press.

Lazonick, W. and M. O'Sullivan (2000), 'Maximising shareholder value: a new ideology for corporate governance', *Economy and Society*, **29** (1), 13–35.

Leibenstein, Harvey (1966), 'Allocative efficiency versus X-efficiency', *American Economic Review*, **56**, 392–415.

Levine, Ross (1997), 'Financial development and economic growth: views and agenda', *Journal of Economic Literature*, **35** (2), 688–726.

Levy, A. and F. Panetta (1996), 'The main trends of real interest rates (1969–1994)', in P. Ciocca and G. Nardozzi, *The High Price of Money. An Interpretation of World Interest Rates*, Oxford: Clarendon Press.

Lindbeck, A. (1993), *Unemployment and Macroeconomics*, Cambridge, MA: MIT Press.

Lindbeck, A. and D. Snower (1987), 'Union activity, unemployment persistence and wage employment ratchets', *European Economic Review*, **31**, 157–67.

Lindbeck, A. D. Snower (1988), *The Insider-Outsider Theory of Employment and Unemployment*, Cambridge, MA: MIT Press.

Lombard, Marc (2000), 'Restrictive macroeconomic policies and unemployment in the European Union', *Review of Political Economy*, **12** (3), 317–32.

Lopez, J. and T. Mott (1999), 'Kalecki versus Keynes on the determinants of investment', *Review of Political Economy*, **11** (3), 291–301.

Lovell, M. (1983), 'Data mining', *Review of Economics and Statistics*, **65** (1), 1–12.

Maddison, Angus (1991), *Dynamic Forces in Capitalist Development. A Long-Run Comparative View*, Oxford: Oxford University Press.

Madsen, J. (1998), 'General equilibrium macroeconomic models of unemployment: can they explain the unemployment path in the OECD?, *Economic Journal*, 108, 850–67.

Malinvaud, Edmond (1984), *Mass Unemployment*, Oxford: Blackwell Publishers.

Marcuzzo, Maria (ed.) (1996), *The Economics of Joan Robinson*, London and New York: Routledge.

Marglin, S. (1984), *Growth, Distribution, and Prices*, Cambridge, MA: Harvard University Press.

Marglin, S. and A. Bhaduri (1990), 'Profit squeeze and Keynesian theory', in S. Marglin and J. Schor (eds), *The Golden Age of Capitalism. Reinterpreting the Postwar Experience*, Oxford: Clarendon.

Marterbauer, M. and E. Walterskirchen (2000), *Einfluss des Wirtschaftswachstums auf die Arbeitslosigkeit. Studie des Österreichischen Instituts für Wirtschaftsforschung im Auftrag der Kammer für Arbeiter und Angestellte für Wien*, Wien: Wifo-Österr. Inst. für Wirtschaftsforschung.

Mayer, Colin (1988), 'New issues in corporate finance', *European Economic Review*, **32**, 1167–89.

Mayer, Colin (1994), 'Stock-markets, financial institutions and corporate performance', in N. Dimsdale and M. Prevezer (eds), *Capital Markets and Corporate Governance*, Oxford: Clarendon Press.

Mayer, C. and I. Alexander (1990), 'Stock markets and corporate performance. A comparison of quoted and unquoted companies', CPER discussion paper.

Mazier, J., M. Basle and J. Vidal (1993), *Quand les crises durent*, Paris: Economica.

McCloskey, D. and S. Ziliak (1996), 'The standard error of regressions', *Journal of Economic Literature*, **34** (1), 97–114.

McConnell, J. and C. Muscarella (1985), 'Corporate capital expenditure decisions and the market value of the firm', *Journal of Financial Economics*, **14**, 399–422.

Meyer, J. and E. Kuh (1957), *The Investment Decision*, Cambridge, MA: Harvard University Press.

Miles, D. (1993), 'Testing for short-termism in the UK stock market', *Economic Journal*, **103**, 1379–96.

Minsky, Hyman (1982), *Can 'it' Happen Again? Essays on Instability and Finance*, Armonk, NY: Sharpe.

Minsky, H. (1985), 'The financial instability hypothesis: a restatement', in P. Arestis and T. Skouras (eds), *Post Keynesian Economic Theory. A Challenge to Neo Classical Economics*, Brighton, Sussex: Wheatsheaf Books.

Minsky, Hyman (1986), *Stabilizing an Unstable Economy*, New Haven, CT: Yale University Press.

Miron, J. (1991), 'Comment', in O. Blanchard and S. Fischer (eds), *NBER Macroeconomics Annual 1991*, Cambridge and London: MIT Press.

Modigliani, F., J. Fitoussi, B. Moro, D. Snower, R. Solow, A. Steinherr and P. Sylos Labini (1998), 'An economist's Manifesto on unemployment in the European Union', *Journal of Income Distribution*, **8**, 163–87.

Modigliani, R. and M. Miller (1958), 'The cost of capital, corporation finance, and the theory of investment', *American Economic Review*, **48** (3), 261–97.

Monastiriotis, Vassilis (1999), 'The economic impact of labour market flexibility: a macroeconomic cross-country analysis for the OECD', paper presented at the Fourth postgraduate Conference, University of Leeds, November.

Morck, R., A. Shleifer and R. Vishny (1990), 'The stock market and investment: is the market a sideshow?, *Brookings Papers on Economic Activity*, **2**, 157–202.

Morin, Francois (2000), 'A transformation in the French model of shareholding and management', *Economy and Society*, **29** (1), 36–53.

Nell, E. (1985), 'Jean Baptiste Marglin: a comment on growth, distribution and inflation', *Cambridge Journal of Economics*, **9** (2), 173–8.

Nell, Edward (1994), 'Minsky, Keynes and Sraffa: investment and the Long Period', in G. Dymski and R. Pollin (eds), *New Perspectives in Monetary Macroeconomics: Explorations in the Tradition of Hyman P Minsky*, Ann Arbor: University of Michigan Press.

Nelson, C. and C. Plosser (1982), 'Trends and random walks in macroeconomic time series', *Journal of Monetary Economics*, **10**, 139–62.

Newbold, P. and C. Granger (1974), 'Spurious regressions in econometrics', *Journal of Economics*, **2**, 111–20.

Nickell, Stephen (1990), 'Unemployment: a survey', *Economic Journal*, **100** (401), 391–439.

Nickell, S. (1997), 'Unemployment and labor market rigidities: Europe versus North America', *Journal of Economic Perspectives*, **11** (3), 55–74.

Nickell, S. (1998), 'Unemployment: questions and some answers', *Economic Journal*, **108**, 802–16.

Nickell, S. and S. Wadhwani (1987), 'Myopie, the dividend puzzle and share prices', Centre for Labour Economics discussion paper 272, LSE.

OECD (1994), *The OECD Jobs Study*, Paris: OECD.

OECD (1996), *Employment and Growth in the Knowledge-based Economy*, Paris: OECD Publications.

OECD (1997a), 'Economic performance and the structure of collective bargaining', *Employment Outlook*, Chapter 3.

OECD (1997b), *Implementing the Jobs Strategy*, Paris: OECD.

OECD (1998a), 'Making the most of the minimum: statutory minimum wages, employment and poverty', *OECD Employment Outlook*, Chapter 2.

OECD (1998b), 'Shareholder value and the market in corporate control in OECD counties', *Financial Market Trends*, **69**, 15–38.

OECD (1999a), 'Employment protection and labour market performance', *OECD Employment Outlook*, Chapter 2.

OECD (1999b), 'New enterprise work practices and their labour market implications', OECD *Employment Outlook*, Chapter 4.

OECD (2002), *Economic Outlook Database Inventory* (EO72 December 2002 Version).

Onaran, Ö. and E. Stockhammer (2004) 'Two different export-oriented growth strategies: accumulation and distribution a la Turca and a la South Korea', *Emerging Markets Finance and Trade* (forthcoming).

Palley, Thomas (1996), *Post Keynesian Economics. Debt, Distribution and the Macro Economy*, London: Macmillan.

Palley, Thomas (1998), 'Macroeconomics with conflict and income distribution', *Review of Political Economy*, **10** (3), 329–42.

Pasinetti, Luigi (1962), 'Rate of profit and income distribution in relation to the rate of economic growth', *Review of Economic Studies*, **30**, 267–79.

Peck, S. and P. Temple (1999), 'Corporate governance, investment and economic performance', in C. Driver and P. Temple (eds), *Investment, Growth and Employment: Perspectives for Policy*, New York: Routledge.

Pesaran, M. and Y. Shin (1998), 'An autoregressive distributed-lag modelling approach to cointegration analysis', in S. Strom (ed.), *Econometrics and Economic Theory in the 20th Century: The Ragnar Frisch Centennial Symposium*, Cambridge: Cambridge University Press.

Phelps, Edmund (1968), 'Money-wage dynamics and labor-market dynamics', *Journal of Political Economy*, **78** (4), 678–711.

Phelps, Edmund (1992), 'A review of unemployment', *Journal of Economic Literature*, **30**, 1476–90.

Phelps, Edmund (1994), *Structural Slumps. The Modern Equilibrium Theory of Unemployment, Interest, and Assets*, Cambridge and London: Harvard University Press.

Phelps, Edmund (1996), 'The structuralist theory of employment', *American Economic Review*, **85** (2), 226–31.

Phelps, E. and G. Zoerrga (1998), 'Natural Rate Theory and OECD unemployment', *Economic Journal*, **108**, 782–801.

Pindyck, Robert (1991), 'Irreversibility, uncertainty, and investment', *Journal of Economic Literature*, **29**, 1110–48.

Pindyck, R. and A. Solimano (1993), 'Economic instability and aggregate investment', in O. Blanchard and S. Fischer (eds), *NBER Macroeconomic Annual 1993*, Cambridge and London: MIT Press.

Pollin, Robert (1991), 'Two theories of money supply endogeneity: some empirical evidence', *Journal of Post Keynesian Economics*, **13** (3), 366–98.

Pollin, Robert (1995), 'Financial structures and egalitarian economic policy', *New Left Review*, **214** November/December, 26–61.

Pollin, Robert (1997), 'Financial intermediation and the variability of the saving constraint', in R. Pollin (ed.), *The Macreoeconomics of Saving, Finance, and Investment*, Ann Arbor, MI: University of Michigan Press.

Pollin, Robert (1998), 'The "Reserve Army of Labor" and the "Natural Rate of Unemployment": Can Marx, Kalecki, Friedman, and Wall Street all be wrong?' *Review of Radical Political Economics*, **30** (3), 1–13.

Pollin, Robert (2000), 'Globalization, inequality and financial instability: confronting the Marx, Keynes and Polyani problems in Advanced Capitalist Countries', PERI Working Paper 8.

Pollin, R., D. Baker and M. Schaberg (2002), 'Securities transaction taxes for financial markets', PERI Working Paper Series 20.

Poterba, J. (2000), 'Stock market wealth and consumption', *Journal of Economic Perspectives*, **14**, 2.

Poterba, J. and A. Samwick (1995), 'Stock ownership patterns, stock market fluctuations, and consumption', *Brookings Papers on Economic Activity*, **2**, 1995, 295–357.

Power, D., G. Epstein and M. Abrena (2003a), 'Individual country technical notes for trends in the rentier income share in OECD countries 1960–2000', PERI Working Paper 58b.

Power, D., G. Epstein and M. Abrena (2003b), 'Trends in the rentier income share in OECD countries 1960–2000', PERI Working Paper 58a.

Prevezer, M. and M. Ricketts (1994), 'Corporate governance: the UK compared with Germany and Japan', in N. Dimsdale and M Prevezer (eds), *Capital Markets and Corporate Governance*, Oxford: Clarendon Press.

Rappaport, Alfred (1986), *Creating Shareholder Value. The New Standard for Business Performance*, New York: Free Press.

Resnick, S. and R. Wolff (1987), *Knowledge and Class. A Marxian Critique of Political Economy*, Chicago and London: University of Chicago Press.

Rima, Ingrid (ed.) 1991), *The Joan Robinson Legacy*, Armonk, NY: Sharpe.

Robinson, Joan (1937), *Introduction to the Theory of Employment*, London: Macmillan.

Robinson, Joan (1956), *The Accumulation of Capital*, London: Macmillan.

Robinson, Joan (1962), *Essays in the Theory of Economic Growth*, London: Macmillian.

Robinson, Joan (1974), 'History versus equilibrium', *Thames Papers in Political Economy*. Reprinted in Joan Robinson, *Collected Economic Papers*, Cambridge MA: MIT Press (1980).

Rodrik, Dani (1998), 'Where did all the growth go? External shocks, social conflict, and growth collapses', NBER Working Paper W6350.

Ross, S. (1973), 'The economic theory of agency: the principal's problem', *American Economic Review*, **63**, 134–9.

Rowthorn, Robert, (1977) 'Conflict, inflation and money', *Cambridge Journal of Economics*, **1** (3), 21–39. Reprinted in Bob Rowthorn, *Capitalism, Conflict and Inflation*, London: Lawrence and Wishart, 1980.

Rowthorn, Robert (1981), 'Demand, real wages and economic growth', *Thames Papers in Political Economy*, Autumn 1–39. Reprinted in *Studi Economici* (1982), **18** 3–54 and also reprinted in M. Sawyer (ed.) (1988), *Post-Keynesian Economics*, Aldershot: Edward Elgar; Brookfield, VT: Gower.

Rowthorn, Robert (1995), 'Capital formation and unemployment', *Oxford Review of Economic Policy*, **11** (1), 26–39.

Rowthorn, Robert (1999a), 'Unemployment, capital–labor substitution, and economic growth', IMF Working Paper 99/43.

Rowthorn, Robert (1999b), 'Unemployment, wage bargaining and capital-labour substitution', *Cambridge Journal of Economics*, **23**, 413–25.

Sarantis, N. (1993), 'Distribution, aggregate demand and unemployment in OECD countries', *Economic Journal*, **103**, 459–67.

Sawyer, Malcolm (2001), 'The NAIRU: a critical appraisal', in P. Arestis and M. Sawyer (eds), *Money, Finance and Capitalist Development*, Cheltenham: Edward Elgar.

Sawyer, Malcolm (2002), 'The NAIRU, aggregate demand and investment', *Metroeconomica*, **53** (1), 66–94.

Scarpetta, Stefano (1996), 'Assessing the role of labour market policies and institutional settings on unemployment: a cross-country study', *OECD Economic Studies*, 26, 43–98.

Schaberg, Marc (1999), *Globalization and the Erosion of National Financial Systems*, Cheltenham: Edward Elgar.

Schianterelli, F. (1996), 'Financial constraints and investment: methodological issues and international evidence', *Oxford Review of Economic Policy*, **12** (2), 70–87.

Schulmeister, Stephan (1996), *Zinssatz, Investitionsdynamik, Wachstumsrate und Staatsverschuldung*, Wien: Österreichisches Institut für Wirtschaftsforschung.

Scott, John (1986), *Capitalist Property and Financial Power. A Comparative Study of Britain, the United States and Japan*, Brighton: Wheatsheaf Books.

Sen, A. and A. Dutt (1993), 'Wage bargaining, imperfect competition and the markup: optimizing microfoundations', *Economic Letters*, **48**, 15–20.

Setterfield, Mark (ed.) (2002), *The Economics of Demand-led Growth*, Cheltenham, UK: Edward Elgar.

Setterfield, M. and J. Cornwall (2002), 'A neo-Kaldorian perspective on the rise and decline of the Golden Age', in Mark Setterfield (ed.), *The Economics of Demand-led Growth. Challenging the Supply-side Vision of the Long Run*, Cheltenham: Edward Elgar.

Shiller, Robert, (2000), *Irrational Exuberance*, Princeton University Press.

Shleifer, Andrei (2000), *Inefficient Markets: An Introduction to Behavioral Finance*, Oxford: Oxford University Press.

Shleifer, A. and L. Summers (1990), 'The noise trader approach to finance', *Journal of Economic Perspectives*, **4** (2), 19–34.

Short, H. (1994), 'Ownership, control, financial structure and the performance of firms', *Journal of Economic Surveys*, **8** (3), 203–25.

Siebert, H. (1997), 'Labour market rigidities: at the root of unemployment in Europe', *Journal of Economic Perspectives*, **11** (3), 37–54.

Sims, Christopher (1980), 'Macroeconomics and reality', *Econometrica*, **48** (1), 1–48.

Sims, Christopher (1986), 'Are forecasting models usable for policy analysis?', *Federal Reserve Bank of Minneapolis Quarterly Review*, Winter.

Sims, C., J. Stock and M. Watson (1990), 'Inference in linear time series models with some unit roots', *Econometrica*, **58** (1), 113–44.

Skott, Peter (1994), 'On the modeling of systemic financial fragility', in A. Dutt (ed.), *New Directions in Analytical Political Economy*, Aldershot: Edward Elgar.

Skott, Peter (1995), 'Financial innovation, deregulation, and Minsky cycles', in G. Epstein and H. Gintis (eds), *Macroeconomic Policy after the Conservative Era*, Cambridge: Cambridge University Press.

Smithin, John (1996), *Macroeconomic Policy and the Future of Capitalism: The Revenge of the Rentiers and the Threat to Prosperity*, Cheltenham: Edward Elgar.

Snowden, B., H. Vane and P. Wynarczyk (1994). *A Modern Guide to Macroeconomics: An Introduction to Competing Schools of Thought*, Northampton, MA: Edward Elgar.

Solow, Robert (1970), *Growth Theory. An Exposition*, Oxford: Oxford University Press.

Soskice, D. and W. Carlin (1989) 'Medium-run Keynesianism: hysteresis and capital scrapping', in Paul Davidson and Jan Kregel (eds), *Macroeconomic Problems and Policies of Income Distribution: Functional, Personal, International*, Aldershot: Edward Elgar.

Steindl, Josef (1952), *Maturity and Stagnation in American Capitalism*, New York: Monthly Review Press.

Steindl, Josef (1981), 'Some comments on the three versions of Kalecki's theory of the trade cycle', in J. Osiatynski (ed.), *Collected Works of Michal Kalecki*, Vol. 2, Oxford: Clarendon Press.

Stiglitz, Joseph (1987), 'The causes and consequences of the dependence of quality on price', *Journal of Economic Literature*, **25**, 1–48.

Stiglitz, J. and A. Weiss (1981), 'Credit rationing in markets with imperfect information', *American Economic Review*, **71**, 393–410.

Stockhammer, Engelbert (1999), 'Robinsonian and Kaleckian growth. An update on post-Keynesian growth theories', Working paper of the Department of Economics of the University of Economics and Business Administration No. 67.

Stockhammer, Engelbert (2004a), 'Explaining European unemployment: testing the NAIRU theory and a Keynesian approach', *International Review of Applied Economics*, **18** (1), 3–24.

Stockhammer, Engelbert (2004b), 'Financialization and the slowdown of accumulation', *Cambridge Journal of Economics*, **25** (5), 719–41.

Stockhammer, Engelbert (2004c), 'Is there an equilibrium rate of unemployment in the Long Run?', *Review of Political Economy*, **16** (1), 59–77.

Stockhammer, E. and O. Onaran (2004), 'Accumulation, distribution and employment: a structural VAR approach to a Kaleckian macro-model', *Structural Change and Economic Dynamics* (forthcoming).

Taylor, Lance (1985), 'A stagnationist model of economic growth', *Cambridge Journal of Economics*, **9**, 383–403.

Taylor, Lance (1996), 'Stimulating global employment growth', in J. Eatwell (ed.), *Global unemployment. Loss of Jobs in the 90s*, Armonk, NY: M.E. Sharpe.

Tease, Warren (1993), 'The stock market and investment', *OECD Economic Studies*, **20**, 41–61.

Tease, W., A. Dean, J. Elmeskov and P. Hoeller (1991), 'Real interest rates: the influence of saving, investment and other factors', *OECD Economic Studies*, **17**, 107–44.

Temple, Jonathan (1999), 'The new growth evidence', *Journal of Economic Literature*, **37** (1), 112–56.

Tietmeyer, Hans (1994), 'Unemployment: a German View', *Reducing Unemployment: Current Issues and Policy Options*, Federal Reserve Bank of Kansas City.

Tinbergen, Jan (1938), 'Statistical evidence on the acceleration principle', *Economica*, **5** (2), 164–76.

Tinbergen, Jan (1939), 'A method and its application to investment activity', in *Statistical Testing of Business Cycle Theories*, Vol. I, Geneva: League of Nations.

Tobin, James (1969), 'A general equilibrium approach to monetary theory', *Journal for Money Credit and Banking*, **1** (1), 15–29.

Tobin, James (1978), 'A proposal for international monetary reform', *Eastern Economic Journal*, **4**, 153–9.

Tobin, James (1997), 'Comment', in R. Pollin (ed.), *The Macroeconomics of Savings, Finance and Investment*, Ann Arbor, MI: University of Michigan Press.

van Ees, H., G. Kuper and E. Sterken (1997), 'Investment, finance and the business cycle: evidence from the Dutch manufacturing sector', *Cambridge Journal of Economics*, **21**, 395–407.

Vickers, Douglas (1992), 'The investment function: five propositions in response to Professor Gordon', *Journal of Post Keynesian Economics*, **14** (4), 445–64.

Visser, J. (1996), 'Unionisation Trends', The OECD Countries Union Membership File, Amsterdam: University of Amsterdam, Centre for Research of European Societies and Labour Relations CESAR.

Watson, Mark (1994), 'Vector autoregressions and cointegration', in R.F. Engle and D.L. McFadden (eds), *Handbook of Econometrics*, Volume IV, 2844–915.

Williams, Karel (2000), 'From shareholder value to present-day capitalism', *Economy and Society*, **29** (1), 1–12.

Wright, Erik (1985), *Classes*, London: Verso.

Wright, Erik (ed.) (1989), *The Debate on Classes*, London: Verso.

Wright, Erik (1997), *Class Counts: Comparative Studies in Class Analysis*, Cambridge: Cambridge University Press.

Zellner, A. (1962), 'An efficient method of estimating seemingly unrelated regressions and tests for aggregation bias', *Journal of the American Statistical Association*, **57**, 348–68.

Index

NEW DIRECTIONS IN MODERN ECONOMICS

Post-Keynesian Monetary Economics
New Approaches to Financial Modelling
Edited by Philip Arestis

Keynes's Principle of Effective Demand
Edward J. Amadeo

New Directions in Post-Keynesian Economics
Edited by John Pheby

Theory and Policy in Political Economy
Essays in Pricing, Distribution and Growth
Edited by Philip Arestis and Yiannis Kitromilides

Keynes's Third Alternative?
The Neo-Ricardian Keynesians and the Post Keynesians
Amitava Krishna Dutt and Edward J. Amadeo

Wages and Profits in the Capitalist Economy
The Impact of Monopolistic Power on Macroeconomic Performance in the USA and UK
Andrew Henley

Prices, Profits and Financial Structures
A Post-Keynesian Approach to Competition
Gokhan Capoglu

International Perspectives on Profitability and Accumulation
Edited by Fred Moseley and Edward N. Wolff

Mr Keynes and the Post Keynesians
Principles of Macroeconomics for a Monetary Production Economy
Fernando J. Cardim de Carvalho

The Economic Surplus in Advanced Economies
Edited by John B. Davis

Foundations of Post-Keynesian Economic Analysis
Marc Lavoie

The Post-Keynesian Approach to Economics
An Alternative Analysis of Economic Theory and Policy
Philip Arestis

Income Distribution in a Corporate Economy
Russell Rimmer

The Economics of the Profit Rate
Competition, Crises and Historical Tendencies in Capitalism
Gérard Duménil and Dominique Lévy

Corporatism and Economic Performance
A Comparative Analysis of Market Economies
Andrew Henley and Euclid Tsakalotos

Competition, Technology and Money
Classical and Post-Keynesian Perspectives
Edited by Mark A. Glick

Investment Cycles in Capitalist Economies
A Kaleckian Behavioural Contribution
Jerry Courvisanos

Does Financial Deregulation Work?
A Critique of Free Market Approaches
Bruce Coggins

Pricing Theory in Post Keynesian Economics
A Realist Approach
Paul Downward

The Economics of Intangible Investment
Elizabeth Webster

Globalization and the Erosion of National Financial Systems
Is Declining Autonomy Inevitable?
Marc Schaberg

Explaining Prices in the Global Economy
A Post-Keynesian Model
Henk-Jan Brinkmon

Capitalism, Socialism, and Radical Political Economy
Essays in Honor of Howard J. Sherman
Edited by Robert Pollin

Financial Liberalisation and Intervention
A New Analysis of Credit Rationing
Santonu Basu

Why the Bubble Burst
US Stock Market Performance since 1982
Lawrance Lee Evans, Jr.

Sustainable Fiscal Policy and Economic Stability
Theory and Practice
Philippe Burger

The Rise of Unemployment in Europe
A Keynesian Approach
Engelbert Stockhammer